The End of the Village

Globalization and Community

Susan E. Clarke, Series Editor
Dennis R. Judd, Founding Editor

Volume 33
The End of the Village: Planning the Urbanization of Rural China
Nick R. Smith

Volume 32
Private Metropolis: The Eclipse of Local Democratic Governance
Dennis R. Judd, Evan McKenzie, and Alba Alexander, Editors

Volume 31
The Migrant's Paradox: Street Livelihoods and Marginal Citizenship in Britain
Suzanne M. Hall

Volume 30
Chasing World-Class Urbanism: Global Policy versus Everyday Survival in Buenos Aires
Jacob Lederman

Volume 29
Gringolandia: Lifestyle Migration under Late Capitalism
Matthew Hayes

Volume 28
Renew Orleans? Globalized Development and Worker Resistance after Katrina
Aaron Schneider

Volume 27
Globalized Authoritarianism: Megaprojects, Slums, and Class Relations in Urban Morocco
Koenraad Bogaert

Volume 26
Urban Policy in the Time of Obama
James DeFilippis, Editor

Volume 25
The Servant Class City: Urban Revitalization versus the Working Poor in San Diego
David J. Karjanen

Volume 24
Security in the Bubble: Navigating Crime in Urban South Africa
Christine Hentschel

Volume 23
The Durable Slum: Dharavi and the Right to Stay Put in Globalizing Mumbai
Liza Weinstein

Volume 22
The Fragmented Politics of Urban Preservation: Beijing, Chicago, and Paris
Yue Zhang

(continued on page 325)

The End of the Village

PLANNING THE URBANIZATION OF RURAL CHINA

Nick R. Smith

Globalization and Community, Volume 33

University of Minnesota Press
Minneapolis | London

The University of Minnesota Press gratefully acknowledges the financial assistance provided for the publication of this book by the Chiang Ching-kuo Foundation for International Scholarly Exchange.

Published by the University of Minnesota Press
111 Third Avenue South, Suite 290
Minneapolis, MN 55401-2520
http://www.upress.umn.edu

ISBN 978-1-5179-1091-4 (hc)
ISBN 978-1-5179-1092-1 (pb)

Library of Congress record available at https://lccn.loc.gov/2020058457

Printed in the United States of America on acid-free paper

UMP BmB 2021

For Yaya

Contents

INTRODUCTION

China's New Era of Urbanization

Even low in the sky, the sun felt close, doggedly clinging to every surface, working under the skin of the city. Waves of heat rippled on bare pavement, as if Chongqing were stirring in its concrete shell, roused by the quickening pulse of rush hour. Workers in soot-stained uniforms filtered out of factory gates into the oppressive humidity of late summer. On their way to the market, the bus stop, or the relief of a lukewarm shower, they dodged trucks laden with motorcycle parts they had just assembled and luxury sedans driven by factory owners who sometimes paid their wages. Apple-green, three-wheeled tuk-tuks stopped by the curb to pick up fares to transit hubs in the nearby towns of Baishiyi and Hangu: "Still room for one more! Two *kuai* apiece!" Along the side of the road, a man staggered under the weight of a wheelbarrow, nearly colliding with a bicycle wobbling in the draft of an oncoming truck. A single brick tumbled into the road, and there was a murmured chorus of concern and support for the bricklayer. A knot of men had gathered under the lengthening shade of a large tree, escaping the heat of the sun while they watched the "social heat" (*renao* 热闹) of one of the busiest intersections in Hailong Village.

An elderly man, Feng Shunde, pulled out a short wooden stool, waving me into the shade. "Tired?" he asked as he sat down. "A little," I admitted, my legs aching from hours walking Hailong's back hills. "It's too hot!" Feng chided. "What are you doing wandering around in the sun?" I looked up at the men seated around us—mostly elderly, a few middle aged. Their conversations hushed as they listened intently for my answer. The owner of the adjacent hardware store pulled up a stool. "Research," I replied simply. "Research!" Feng enunciated the word with an exaggerated

Chongqing accent for the benefit of our audience. Then he added, "Researching what?" I offered the most straightforward answer: "Urban–rural coordination" (*chengxiang tongchou* 城乡统筹), a national policy program for which both Chongqing Municipality and Hailong Village were experimental sites.

From across the circle, one of the other men, Xu Jianguo, erupted, incensed: "Urban–rural equal pay? What equality? What pay?" Chongqing's residents are famous for their fiery rhetoric, but Xu's invective caught me by surprise. It seemed he had misheard me, mistaking "urban–rural coordination" (*chengxiang tongchou* 城乡统筹) for its near homophone, "urban–rural equal pay" (*chengxiang tongchou* 城乡同酬).[1] Laughing, Xu's neighbors pointed out his apparent mistake as they tried to calm him down, but Xu refused to be placated and waved them off: "I know what he said. It doesn't matter how you say it—it's just a way to swindle us villagers." At this point, it seemed the knot of men drew a little tighter and the laughter grew a bit less jovial. Several of the men cast nervous glances toward the owner of the hardware store and, behind the counter, his wife, a senior cadre in Hailong Village's party branch.

Xu Jianguo had more reason to complain than most. Unbeknownst to me, I had just stumbled through his living room, or what was left of it. In Hailong's interior, where Xu's house had once stood, migrants from Hechuan now scavenged through the rubble, cleaning and stacking bricks into neat cubes of reclaimed building material. The house Xu had built with his own hands was being sold off, brick by brick. Like other villagers whose houses had been demolished, Xu was promised an apartment in the new village development, dubbed Hailong City, the centerpiece of the village's much-heralded experiment in urban–rural coordination. Village plans called for the development to be built on the very site of Xu's house, but nearly a year had passed since the bulldozers had come and no visible progress had been made. In the meantime, Xu's life was in limbo. The housing subsidy he received from the village development corporation did not even cover the monthly rent he paid to stay in Hailong, where he relied on the support of friends and family to make ends meet. And with the development of Hailong City, it was unclear how long the village and its mutual support networks would survive. With nowhere to put down roots, Xu felt like a stranger in his own community. He lived much like the thousands of migrants who sojourned in Hailong, though they still had houses they could return to in their home villages. Xu had nothing, his past erased and his future uncertain.

According to China's leaders, urban–rural coordination was intended to help rural residents like Xu Jianguo, not harm them. The program was introduced in the early 2000s in an effort to improve the welfare of rural people and resolve China's burgeoning rural development crisis, which threatened to foment widespread social instability during the 1990s. In the narrative put forward by the party–state, the crisis was a natural and temporary result of China's rapid development during the post-1978 reform era. Rooted in the Chinese Communist Party's understanding of Marxism, urban–rural coordination grew out of the view that "social development is a kind of natural historical process . . . that must follow definite and objective laws" (Ma 2006, 35–36).[2] One of these "objective laws" was uneven development and the resulting opposition between city and countryside, which was expressed as urban–rural inequality. As President Hu Jintao (2004) argued, all nations extract resources from rural areas to support the early stages of industrialization and urbanization. Likewise, Premier Wen Jiabao insisted that "rural and urban are an organic unity, [and] urban development cannot be separated from rural development, [but] urban development also will not naturally promote rural development" (Wen 2003, 11). To overcome the natural imbalances between urban and rural areas, China's leaders proposed urban–rural coordination, which would use "scientific planning" to extend the benefits of urbanization beyond China's cities, raising rural standards of living and reducing urban–rural inequality even while maintaining urban growth (Ma 2006, 56–57; Wen 2003). Echoing the ambitions of the rural commune movement under Mao Zedong, party leaders portrayed this redistributive program as a step toward the utopian social relations of communism, in which all people would fully share in the benefits of development and the opposition between city and countryside would be eliminated (Chen 2009, 16–17, 56; Hu 2004). Through urban–rural coordination, the party–state promised to transform urbanization from a zero-sum proposition of urban prosperity and rural exploitation into a win–win for both China's cities and its countryside.

Notwithstanding the rhetorical claims of China's leaders, urban development is never win–win, a fact that Xu Jianguo's poetic substitution of "equal pay" for "coordination" so effectively exposed.[3] Nor are China's trenchant urban–rural inequities an inevitable or natural outcome of a particular stage of economic development, as party leaders claimed.[4] Nowhere are the inequality and artifice of urbanization more apparent than in contemporary China, where the Chinese Communist Party (CCP) has pursued one of the largest urbanization projects in human history. Rather than an inevitable outcome of a natural process of development, China's urban–rural inequities are actively produced by the party–state's own administrative separation of urban and rural areas, a policy that systematically excludes rural areas and populations from many of the benefits of urban development. With stark divisions in the administration of land, population, and governance, this binary system has formed the bedrock of Chinese society for nearly 70 years, starting in the socialist era and continuing into the post-1978 reform era. Under reform, however, the party–state maintained this de jure system of urban–rural separation while also encouraging the de facto integration of urban and rural sectors. The dynamic tension between de jure separation and de facto integration allowed the extraction of resources from rural areas to support urban development, resulting in both supercharged urbanization and incipient rural collapse. By the late 1990s, the party–state's bifurcated approach to development was beginning to falter, with mass protests sweeping China's countryside and the Asian financial crisis threatening its cities. At its heart, the rural development crisis was a result of the persistent tension between China's de jure urban and rural categories and its de facto processes of urban–rural interpenetration, and it was in response to this political contradiction that urban–rural coordination was formulated.

Xu Jianguo's outburst voiced suspicions shared by many of his fellow villagers—that they would once again end up on the losing end of social reform, and that urban–rural coordination would prove to be just another political tool for exploiting rural people and resources. Urban–rural inequality was so deeply embedded in China's social and political fabric that any adjustment to the system of urban–rural difference would pose a threat to personal and professional interests throughout the Chinese polity. As a path-dependent result of previous rounds of reform and transformation, China's social contract has for decades been rooted in the nation's binary system of urban–rural separation: the state takes a more extensive and direct role in the political, economic, and social life of urban areas, while rural areas are primarily governed by village collectives that are formally outside the bounds of the state (though nonetheless subject to party discipline).[5] In urban areas, for instance, registered residents are given access to state-sponsored public services and welfare goods, which municipal governments increasingly fund through the sale of use rights to state-owned urban land. By contrast, in lieu of formal social welfare, rural residents are given use rights to collective-owned land, and resource redistribution is predominantly organized through village-scale mechanisms controlled by villagers and village cadres. While this de jure system of urban–rural separation is unequal and provides the basis for the exploitation of rural areas to support urbanization, the de facto integration of urban and rural areas also gives rural people opportunities to pursue survival strategies that take advantage of urban processes and hybridize urban and rural resources (for instance, through migration and entrepreneurship). Even the CCP relies on these systemic disjunctures for its survival. Eliminating the de jure system of urban–rural separation might result in a wave of rural-to-urban migration, overwhelming and destabilizing China's cities. And disentangling the de facto system of urban–rural interpenetration might starve cities of cheap labor and land, threatening the sustainability of economic growth. The same tensions between categories and processes that precipitated China's rural development crisis and threatened social stability thus also formed the basis of both rural people's lives and livelihoods and the CCP's continued authority and legitimacy. In short, any change to China's urban–rural relations would mean rewriting the nation's social contract and the institutional rules that govern economic and political life.

With the stakes so high, urban–rural coordination was bound to be messier and more contentious than China's leaders hoped. While there was broad agreement that the rules governing China's urban–rural relations should change, there was significantly less agreement on what the new rules should be. As the challenges facing rural China mounted, a host of different diagnoses and proposed solutions were put forward, from the new rural reconstruction movement advocated by elite scholar-activists to the impromptu workarounds jury-rigged by villagers. The party–state's relative monopoly on political power meant that its chosen strategies enjoyed distinct advantages, but even here, the internal fragmentation and heterogeneity of the party–state resulted in a wide diversity of practices enacted under the banner of urban–rural coordination. Like other national policy initiatives, urban–rural coordination relied on the interpretation of local governments for its implementation, meaning that the soaring rhetoric and open-ended policy priorities of the central party–state's urban–rural coordination program were ultimately refracted through the initiatives, interests, and concerns of lower-level cadres. By representing urban–rural coordination as a technical process that would rebalance the "natural" unevenness of urban development, the Chinese party–state obscured these contentious politics (cf. Ferguson 1990; Flyvbjerg 1998). This reflected the party–state's larger pursuit of a "harmonious society" (*hexie shehui* 和谐社会) free of social conflict. Through such depoliticizing rhetoric, the party–state sought to prevent precisely the kind of "unharmonious" suspicions raised by Xu Jianguo's demand for "equal pay."[6]

This book peels back the party–state's depoliticizing rhetoric by investigating some of the earliest efforts to interpret and implement urban–rural coordination at the local level. These early efforts included both Chongqing, a provincial-level municipality in China's late-developing west formally designated as one of the first two national policy experiments in urban–rural coordination, and Hailong, an administrative village on Chongqing's western periphery, where local cadres pursued an alternative version of urban–rural coordination that became a nationally recognized experimental model. By attending to the narratives and practices that planners, cadres, and inhabitants in Chongqing and Hailong used to respond to the crisis of rural development and make sense of urban–rural coordination, this book reaches past the depoliticizing rhetoric of national policy to explore the contested processes through which this new approach to development landed on the ground.

This investigation reveals an epochal shift in China's developmental model, from a state policy of urban–rural separation toward the active integration of rural areas into state-led processes of urbanization. In essence, urban–rural coordination has involved the replacement of de facto urbanization with de jure urbanization, extending state-led forms of urban development to rural areas and displacing existing informal entanglements in urban processes. Taken to its logical conclusion, this inversion in Chinese policy means the near-total urbanization of China's population and territory and the incipient end of the village as a meaningful form of sociospatial organization in contemporary China. Villages have long played an important role in resolving the contradictions of China's urban–rural relations and in ensuring the welfare of rural people, but urban–rural coordination envisions new, state-centric solutions to these problems that leave little room for the grassroots village institutions that structure rural lives and livelihoods. What has replaced these village communities is a decidedly more urbanized rurality—both conventional urbanization, as the party–state concentrates rural populations in towns and cities, and urbanization in a more diffuse sense, as depopulated rural territories are transformed into industrialized agriculture and touristic playscapes shaped by urban needs and sensibilities. The result is the transformation of villages into rural simulacra, which may still have a rural aesthetic and may even be formally categorized as rural villages, but which increasingly function as extensions of an urban way of life rather than as the sociospatial milieux that support villagers' survival. Thus, urban–rural coordination has not so much eliminated the disjuncture between China's de jure urban and rural categories and its de facto processes of urban–rural interpenetration as reconstituted this mismatch in new ways that are more easily controlled by the party–state. As the competing approaches to urbanization unfolding in Hailong indicate, the precise details of China's new social contract are not yet settled, and there are many more versions playing out in diverse locales across the Chinese polity. However, the broad contours of this emergent urban future are becoming clearer, as rural people and places are more tightly integrated into urban processes dominated by the political and economic discipline of the party–state.

The Origins of China's Rural Development Crisis

While China's rural development crisis came to a head in the late 1990s, its origins go back far earlier—to the pragmatic developmentalism of Deng Xiaoping, the socialist managerialism of Mao Zedong, and beyond. The political production of urban–rural difference can be traced back to China's earliest cities, which often existed by virtue of their administrative designation, with city walls spatially inscribing the social distinction between an urban political elite and the rural and suburban populace

(Lewis 2006, 150–70; Wheatley 1971).[7] After China's defeat in the opium wars (1839–42, 1856–60), the isolation of foreigners and their trade in treaty ports created concentrations of economic activity and social privilege, feeding the production of urban–rural difference during the late nineteenth and early twentieth centuries (Esherick 2000, 10–11; Mann 1984; Murphey 1974). But it was not until the 1950s that the socialist regime erected indelible barriers between urban and rural China. The CCP imposed strict limits on urban growth, food prices, and rural–urban migration to maintain control over population centers and reduce the consumption costs of rapid industrialization. Most famously, the "household registration" (*huji* 户籍 or *hukou* 户口) system divided the population into agricultural (rural) and nonagricultural (urban) segments, conditioning people's access to housing, food rations, and other welfare goods. The separation of urban and rural populations privileged urban areas, treating the rural as a labor reservoir and a source of cheap agricultural produce to support industrial production (Chan 1994, 60–82; Kirkby 1985, 14–21).[8]

After the beginning of the reform era in 1978, Deng Xiaoping's pragmatic acceptance of urban–rural division was central to the success of the CCP's agenda of liberalizing the economy while maintaining its political hegemony. The separation between urban and rural sectors allowed China's leaders to pursue reform along separate tracks, without fear that changes to one sector of society might destabilize the other (Wallace 2014). For instance, the strictures of the household registration system kept rural-to-urban migrants from overwhelming China's cities with demands for expensive, state-sponsored welfare goods, while the separation of rural and urban land forestalled widespread rural landlessness and agricultural collapse.[9] Local governments were seated in China's cities and towns, composing an urban network of governmental authority. Administratively designated rural areas were governed by rural collectives, ambiguously defined grassroots organizations that trace their institutional genealogies back through the brigades and communes of the socialist era to the lineage organizations, village solidarity, and consanguinity that predated liberation (He 2003; Fei [1948] 1992). Formally autonomous from the Chinese government but still subject to the disciplinary authority of the CCP, rural collectives were largely left to fend for themselves. In many respects, China thus underwent two separate programs of reform in the 1980s, one rural and the other urban. Early reforms, such as the implementation of the household responsibility system and the establishment of township and village enterprises (TVEs), largely benefited rural areas, leading to rising rural incomes, labor surpluses, and grassroots forms of rural urbanization.[10] But as the 1980s progressed, national leaders began instituting a series of more sweeping reforms that consolidated the party–state's control of China's cities.[11] By the end of the decade, the Chinese party–state was decidedly urban.

Economic and political retrenchment in the 1990s eroded the rural development gains of the 1980s in favor of state-led, city-centered development (Huang 2008; Ren 2013). Structural reform of the TVE sector resulted in a wave of firm closures and consolidations, undermining the initial dynamism of rural urbanization (Huang 2008). Concurrently, the "cities leading the counties" program reinforced urban dominance by placing large rural hinterlands under the direct control of municipal governments (Cartier 2005; Chan 1994, 105; Ma 2005). The party–state loosened restrictions on migration to large cities but maintained limits on the transfer of household registration. Rural migrants could thus participate in urban labor markets, providing cheap labor for China's expanding manufacturing sector (Chan 2010), but they were excluded from urban welfare and public services, meaning that the costs of their social reproduction were borne by their home villages. These reforms paralleled a fiscal recalibration within the Chinese government, in which the center claimed a larger portion of tax receipts and local governments were granted greater discretionary control over land, producing incentives for municipalities to expand urbanization through the expropriation of collective-owned rural land (Rithmire 2015). Fueled by the extraction of labor, land, and other resources from rural areas, China experienced a period of supercharged urbanization, with rapid increases in the number of cities, the extent of urbanized land, the size of the urban population, and the gap between urban and rural incomes (Chan 2012; Lin 2009; Park 2008).

The simultaneous inclusion of rural areas in processes of urban transformation and their categorical exclusion from sharing in the benefits of those processes precipitated a growing rural crisis. The mass migration of the rural working-age population left behind "hollow villages," populated only with small children and the elderly, saddled with the costs of workers' social reproduction, and consequently plagued by a slew of social problems, including high rates of poverty and suicide, a dearth of grassroots leadership, and declining agricultural productivity (Thøgersen 2012). In periurban areas and in China's fertile coastal regions, land enclosure and "development zone fever" drove a precipitous decline in the quantity and quality of arable land (Lin 2009). As these crises came to a head in the late 1990s, and as rural wealth rapidly diminished in real terms, widespread protests over agricultural taxes erupted and rural development reemerged as a focus of public discourse. Decrying the city-centered policies of the past decade, scholars and pundits pointed to the persistence of the "three rural problems" (*san nong wenti* 三农问题): the inefficiency of agriculture, the insufficiency of village infrastructure, and the unsustainability of farmers' incomes (Day 2008; Wen 2000). Meanwhile, government policy makers fretted over the nation's declining agricultural capacity, which threatened China's political commitment to agricultural self-sufficiency. Since the 1950s, rural areas had served as a seemingly limitless reservoir of labor, land, and resources feeding China's cities and ensuring their stability. By the late 1990s, the rural reservoir seemed to be drying up, threatening China's urban juggernaut.

Just as China's leaders were recognizing the mutual interdependence of urban and rural development and the need to reinvest in rural areas, the importance of continued urbanization intensified. In 1997, the Asian financial crisis threatened to destabilize the Chinese economy. The central government responded by doubling down on infrastructure investment and stimulating the emerging real estate sector, resulting in a renewed intensification of urban development in the late 1990s. Faced with the economic threat of the Asian financial crisis, the party–state could hardly afford to stop exploiting rural areas, which supplied the cheap labor that ensured the international competitiveness of Chinese manufacturers and the cheap land that ensured the fiscal health of Chinese municipalities. As a result, the ratio of rural to urban per capita income continued to decline and the conversion of rural land to urban uses continued to increase in the years following 1997 (Lin 2009; Luo 2006; Park 2008). China's leaders thus faced an impossible choice: they relied on urbanization, which served as the engine for both the Chinese economic miracle and the CCP's political legitimacy, but continued urbanization risked destabilizing both rural and urban areas.

The National Policy Response: Urban–Rural Coordination

Confronted with the contradiction between urban and rural development as they took office in 2003, President Hu Jintao and Premier Wen Jiabao placed rural development and urban–rural relations at the center of their national policy agenda. The formal announcement of urban–rural coordination in October 2003 during the Third Plenum of the 16th Party Congress signaled a new approach to policy under Hu and Wen (CCP Central Committee 2003), and in the first annual Number One Document dedicated to rural issues, party leaders reemphasized its importance (State Council 2003).[12] Many of the principles underlying this initiative had circulated among Chinese scholars and policy makers since the early 1980s (Feng 1983). As China's reformers debated the relative merits of city-centered growth and rural urbanization (Kirkby 1985), some adherents of the latter approach advocated "urban–rural coordinated development" (*chengxiang xietiao fazhan* 城乡协调发展) (Fei 1991; Wu, Zou, and Ju 1988; Zhou and Zhang 1991; cf. Zhou 1997). Whereas these proposals often emphasized grassroots approaches and privileged the self-organized initiatives of rural residents, Hu and Wen advanced a state-led model of development. In this respect, urban–rural coordination is more reminiscent of the first two decades of communist rule (1949–69), when socialist land reform and the collectivization movement brought initial gains in prosperity (through the redistribution of landlords' property) combined with increasing dependence on the party–state (through the collectivization of both production and consumption). The consolidation of party–state control over China's rural areas resulted in one of the worst man-made disasters in world history, the Great Leap Forward, when tens of millions of rural people died of starvation (An, Li, and Yang 2001; Lin 1990). The liberalization of the post-1978 reform era loosened the party–state's direct control over rural areas (Chen 2014; He 2007), resulting in what might best be termed a policy of neglect—whether benign (as in much of the 1980s) or otherwise (as in much of the 1990s). For better or worse, rural villages were often left to find their own way. Urban–rural coordination signaled a return to the party–state's direct dominance of China's rural territories and populations, though in a new, urbanized form that barely resembles the socialist transformation of the 1950s and 1960s. Whereas the dramatic upheavals of collectivization grafted socialist institutions onto rural villages that were left largely in place, urban–rural coordination may ultimately leave little of rural China's existing social and spatial fabric intact.

Broadly speaking, urban–rural coordination is an effort to resolve China's rural development crisis by redirecting urban resources toward rural development.[13] The Leninist origins of the CCP have instilled a deep-seated paternalism toward China's rural people, who are assumed to be incapable of solving their own problems and thus reliant on the intervention of the party–state. This is reflected in the cadre training manual for urban–rural coordination: "Obviously, in resolving the 'three rural' problems, . . . if rural people and rural villages were to rely just on their own strength it would be impossible to achieve; it is necessary to coordinate the strengths of the entire nation and the entire society" (Ma 2006, 82). In the Fourth Plenum of the 16th Party Congress, Hu Jintao described the shift from resource extraction to resource provision as a natural progression in China's trajectory of development: like other industrializing nations, China relied on agriculture to subsidize the early stages of industrialization, "but after industry develops to a certain point, it is also common that industry repays agriculture and cities support the countryside" (qtd. in Chen 2009, 183–84). At the 2004 Central Economic Work Conference, Hu (2004) argued that China had already entered this latter stage of development, coining the phrase that is most often used to summarize urban–rural coordination: "industry promotes agriculture, cities carry the countryside" (*yi gong cu nong, yi cheng dai xiang* 以工促农、以城带乡).

To achieve this transformation, China's leaders returned to the principles of scientific rationality deployed by Deng Xiaoping 20 years earlier at another critical juncture in China's development trajectory. This approach was encoded in the term "coordination" (*tongchou* 统筹), which combines the characters for "unite" (*tong* 统) and "plan" (*chou* 筹).[14] It was also made clear by the larger "scientific development platform" (*kexue fazhan guan* 科学发展观), of which urban–rural coordination was a part.

As Wen Jiabao argued, urban–rural coordination emerges from "the party's scientific understanding of the laws of economic development for agriculture and villages" (2003, 3). In cadre training materials, urban–rural coordination also was described in terms reminiscent of comprehensive rational planning: "Urban–rural coordination takes a macro-view of the whole situation of the nation's economic and social development to comprehensively consider and produce a unified plan for urban and rural economic and social development" (Chen 2009, 185). According to this vision, the coordinated planning of urban–rural relations would overcome the divisions that threatened China's stability, enabling the free and harmonious circulation of people, capital, goods, and ideas, and finally allowing all Chinese people to share in the benefits of urbanization.

In a nation where the urban–rural divide has been a continuing source of injustice and inequity for decades, the toppling of these barriers promised real gains in rural prosperity. For instance, in one of the first national initiatives announced under the program, China abolished agricultural taxes, dramatically improving the financial situation of many farming households and addressing a widespread complaint that had roiled rural China with protests during the 1990s (Li and O'Brien 1996). But this reform also undermined the efficacy of village governance and eliminated villages' main source of funding, leaving many villages socially atomized and ridden with debt (Chen 2014; He 2007). In 2005, this gap was partially filled by the "socialist new countryside" (*shehuizhuyi xin nongcun* 社会主义新农村), a campaign under urban–rural coordination that directed increased fiscal transfers toward rural areas to support investments in infrastructure and other public goods (Ahlers and Schubert 2010; Su 2009). But these fiscal transfers made villages increasingly dependent on the financial largesse of local governments confronting their own budgetary shortfalls (Chen 2014). The way such investments were structured also contributed to rising levels of indebtedness among rural households, the appropriation of rural resources by local governments, and a push for the consolidation and liquidation of villages and the permanent migration of rural people to urban areas.[15] With few exceptions, such as the "one village, one product" program and its support for village-scale competition in the agricultural marketplace (Smith 2019b), national interventions generally have not focused on enabling rural areas to catalyze their own development. Instead, advances in rural prosperity have coincided with the weakening of village-scale institutions that once guaranteed rural social welfare and helped resolve China's urban–rural contradictions.

The existential threat to China's villages is inherent in the logic of urban–rural coordination. Path-dependent outcomes of previous rounds of crisis and reform, village-based institutions have evolved to accommodate the uncertainties and inequities of the nation's binary mode of development.[16] However imperfectly, it has been China's villages that have absorbed the inevitable irrationalities of rapid urbanization and ensured continued urban expansion, through, for instance, the maintenance of low-cost land banks and the social reproduction of migrant labor. Urban–rural coordination displaced this patchwork of village-scale strategies and safety nets and substituted an array of state-prescribed solutions that made rural residents more dependent on the welfare programs and redistributive justice of the party–state, potentially creating a new urban underclass of the formerly rural (Day 2008). By disconnecting residents from their village support networks, urban–rural coordination also atomized them, undermining their ability to assert collective rights in the context of sociospatial transformation (cf. Karl 2010; Ren 2013). In effect, urban–rural coordination represented a dramatic expansion of party–state power. The transformation of China's rural society and the "end of the peasant" were already implicit in the rapid urbanization of the 1990s (Li 2005). Rather than wait for the eventual collapse of rural society and the potential social unrest that might ensue, urban–rural coordination accelerated it, ensuring that village communities fall apart in ways that can be controlled and managed by the party–state.

Urban–rural coordination thus entails the end of the village as a meaningful form of social organization, collective action, and economic survival in contemporary China.[17] Between 2000 and 2010, the number of "administrative villages" in China declined from 735,000 to 581,000, and the number of "natural villages" dropped from 3.6 million to 2.6 million—reductions of between 20 and 30 percent.[18] But the true implications of urban–rural coordination are not reflected in these statistics, and the end of any individual village may not necessarily mean its outright demolition and liquidation. The "rural villages" represented in state statistics are sometimes little more than organizational ciphers, mechanisms used to consolidate land parcels or distribute shareholding dividends. These rural simulacra are villages in name only, evacuated of their sociospatial substance and oftentimes emptied of their inhabitants, who are increasingly pulled into China's cities and towns or resettled in consolidated new towns (Bray 2013b). In their place, China's rural territories have been transformed into industrialized farms, nature reserves, and amusement parks populated by tourists and wage laborers (Chen, Zinda, and Yeh 2017; Wilczak 2017). While this outcome is still only a utopian (or dystopian, depending on one's viewpoint) vision, agricultural policy has already encouraged the "vertical integration" of farming under the control of large agribusinesses rather than village small holders (Trappel 2016), and China's first national land use plan has already designated entire counties as ecological protection zones, severely restricting the possibility of in situ village-led development (Shue 2017). The existential threat posed to villages means that urban–rural coordination has been hotly contested by village cadres and inhabitants, whose survival depends on the continuity of village institutions. But in an ironic turn, some of the efforts that are meant to save villages and their institutions may also hasten their demise. For instance, cadres who seek to develop village resources can end up prioritizing profits over villagers' welfare and inhabitants committed to strengthening their thinning mutual support networks may ultimately depart the village in favor of more vibrant communities. The diversity of local circumstances, the variation in approaches to urban–rural coordination, and the intense contestation over its consequences mean that the end of the village is far from a foregone conclusion, but the overwhelming political and economic power that the party–state has brought to the implementation of urban–rural coordination ensures that the social contract of semiautonomous self-reliance and collective welfare that has heretofore defined village life is slowly disappearing.[19]

As the social functions that villages once served are eliminated, an increasingly urban future is taking their place. By actively integrating rural territories and populations into state-led urbanization processes, urban–rural coordination clears the way for the party–state to extend the city-centric successes of the 1990s—including both their economic dynamism and the CCP's political hegemony—to rural areas, and by implication to the entirety of China's national territory (Bray 2013a).[20] Indeed, accelerating urbanization was an explicit objective of urban–rural coordination (Luo 2006; Ma 2006). Only continued urbanization, it was argued, could provide the resources necessary to support further rural development—the proposed win–win of urban–rural coordination (Chen 2009, 186). The ultimate goal of this process is something called "urban–rural unification" (*chengxiang yitihua* 城乡一体化), whereby rural life becomes indistinguishable from urban life (Ma 2006, 94).[21] While this urban vision is sometimes expressed in the form of new towns and apartment buildings, the urbanization of rural China does not always resemble the tall buildings and crowded plazas that have become hallmarks of Chinese urbanity. Indeed, urban–rural coordination sometimes appears to produce quite the opposite of conventional urbanization. By shifting population and resources out of villages and into cities, urban–rural coordination makes the urban more urban and the rural more rural, thus widening the urban–rural gap rather than closing it (Abramson and Qi 2011; Cheung 2012; Wilczak 2017). But this rural intensification is itself a form of urbanization. In what has been characterized as the "recasting" or "reappraisal" of rural China (Chen, Zinda, and Yeh 2017; Griffiths, Chapman, and Christiansen 2010), the rural territories that urban–rural coordination leaves behind have been refracted through an urban lens and reconceived according to the urban sensibilities of the party–state's planners and policy makers. For example, these urban reimaginings of the rural might take the form of "operational landscapes" (Brenner and Schmid 2015), in which hinterlands once inhabited by villages are more tightly entwined in industrialized networks of extraction that concentrate their agricultural and ecological outputs in China's cities. In other instances, they might appear as "rural idylls" (Williams 1973), in which nostalgia for an imagined rural past is repackaged for the cultural and social consumption of urban elites. Alongside the densification and expansion of cities and towns, these processes of rural reification—what I term "urbanization by other means"—are producing an even more fundamental transformation of rural China.

These tendencies toward the expansion of state-led urbanization are further reflected in the national policy programs that have followed urban–rural coordination. Since President Xi Jinping and Premier Li Keqiang succeeded Hu Jintao and Wen Jiabao in 2013, the term "urban–rural coordination" has lost its prominence in national policy. But the underlying agenda of urban–rural coordination has been repackaged as the "National Plan for New-Type Urbanization" (*guojia xinxing chengzhenhua guihua* 国家新型城镇化规划) released by Xi and Li in 2014.[22] This wide-ranging document incorporates many of the key elements of urban–rural coordination into the nation's first explicitly articulated urbanization program. Like urban–rural coordination, the national urbanization plan proposes to break down the barriers that still separate urban and rural sectors, including the management of China's population, land, and governance. The main difference is that the national urbanization plan has more explicitly foregrounded the ultimate goal of these policies: the expansion of the party–state's program of urbanization to encompass rural territories and populations.[23] Meanwhile, many parts of the national urbanization plan that have been highlighted as distinctive departures—such as support for mass urban migration and the linking of rural urbanization to the growth of domestic consumer demand—can also be found in the earliest articulations of urban–rural coordination (Ma 2006, 82). New-type urbanization is therefore best understood as an intensification of the policies begun under urban–rural coordination, and its forthright rhetoric—its bold call for a new type of urbanization that encompasses rural areas—reflects the extent to which the underlying goals of urban–rural coordination have taken root in the party–state.

Experiments in Urban–Rural Coordination: Chongqing and Hailong

While national policy sets the direction and tone of social transformation in China, the size and complexity of the Chinese polity mean that urban–rural coordination is not a monolithic enterprise, and its ultimate outcome is far from a foregone conclusion. Like all of the national government's policy priorities, urban–rural coordination relies on interpretation and implementation by cadres at each level of the locally fragmented party–state, all of whom have their own interests and agendas that do not always conform to those of the national leadership (Lieberthal and Oksenberg 1988). While principals at higher levels of the party–state

	China	Chongqing	Hailong
2002		Huang Zhengdong named party secretary Wang Hongju named mayor	Administrative village formed through merger Yan Jing named party secretary
2003	Hu Jintao named president Urban-rural coordination first announced	Work begins on 2007 master plan	Land management corporation formed First manufacturers move to village
2004	First annual Number One Document released		
2005	Socialist new countryside launched Abolition of agricultural taxes announced	Wang Yang named party secretary Second ring road opens	
2006			Chongqing party secretary first visits village
2007	Urban-Rural Planning Law revised	Chongqing designated as pilot area for urban-rural coordination Bo Xilai named party secretary Master plan approved	New village center built, including Hailong Square and Easy Street
2008		Land reform launched	
2009		Rural planning division founded Second ring road completed	
2010		Huang Qifan named mayor Household registration reform launched	Central party research team writes report on village's development
2011		Master plan revised	Village "relaunch" announced Village development plan approved Work on statutory plan begins
2012		Bo Xilai removed as party secretary; succeeded by Zhang Dejiang (interim) Sun Zhengcai named party secretary	Demolition for Hailong City begins in earnest

	China	Chongqing	Hailong
2013	Xi Jinping named president Beautiful countryside initiative launched Belt and Road Initiative announced		Statutory plan approved Construction of Hailong City begins Shareholding cooperative formed
2014	New-Type Urbanization plan released		
2015			Hailong Avenue completed
2016		Zhang Guoqing named mayor Chengdu-Chongqing regional plan released	
2017		Chen Min'er named party secretary	
2018	Rural revitalization initiative launched		Residents move into first phase of Hailong City

Figure 1. Timeline of Urban–Rural Coordination. This timeline records key policies and events for the implementation of urban–rural coordination at three scales: China (national), Chongqing (municipal), and Hailong (village). It begins in 2002 with the founding of Hailong Village (the year before the national announcement of urban–rural coordination) and ends in 2018 with the completion of the initial phase of Hailong City.

hierarchy often have the power to enforce strict compliance, they also rely on the cooperation and discretion of distant agents, whose control over local political and economic resources can enable them to stall, subvert, or otherwise manipulate policy initiatives to their own ends (Lieberthal and Oksenberg 1988). Even China's citizens, who are sometimes represented as relatively powerless, have tools of resistance that allow them to exact concessions from the local party–state or changes in policy implementation (O'Brien and Li 2006; cf. Scott 1976). Moreover, when major reform programs like urban–rural coordination destabilize the existing rules of the game—for instance, by disassembling the conceptual binary that has defined Chinese society for generations—it opens a window for other actors to advance their own preferred alternatives. This is particularly so given China's long tradition of making policy through experimentation, in which national policy is formulated iteratively through

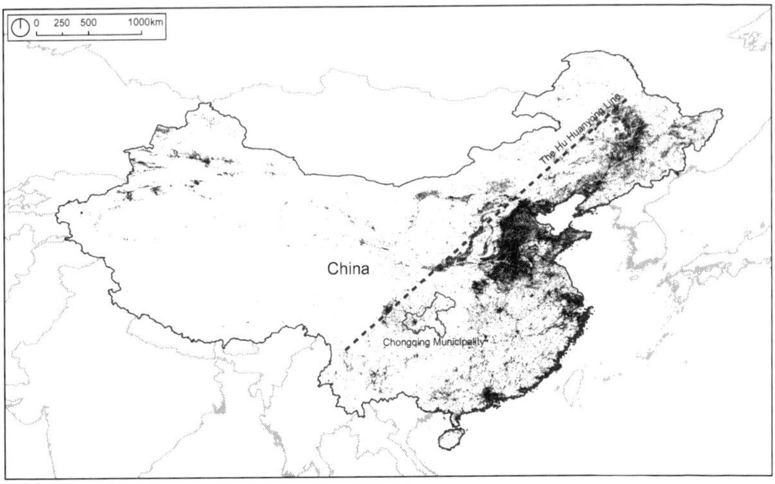

Figure 2. Chongqing Municipality and the Hu Huanyong Line. Chongqing, a provincial-level municipality, is located in China's mountainous southwestern interior. Chongqing lies near the Hu Huanyong Line (first postulated by the eponymous geographer in 1935), which divides the nation's territory roughly in two. Nearly 95 percent of China's population lives to the east of the line. The shaded areas of the map represent built-up areas as of 2010.

the selective adoption of repeated, parallel local experiments (Heilmann 2011; Heilmann and Melton 2013). The complicated process of policy implementation is therefore open-ended and underdetermined, and it is at the stage of experimentation, as local actors first grapple with the implications of urban–rural coordination and before the new rules of urbanization are settled, that the messy trade-offs and political choices involved with the program become clearest.

This book investigates the process of interpretation, implementation, and contestation by which urban–rural coordination is made a reality on the ground. This means turning away from the rarefied air of national policy makers in Zhongnanhai and toward the stifling summer heat of Chongqing, where some of the earliest and most consequential experiments in urban–rural coordination took place. In 2007, China's State Council designated the western municipalities of Chongqing and Chengdu as the first two experimental areas for urban–rural coordination (Figure 2). As a provincial-level municipality, a status granted to only three other cities in China, Chongqing is under the direct supervision of

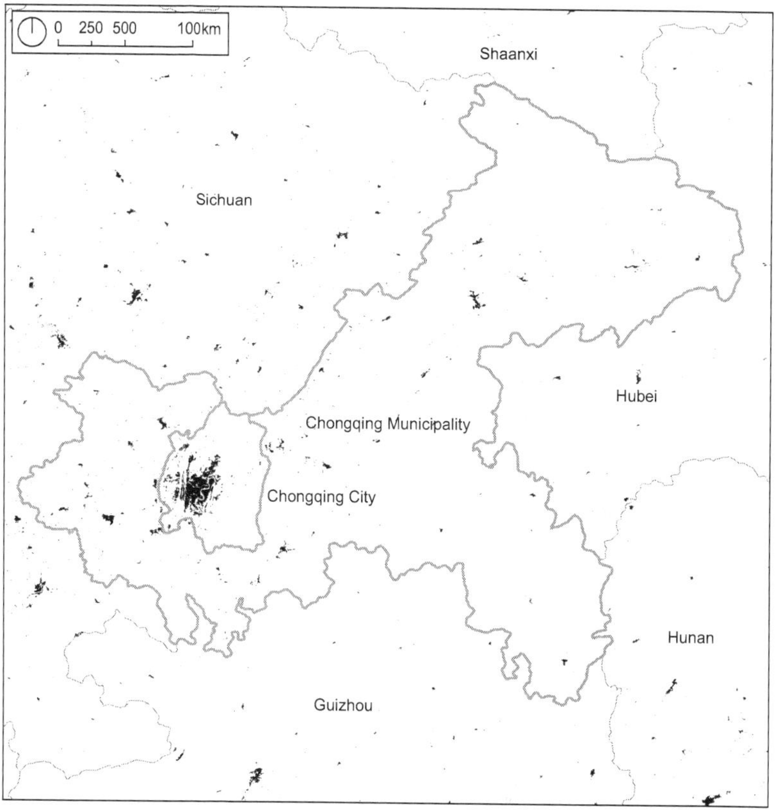

Figure 3. Chongqing Municipality and Chongqing City. The city of Chongqing is located in the southwest of the municipality and includes the majority of Chongqing's urbanized areas. The shaded areas of the map represent built-up areas as of 2010.

the State Council and enjoys significant development powers over a wide hinterland. Measured by its jurisdictional boundaries, Chongqing is one of the world's largest cities, covering more than 82,000 square kilometers (approximately the size of Ireland) and including more than 30 million people. Even the eponymous municipal seat comprises 5,500 square kilometers and about 7 million people (Figure 3), a population approximately equivalent to Hong Kong's but spread across an area nearly five times the size. Chongqing's scale makes it the largest of China's early experiments in urban–rural coordination; moreover, as Chongqing officials are fond of arguing, Chongqing is like a microcosm of China. In the words of one

Chongqing planning official, "All of the nation's problems are concentrated here, and the gap between urban and rural is extremely wide. So, the results of our experiments should be applicable for the entirety of the country. If Chongqing can coordinate urban and rural, all the other parts of China should be able to do it too."[24] Most prominent among these experiments were Chongqing's two marquee reform programs: land reform and household registration reform. The former bypassed the administrative firewall that separates urban and rural land by providing a market for the transfer of development rights from rural areas to urban areas, while the latter challenged the administrative separation of rural and urban people by offering rural people a way to convert their rural registration to urban status. Chongqing's experiments in urban–rural coordination also included less prominent recalibrations of China's urban–rural relations, such as new mechanisms for the distribution of investment capital to rural areas and the expansion of urban planning processes to rural villages. The municipality also sought to address urban–rural imbalances through accelerated sociospatial transformation, for instance by concentrating the majority of its population in a "one-hour circle" around the main city of Chongqing while depopulating its rugged hinterland.

China's experimental policy making also appears in a different, grassroots form exemplified by Hailong Village, a rapidly transforming administrative village on Chongqing's urban–rural edge (Figure 4). In this version of experimentation, entrepreneurial local cadres push the boundaries of established practice, experimenting with policy without necessarily receiving an official remit to do so. In some cases, these policy entrepreneurs actively seek to legitimize their experimental practices by representing them as part of the latest national policy platform. In other cases, the experiment is "discovered" by higher-level leaders and retroactively branded as a model for emulation and propagation. Hailong Village pursued both avenues of grassroots policy experimentation. Village cadres sought to legitimize their entrepreneurial responses to China's rural development crisis by appealing to the authority of urban–rural coordination and rescaling Chongqing's own policy experiments to the level of the village. Their success in driving the village's rapid urbanization also drew the attention of highly placed provincial and national leaders, including both Bo Xilai (then Chongqing's party secretary and a candidate for China's Politburo Standing Committee) and Xi Jinping (then China's

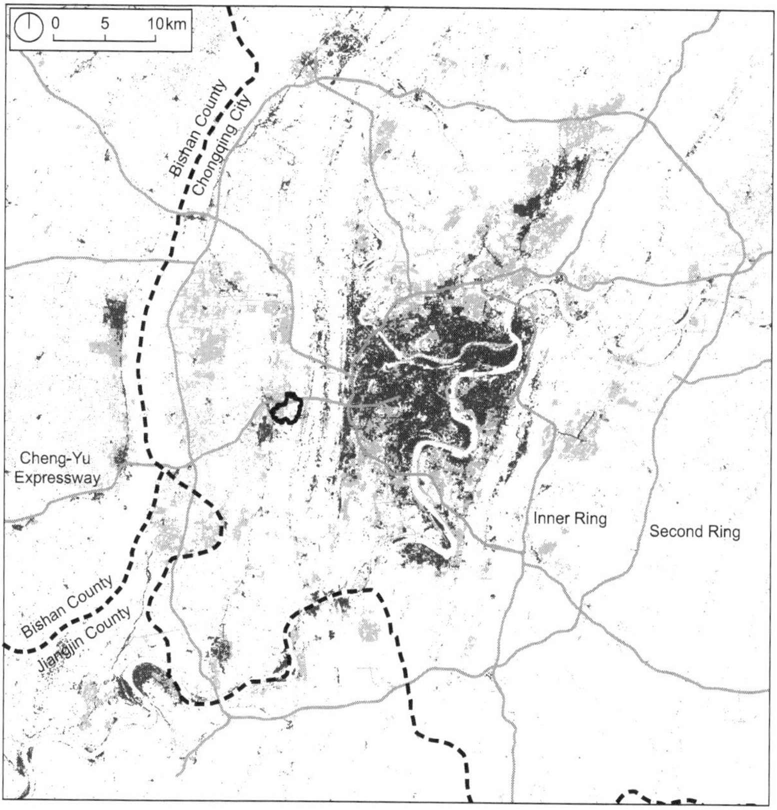

Figure 4. Chongqing Morphology. The primary axes of growth in Chongqing are in the west and north of the city, where land is relatively flat. Hailong Village (outlined with a solid black line) is located on the rapidly expanding western periphery, adjacent to the Cheng-Yu Expressway. Built-up areas from 2000 are represented in dark gray, while newly built-up areas in 2010 are represented in light gray.

vice president), resulting in the establishment of Hailong as an experimental site for grassroots village development in the context of urban–rural coordination.

If Chongqing is a microcosm of China's urban–rural system, then Hailong is a microcosm of the nation's urbanization process, transforming from agricultural to industrial to tertiary within the span of just a decade. The village is approximately 400 hectares in size, located 22 kilometers to the west of Chaotianmen, the tip of the Yuzhong peninsula and the symbolic center of Chongqing. Administratively, it is part of Baishiyi Town in Jiulongpo District, both of which were also designated strategic sites for Chongqing's urban–rural coordination program (Figure 5). From the east of Hailong rises Zhongliang Mountain (Figure 6), a north–south ridge that divides the historical extent of downtown Chongqing from its relatively flat western periphery, now an area of rapid urban expansion dubbed West City. Like other villages across China's mountainous western interior, Hailong missed the golden era of rural growth experienced by coastal villages in the 1980s. In the late 1990s, a newly completed expressway tunnel meant that Hailong was suddenly just a 20-minute drive from central Chongqing. But by 2001, Hailong was still a collection of impoverished agrarian settlements with fewer than 2,000 residents, most of whom had migrated to China's coastal provinces in search of work.[25] In many ways, Hailong thus epitomized the rural development crisis of the late 1990s and early 2000s. By 2011, a decade of industrialization had turned its relatively flat western third into a densely settled industrial estate (Figure 7). Population increased to 16,266, including 2,877 registered villagers and 13,389 long-term migrants, most of whom hailed from other parts of Chongqing and neighboring Sichuan.[26] Hailong's rapid urbanization during the initial decade of urban–rural coordination makes it a particularly revealing case for investigation, as does its liminal condition at Chongqing's urban–rural edge, where the disjuncture between urban and rural categories and the unruly reality of urbanization processes is most apparent (Roy 2011). The friction of the urban–rural edge exposes the instability and mutual constitution of urban and rural categories, creating seams within which actors can experiment with newly emergent forms of sociospatial transformation (Simone 2010). These were the opportunities navigated by village inhabitants—often forgotten in elite-led processes of experimentation—who found creative new ways to stay afloat amid Hailong's turgid and ever-shifting landscape.

Investigating China's Urban–Rural Relations under Urban–Rural Coordination

This book intervenes in a growing Anglophone literature that explores the implementation of urban–rural coordination and its subsidiary programs. Some of these studies praise the economic necessity, social comprehensiveness, and political progressivism of the experimental initiatives in Chongqing and Chengdu (Cui 2011; Gore 2012; Huang 2011; Liu et al. 2016; Ye and LeGates 2013). Other scholars focus on individual policies, such as

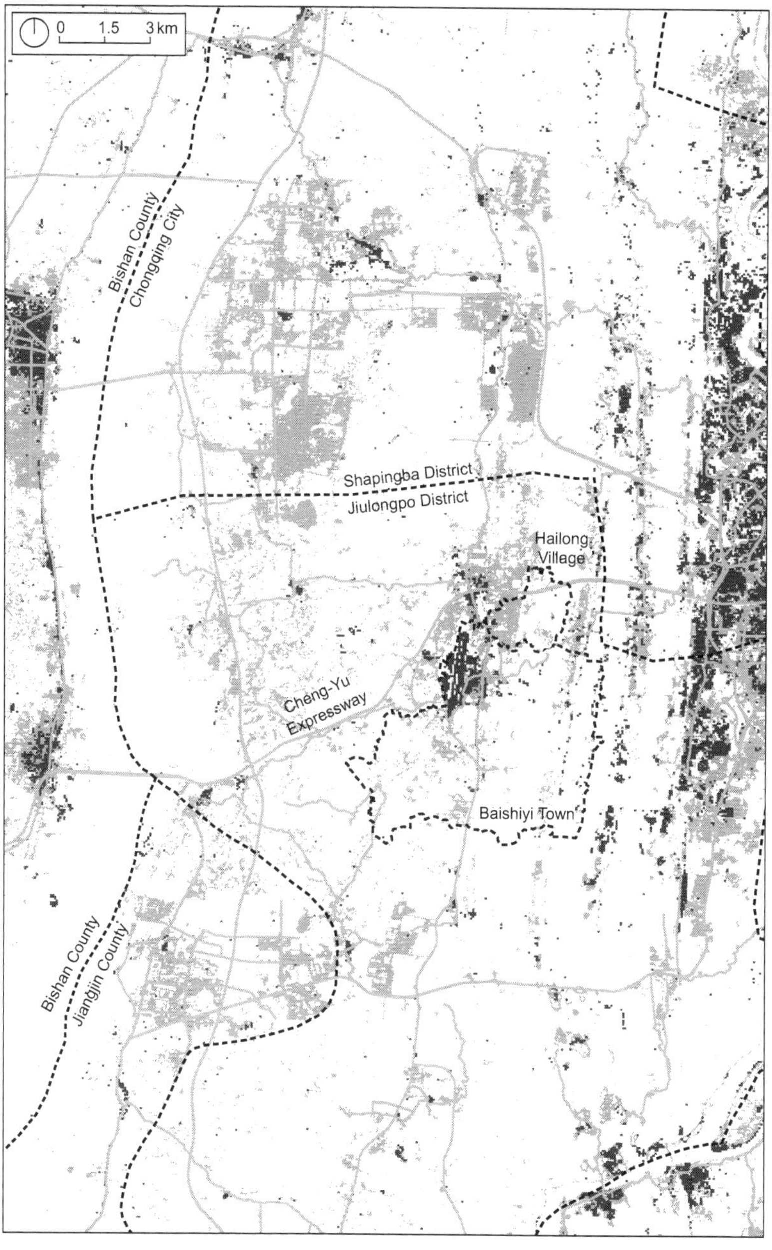

Figure 5. Hailong Village and West City. The administrative village of Hailong is located in Baishiyi Town, Jiulongpo District. Its development has been part of a faubourg-style expansion at the exit of the Zhongliang Mountain tunnel. Further north, recent urban development shows the planned expansion of West City through the construction of the University Town and the Xiyong Free Trade Zone. Built-up areas from 2000 are represented in dark gray, while newly built-up areas in 2010 are represented in light gray.

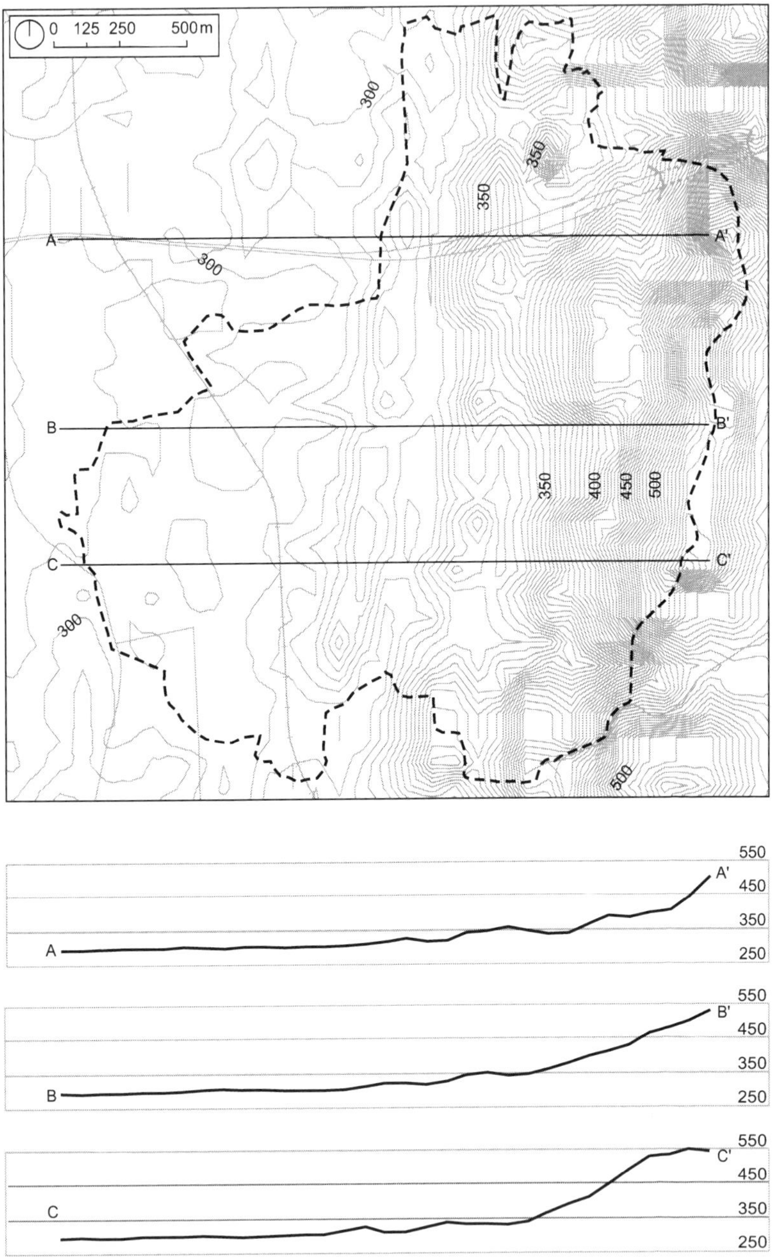

Figure 6. Village Topography. Hailong's western third is relatively flat with steeper land to the east, rising up to Zhongliang Mountain. Two smaller ridges run down the middle of the village, separating the more accessible west of the village from the hillier interior.

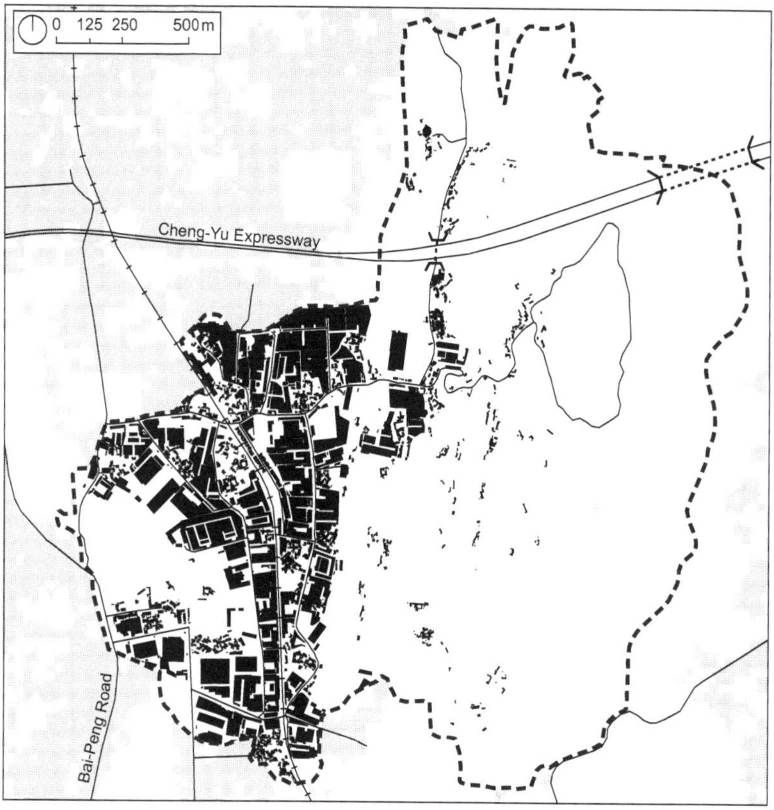

Figure 7. Village Settlement (2010). This figure–ground drawing shows Hailong's built fabric in black and the approximate extent of surrounding development in gray. Development has been concentrated in the flatter and more accessible western third of the village. The Cheng-Yu Expressway bisects Hailong's northern section.

land reform (Huang et al. 2014; Shi and Tang 2020), household registration reform (Cai 2011; Wang 2010), public housing (Zhou and Ronald 2017), village consolidation (Huang et al. 2013), and the socialist new countryside (Ahlers and Schubert 2010; Su 2009). While these authors offer important evidence to contextualize the analysis pursued here, the resulting picture is necessarily fragmentary and leaves the larger implications of urban–rural coordination for rural lives and livelihoods unexamined. This results in part from a tendency to adopt the party–state's own representation of urban–rural coordination, its objectives, its implementation, and the internal relations of its various parts.[27] By contrast, a range of more critical engagements with urban–rural coordination have treated party–state rhetoric as a set of claims to be interrogated and tested. Much as this book aims to do, these authors have scrutinized the gaps between the stated objectives and the actual outcomes of individual policies; the uneven implementation of urban–rural coordination, as different actors manipulate new policies in service of their own interests and objectives; and the cumulative effects of parallel programs that interact in unpredictable ways. Many of these contributions suggest outcomes that resonate with the findings discussed in the following pages. These include, for instance, the emergence of new understandings of the rural that increasingly reflect urban positionalities (Bray 2013b; Chen, Zinda, and Yeh 2017; Wilczak 2017), the widening and stiffening of the sociospatial gaps between urban and rural areas (Abramson and Qi 2011; Cheung 2012; Wilczak 2017), the decreasing governance capacity and social cohesion of village communities (Chen 2014; Looney 2015; Yep and Forrest 2016), the growing exploitation of village residents by local governments (Chuang 2014; Zhang 2018), and the intensifying efforts of diverse actors to manipulate these shifting conditions in their own interests (Zeuthen 2012). Taken together, these critical engagements with urban–rural coordination point toward a more fundamental and wide-reaching transformation that this book seeks to document: in a polity that has been built on the assumption of urban–rural difference, changing the terms of urban–rural relations means changing the very foundations of society.

In pursuit of a holistic account of China's ongoing transformation, this book contextualizes the implementation of urban–rural coordination in a more expansive set of questions about the evolution of urban–rural relations in contemporary China. During the early reform era, investigations of China's urban–rural relations were often framed by the "urban bias" hypothesis in the wider field of development studies, focusing on both the inequalities produced by socialist policy and the rural prosperity promised by economic reform (Kirkby 1985; Nolan and White 1984; Zweig 1987). The inherently problematic nature of China's urban–rural relations did not gain traction in the Anglophone literature until the mid- to late 1990s (Chan 1994; Guldin 1996, 1997a), as accelerating urbanization precipitated increasingly evident urban–rural imbalances, including many of the same contradictions and crises that ultimately inspired urban–rural coordination. This was when terms such as "urbanization from below" (Ma and Fan 1994) and "village-in-the-city" (Xiang 1999) first entered the English lexicon. Derived from parallel shifts in Chinese usage (Gu and Li 1998; Yang 1996), these new terms described emergent patterns of rural transformation that did not fit the dominant, city-centric narrative of Chinese urbanization or the state-defined urban and rural categories on which that narrative was based.[28] Defining urbanization in China became newly problematic, as researchers highlighted the insufficiency of the state's sharp categorical and statistical divisions, which no longer reflected the indeterminacy and hybridity of people's lives (Chan 1994; Guldin 1997b, 265; 2001, 126; Hoffman and Liu 1997, 155–56; Zhang and Zhao 1998). Yet China's administrative distinctions between urban and rural continued to produce indelible consequences, especially for the millions of migrants living on both sides of the urban–rural divide (Chan 1994; Solinger 1999). The mismatch between China's urban categories and its urban processes thus resulted in an increasingly apparent contradiction: China's urban and rural categories *over*-determine livelihoods and life chances, but they simultaneously fail to capture the *under*-determined nature of urbanization as a set of social and material processes.[29] Though not always explicitly stated, the effort to resolve this contradiction and restore conceptual coherence to Chinese urbanization has served as one of the primary motivations for an entire generation of urban scholarship, just as a similar set of tensions has inspired the party–state's program of urban–rural coordination.

To resolve the contradiction between China's urban categories and processes scholars have variously redefined, complicated, and recombined China's existing categories to more accurately reflect the sociospatial complexity of urbanization. Much of this literature does not explicitly mention urban–rural coordination or its subsidiary programs. Nonetheless, insofar as these strategies engage with the same fundamental problematic—that is, the imbalance in China's urban–rural relations—they point toward some of the potential avenues (and pitfalls) for investigating urban–rural coordination and its larger implications. The first of these strategies redefines the rural as a distinct mode of social and economic organization producing processes of urban transformation equivalent to and distinct from those originating in China's cities

(Guldin 2001; Lin 2009). This approach thus starts from China's existing urban and rural categories and the indelible divide they produce in Chinese society while reconceptualizing this divide as a distinction between two different urban processes rather than between fixed urban and rural states. The result is a bifurcated mode of urbanization, variously framed as an opposition between "top-down" and "bottom-up" urbanization (Lin 2009, 11; Tian, Ge, and Li 2017), city-based urban expansion and rural urbanization in situ (Guldin 2001; Zhou 1997; Zhu 2002), "citization" (*chengshihua* 城市化) and "townization" (*chengzhenhua* 城镇化) (Guldin 2001), or state-led and society-driven urbanization (Lin 2007).

A related strategy complicates the urban–rural binary by emphasizing the internal heterogeneity of the rural and the varied ways in which urbanization unfolds outside of cities. This includes spatial typologies that distinguish "developed" or coastal areas from "undeveloped" regions in China's interior (Guldin 2001, 16), "inner suburbs" (*jinjiao* 近郊) from "outer suburbs" (*waijiao* 外郊) (Zhou and Logan 2008), or "villages-in-the-city" (*chengzhongcun* 城中村) from "villages beside the city" (*chengbiancun* 城边村) and "villages outside the city" (*chengwaicun* 城外村) (Wang, Wang, and Wu 2009). By internally differentiating the rural along a continuum of urban proximity, it thus becomes possible to analyze more precisely the diversity of ways in which rural areas experience and respond to processes of urbanization (Hsing 2010, 186–87).

Finally, a third strategy recombines China's existing urban and rural categories "to overcome black/white, either/or portrayals of urban transformation" and more faithfully account for the indeterminacy of transformative processes (Kipnis 2016, 10). For instance, by likening China's urban–rural relations to the interdependence of yin–yang relations, some scholars have argued for the mutual embeddedness of urban and rural as entangled polarities in a larger "urban-*cum*-rural" unity that is always in the process of becoming (Kipnis 2016, 14; Tang 2019, 473–74). Others have argued for "*desakotas* with Chinese characteristics" (Guldin 2001, 18; Heikkila, Shen, and Yang 2003), borrowing a neologism that describes the disappearance of the urban–rural binary through a recombination of the Indonesian terms for "village" *(desa)* and "town" *(kota)* (McGee 1991). More concretely, this approach is often articulated in relation to rural–urban migration and leads to predictions that China's old categorical divisions between urban and rural populations will break down or disappear in the face of the processual continuity and complexity of urban transformation (Cai 2011; Guldin 1997b, 272; 2001, 131; Kipnis 2016, 230; Wang 2010).[30]

As municipal officials, village cadres, and village inhabitants in Chongqing and Hailong grappled with the implications of urban–rural coordination, they pursued analogous strategies of categorical redefinition, complication, and recombination. Unlike scholars of Chinese urbanization, however, these actors were not trying to address the tension between categories and processes as a problem of analysis but as a problem of practice.[31] This distinction has at least two important implications for understanding urban–rural coordination. First, whereas analytical engagements with China's urban–rural relations are necessarily limited to conceptual refinement, the actors in Chongqing and Hailong responded to urban–rural coordination dialectically, through both the recalibration of China's urban and rural categories and the transgressive transformation of the sociospatial landscape, including material and embodied practices of production, inhabitation, and mobility. Second, unlike the three analytical strategies outlined above, each of which aims to close the representational gap between China's urban categories and its urban processes, the actors in Chongqing and Hailong were not primarily concerned with eliminating or resolving this disjuncture but rather with manipulating and reshaping it in their own interests. This instrumentalization of urban–rural relations means that a shift in analytical perspective is required for the study of urban–rural coordination. First, urban–rural coordination demands a wider analytical lens, one that investigates both China's urban categories and its urban processes as potential sources of their mutual disjuncture. And second, instead of looking at the disjuncture as a problem requiring resolution, it is necessary to investigate the production of the disjuncture as an ongoing process through which the rules governing social life in contemporary China are made and remade. Thus, rather than proposing an alternative analytical strategy for resolving the contradictions inherent in China's urban–rural relations, this book investigates the ways in which those on the ground themselves responded to these contradictions and thereby produced the conditions of possibility for new (and newly contradictory) forms of Chinese urbanization.[32]

This shift in analytical approach leads to one of the central claims advanced in this book, the full implications of which I return to in the conclusion: the tension between China's urban categories and its urban processes is an important generative force in the production of urbanization, a dynamic I refer to as "disjunctural urbanization." Implicit in much of the scholarship on China's urban–rural relations is a shared assumption that the nation's urban and rural categories should faithfully describe its processes of sociospatial transformation. But the instrumentalization of urban–rural relations under urban–rural coordination exposes this mismatch between categories and processes as a feature of urbanization, not a bug. During the 1990s, it was the disjuncture between China's de jure categories of urban–rural separation and its de facto processes of urban–rural integration that drove accelerating urbanization. This process of rapid urbanization also produced trenchant inequities and instabilities that party–state leaders sought to address through urban–rural coordination, but this did not necessarily mean eliminating the mismatch between categories and processes altogether. Under urban–rural coordination, the actors in Chongqing and Hailong competed (and sometimes collaborated) to restabilize the mismatch between categories and processes in their own interests. On the one hand, these actors sought to extend urban processes of sociospatial transformation in order to bring together new combinations of resources that could benefit their agendas of personal and professional advancement. On the other, they tried to ensure their control over those resources by concentrating them within areas defined by categorical divisions that would exclude alternative forms of collective action. Contingent as they were on actors' relative power, these strategies achieved varying levels of efficacy and intersected in unpredictable ways, resulting in new disjunctures and newly uneven landscapes of opportunity that redistributed access to resources. These combinations of extension and concentration thus produced the fundamental politics of extraction and accumulation that are at the heart of urbanization everywhere (Brenner and Schmid 2015; Lefebvre [1970] 2003). This happened not in spite of the infidelity of China's urban and rural categories but rather precisely because those categories did not accurately describe the continuity and complexity of the sociospatial landscape. Far from an effort to eliminate the urban–rural contradictions arising from rapid development, urban–rural coordination is a process through which those contradictions are remade, resulting in new distributions of resources, new modes of collective action, and new forms of urbanization.

Overview of the Book

In what follows, I take a vertical slice through the Chinese polity, exploring three distinct layers of experimentation in the practices of municipal officials, village cadres, and village inhabitants, as well as their strategic interscalar encounters. These experimental practices constituted intersecting efforts to respond to China's rural development crisis and to harness the process of transformation launched by urban–rural coordination. I place these different efforts in a comparative framework that reaches across scales rather than across locales (Nader 1972; Robinson 2014), working to achieve analytical equivalence between actors despite the stark inequalities in their relative power and the efficacy of their strategies. In engaging these intersecting responses to urban–rural coordination, I present an account that moves between the vehicles and meeting rooms of municipal officials, the offices and banquet tables of village cadres, and the homes and workplaces of village inhabitants. Over the course of 18 months of fieldwork between 2010 and 2015, I conducted more than 200 interviews, including 33 conversations with planners and municipal officials, 45 with Hailong cadres, and 121 with Hailong inhabitants.[33] Grounded in an appreciation of the messy indeterminacy of social experience (Herzfeld 2005, 217), where decisive and consistent evidence is often elusive and authority is always contested, this book foregrounds the textual and oral narratives actors used to make sense of their transforming contexts. This means sharing theoretical and ethnographic authority with my interlocutors, allowing them room to advance their own understandings of what is unfolding while simultaneously maintaining a realistic skepticism of the persuasive intent and representational fidelity of their accounts. I therefore attend not just to what is said but also to how, where, and when—not to mention what is left unsaid. I also look beyond the discursive to address actors' practices and spaces through participant observation and spatial analysis. Participant observation coexisted with more formal conversations and included a range of idle moments and organized activities, such as the everyday (meals, games, and chores), the professional (meetings, field visits, and work), and the celebratory (festivals, outings, and weddings).[34] I also pursued a parallel track of spatial analysis, including actors' spatial representations and my own survey of Hailong's sociospatial transformation.[35] This spatial evidence is interwoven with the ethnography produced through interviews and observation, supplying a visual account that both complements and speaks back to the textual narrative. The result is a contingent interpretation of the experimental implementation of urban–rural coordination in Chongqing and Hailong—contingent on the perspectives various actors chose to share during my fieldwork, on the existing scholarship and theory available to guide my analysis of the evidence, and on my own peripheral positionality as a temporary visitor with biases and preconceptions borne from outside China.

The first three chapters of the book consider the different challenges municipal officials, village cadres, and village inhabitants faced as they responded to China's rural development crisis and tried to make sense of urban–rural coordination, following their distinct narratives of transformation and their visions for China's urban future. Chapter 1 begins with the municipal planners and policy makers responsible for implementing Chongqing's urban–rural coordination programs. In destabilizing the urban–rural binary, urban–rural coordination threatened the very foundations of Chinese urban development and planning practice, which starts from the assumption of urban–rural separation. In response, Chongqing's planners and policy makers sought to reconceptualize rural villages as extensions of the existing urban system. These municipal officials complicated the rural by disciplining villages into functional typologies on the basis of their ability to provide products and services for urbanites. In chapter 2, Hailong's cadres confront their declining political authority as part of the rural development crisis, which they traced to China's bifurcated land system and the de-collectivization of village landholdings in the early 1980s. Adapting earlier experiments from China's coastal provinces, Hailong's cadres thus sought to re-collectivize village land, appropriating the land's value for redistribution among themselves and their clients and redefining the rural as a site of economic dynamism independent of the city. This bootstrapping approach to development resulted in a village-scale growth machine that allowed cadres to rebuild their authority by capturing land rents that could be invested in political patronage and urban spectacle. In chapter 3, Hailong's inhabitants—including both registered villagers and migrants from outside the village—grapple with their persistent exploitation within the system of urban–rural differentiation, developing adaptive responses that navigated the seams of urban–rural difference. Rather than embarking on a linear path of transformation from rural to urban, residents recombined China's urban and rural categories, entangling diverse people, resources, and locales into complex webs of urban–rural interdependence that were concretized through the spatial form of village communities and the spatial practices of village residents. By disconnecting residents from these networks and normalizing them into predefined urban (or rural) roles, municipal and village experiments in urban–rural coordination threatened these adaptive responses to marginality. In each of these chapters, actors navigate the implementation of urban–rural coordination by simultaneously pursuing novel forms of sociospatial transformation that bring together new combinations of resources and recalibrating urban and rural categories to ensure their ability to control the concentration and deployment of those resources.

The subsequent three chapters investigate how the practices of these different actors intersect in Hailong's sociospatial transformation, moving from the scale of the municipality and the process of planning, to the administrative village and its redevelopment projects, and finally to village communities and inhabitants' responses to displacement. Chapter 4 follows Hailong's "relaunch" and the ensuing village planning process, which sought to build on the support of national leaders by turning Hailong into a national model for village development. Serving to coordinate the interests of rival party–state actors, this process unfolded as a function of intraparty politics, with resources and powers bartered for discretionary control over planning outcomes. The eventual compromise between village cadres and municipal officials exposed both the political artificiality and the material efficacy of China's urban–rural divisions by dividing Hailong in two, half urban and half rural, with each half subject to a separate master plan. In chapter 5, village cadres navigate the gaps opened up through urban–rural coordination by creatively repurposing the municipality's reform policies in ways that simultaneously undermine municipal objectives. This included both the transformation of the village's collective landholdings into real estate, securing a partial escape from the conventional constraints on rural urbanization, and the transformation of Hailong's villagers into shareholders, replacing moral claims to rural welfare with financial stakes in village development. Together, these two initiatives provided the basis for the realization of Hailong City, through which cadres sought to redefine the village as a real estate enterprise and transcend China's urban–rural contradictions in a single, self-contained site. As village cadres began implementing their vision for Hailong City, including the demolition of existing neighborhoods, many inhabitants reacted with fear and trepidation. Chapter 6 explores villagers' responses to the end of the village and the displacement of both the village's institutions and its inhabitants. Villagers expressed their feelings through the language of ghosts, which indexed both villagers' nostalgic desires to return to the relationships and practices disallowed by Hailong's new form of urbanization and the traumatic disorientation that followed their exclusion from the decision-making processes that were reshaping the village. Villagers' "ghost talk" prescribed alternative strategies for responding to the disruptions of urban–rural coordination. Ultimately, most villagers chose exit, abandoning the disappearing village and reconsolidating their social worlds through their extended networks. Though the specifics of Hailong's experience are singular, the incipient end of villages as sites of grassroots social organization and their replacement by new corporate and market mechanisms largely controlled by the party–state is a potential future that rural people confront throughout China.

To conclude, I consider the implications Hailong has for broader understandings of urbanization, both in mainland China and beyond. Far from a natural outcome of development, Hailong's urbanization emerges as a politically contested process that conditions the lives and opportunities of inhabitants. To understand the process of urban–rural coordination, it is therefore necessary to recognize both the politics of China's urban and rural categories, which indelibly shape the conditions of possibility for urbanization, and the politics of sociospatial transformation, which inevitably exceeds the limits set by those categories. Making sense of Chinese urbanization thus requires more than the analytical refinement of conceptual categories. It calls for critical interrogation of the dialectical relationship between categories and processes and the social and political effects their disjunctures produce. While this approach is particularly suited to the study of China, where the party–state's hegemonic urban–rural categories and its dogged pursuit of rapid urbanization have produced persistent and unavoidable contradictions, similar dynamics can also be found in the wider field of urban studies and elsewhere among the rapidly urbanizing countries of Asia. This discussion therefore suggests a new Asian agenda for urban scholarship that foregrounds the dialectical tension between urban categories and urban processes as a central generative force in urbanization.

CHAPTER 1

Urbanization by Other Means

Planning under Urban-Rural Coordination

"Zoom out! Zoom out!" Duan Leishi, usually so soft spoken and sometimes stuttering, grew surprisingly strident as he gripped the steering wheel with one hand and gestured at the digital map with the other. I was trying to zoom in to display Hailong on Duan's tablet as the village passed by in a blur through the window. Hailong disappeared as we accelerated out of the Zhongliang Mountain tunnel and down the Cheng-Yu Expressway, finally breaking free of the traffic of old Chongqing and bursting into Chongqing's expanding future, dubbed West City. From Duan's admonishing tone, it was clear that my myopic focus on the village was missing the planner's-eye view that the map on his tablet computer offered. Off from work as a vice director in one of Chongqing's district planning bureaus, Duan was taking me on a weekend tour of the city; the digital map's synoptic aerial view was meant to guide me through our automotive journey. The outing was not a typical tour of Chongqing but rather a tour of Chongqing as imagined by its planners and policy makers. We would not be visiting any landmarks or noteworthy neighborhoods. We would not even be viewing the 892 square meter scale model of the main city, symbolically placed at the very tip of the Yuzhong peninsula. Duan insisted the model was too small—too zoomed in—to show Chongqing's planned future. Instead, Duan was taking me on a three-hour tour of Chongqing's two ring roads, the "inner ring" (*neihuan* 内环) and the "second ring" (*erhuan* 二环). The ring roads, Duan argued, would give us an introduction to what Chongqing was really about. We were on our way to the axis mundi of Chinese planning and policy.

As we exited from the Cheng-Yu Expressway and merged onto the second ring, Duan began to explain why he had brought me there: "This highway is the future boundary of the city." Chongqing's planners and policy makers referred to the city's "second ring era" (*erhuan shidai* 二环时代) to describe their plans for urban expansion—a fourfold increase in urban land use focused on the area between the two ring roads.[1] An important part of this peripheral expansion was "West City" (*xi cheng* 西城), a catchall term for a collection of new urban centers being built on the relatively flat land to the west of the historical city. This new city included existing settlements, such as Baishiyi and Hailong, as well as entirely new districts, such as the High Tech Zone and University Town, the outer limits of which were already pushing up against the second ring. Using the second ring road as a boundary for the city's expansion was not simply a rhetorical device. The municipality's 2007 master plan had drawn the urban construction boundary, which divided the city's urban interior from its rural hinterland, along the path of the second ring (Figures 8 and 9). Functioning much like a statutory growth boundary, the urban construction boundary defined the morphological limits of formal urban development, the remit of urban planning processes (because urban planning only covers formally urban land), and the proposed extent of state land ownership (because all urban land is state owned). In many of China's master plans, however, the urban construction boundary is little more than a red line drawn on a map and is regularly transgressed. As Duan Leishi described, Chongqing's new urban construction boundary would be different: the second ring would provide a "material boundary" (*shiti bianjie* 实体边界), manifested in the form of the eight-lane highway we were driving down.

As we drove along the second ring road, Duan Leishi carried on a debate with himself, acting as both critic and defender of the planning profession and the efficacy of the urban construction boundary. Educated at elite universities in both China and the United States, Duan was well versed in the arguments used to criticize Chinese planning; but he was also a senior planning official tasked with plan implementation, which made him committed to the profession's goals. This internal conflict was reflected in the importance Duan attached to the "material boundary" of the second ring road, which he hoped would overcome the shortcomings of China's urban planning. Like many Chinese planners, Duan criticized

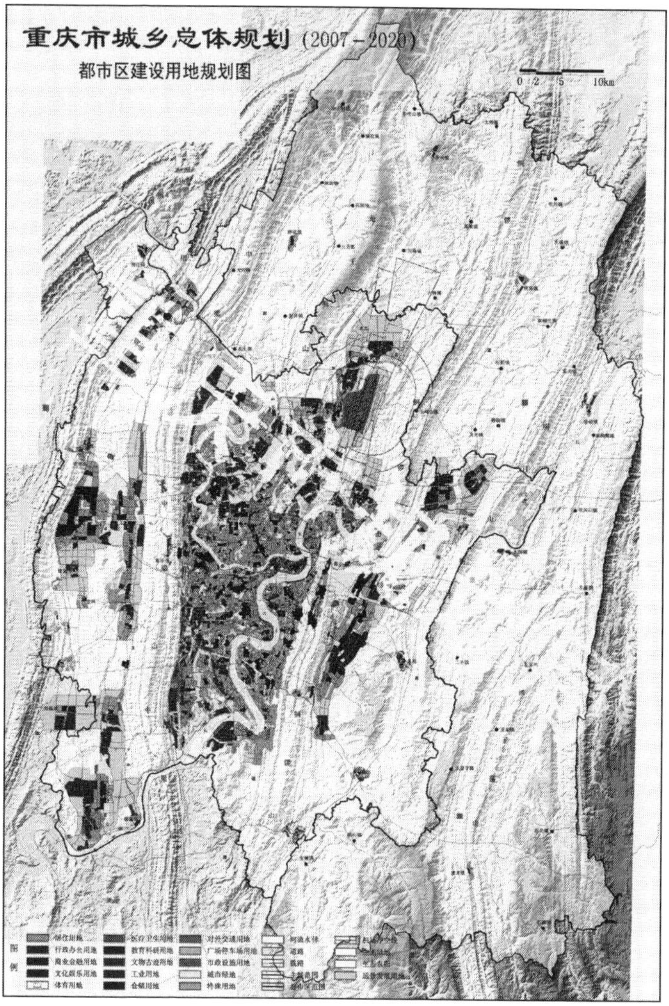

Figure 8. Chongqing's 2007 Master Plan: Metropolitan Area. The land use plan for the main city of Chongqing identified new areas for periurban expansion, particularly in Chongqing's west. Courtesy of Chongqing's municipal planning bureau (http://www.cqupb.gov.cn/2008new/ghzs.aspx).

Chinese planning for its inability to control urban development (Zhao 2008; Zhu 2005; see also Leaf 1998). For evidence of this, planners have pointed to master plans that are out of date as soon as they are released, with the frequent transgression of urban construction boundaries cited as

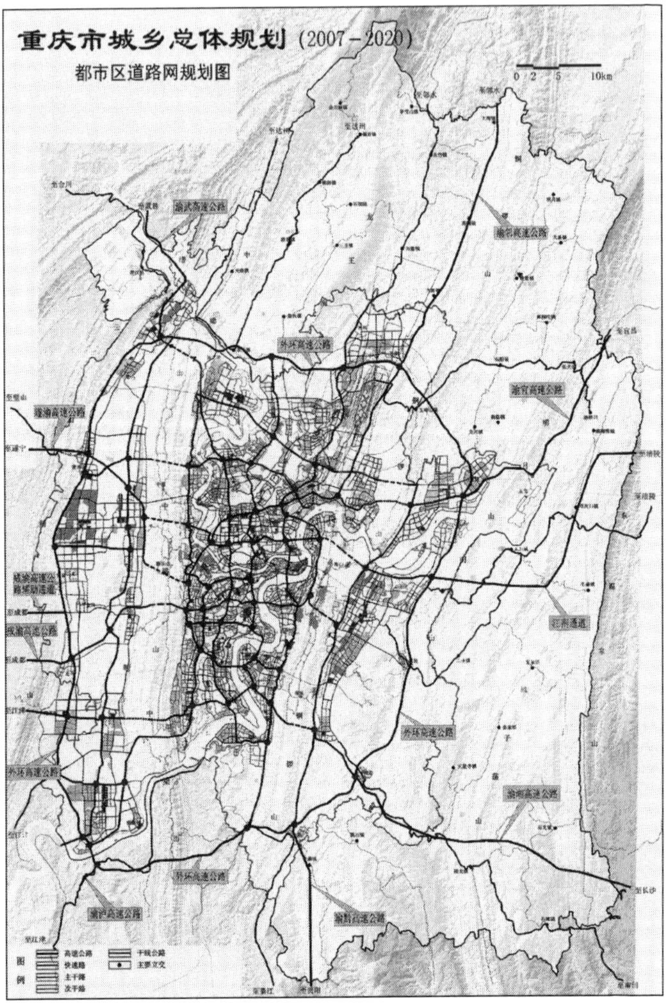

Figure 9. Chongqing's 2007 Master Plan: Road Network. The transportation plan shows the expanded second ring road encircling the main areas of new urban development. Courtesy of Chongqing's municipal planning bureau (http://www.cqupb.gov.cn/2008new/ghzs.aspx).

the most visible examples (Chen 2003; Ng and Wu 1995, 291). Concerns about planning efficacy emerged in the late 1990s and early 2000s as part of a larger self-critique among planners regarding their role in Chinese society and the absence of clearly defined "planning ethics" (*guihua daode*

规划道德 or *guihua lunli* 规划伦理) to guide their practice (Leaf and Hou 2006, 569). Struck by their inability to constrain the supercharged urbanization of the 1990s, planners questioned their complicity in the resulting social problems and contradictions, including China's growing urban–rural inequities (Leaf and Hou 2006, 568–659; Xu 2004; Zhang 2004). Thus, it was no coincidence that the planning ethics debate arose at the same time as urban–rural coordination, which also responded to the monomaniacal commitment to urbanization and economic growth that dominated the 1990s.

In search of a resolution to this crisis of professional identity, many of China's planners turned to principles of "scientific rationality" (*kexue lixing* 科学理性) as the most reliable basis for planning ethics (Dai 2004; Guo 2004; Xu 2004). Echoing arguments that China's rapid urbanization has resulted from a process of marketization during the reform era (Naughton 1995; Zhu 1999), and drawing on European and American precedents of comprehensive rational planning (Klosterman 1985; Skjei 1976; Webber 1963), many Chinese planners concluded that their societal role is to regulate and control the market (Shi 2004; Zhu 2005). Grounded in the new discipline of "urban science" (*chengshi kexue* 城市科学), planners thus sought to establish objective and universal laws of market-driven urbanization to ensure the predictive accuracy and "scientific quality" (*kexue xing* 科学性) of urban plans (Chen 2003; Shi 2003). Where planning diverged from these principles, China's planners often blamed the political intervention of party–state leaders, who manipulate planning processes to prioritize economic development over regulatory control (Guo 2004; Han and Liu 2009; Xu 2004). Here again, Chinese planners invoked the impartial objectivity of scientific expertise as an ethical basis for curbing the "irrational" (*fei lixing* 非理性) politicization of planning (Guo 2004; Xu 2004; Zou 2003; see also Bray 2013a).

Duan Leishi subscribed to the aspirations of scientific rationality, but he also worried that it might be a misguided basis for planning ethics. These concerns grew out of a different set of precedents from mid-twentieth-century Europe and North America, where the excesses of comprehensive rational planning and urban renewal sparked a grassroots backlash and a similar crisis of professional identity within planning (Davidoff 1965; Friedmann 1973; Jacobs 1961). For instance, some Chinese planning scholars argued that China's "professional planners should recognize the political nature of planning and acknowledge that the situation cannot be fully understood by scientific analysis alone" (Ng and Wu 1995, 288). Others emphasized that planners have a professional responsibility to serve the interests of their clients: government leaders (Zhao 2002). Similar sentiments were widely shared among senior Chinese planning officials, who complained that in China, where planning is a governmental function that serves to support economic growth, planning is inherently political, and scientific rationality is therefore an unrealistic theoretical ideal (Wu 2015; Zhao 2013). In Europe and North America, the tension between science and politics resulted in a turn toward democratic participation in planning (Healey 1996; Innes 1996), and planning scholars have advocated a similar embrace of participatory practices in China (Dai 2000; Liu et al. 2005; Ng and Wu 1995; Wang and Li 2009). In China's one-party authoritarian system, where local governments have few incentives to respond to citizens (Zhao, Liu, and Zhuang 2009), this has resulted in widespread tokenism and outright manipulation, leading some to conclude that Chinese planning cannot be fixed without systemic democratic reform (Leaf and Hou 2006, 574).[2]

For practicing planners like Duan Leishi, it is not a question of choosing between science and politics or finding some means of escape like participation or revolution. To practice planning in contemporary China is to navigate the dynamic tension between science and politics, to play one against the other. Like other planners in Chongqing, Duan was quick to label problematic planning outcomes as "insufficiently scientific" (*bugou kexue xing* 不够科学性). As I got in Duan's car in Three Gorges Square, he grumbled about the sacrifice he had made in coming to pick me up: "Shapingba has the worst traffic of any district in the city. There's traffic when you come, and there's traffic when you go!" Duan explained that the last director of the municipal planning bureau was corrupt and had changed the square's planning to allow overbuilding in the area, pushing traffic volume beyond the road network's scientifically determined carrying capacity. An hour later, we drove along the second ring road and looked out on a phalanx of apartment towers and construction sites advancing on the "material boundary" of the highway, with a scattering of self-built village homes standing between us and the battle line of backhoes. Duan admitted that there might be more to it than that: “Planning isn’t just a technical problem. . . . Numbers, statistics, spatial distributions, beautiful diagrams—we spend a lot of time on those things. We spend too much time on those things. In truth, we have overlooked many social and economic problems that planning should pay attention to.” For Duan, as for many of China’s planners, science and politics was not an either/or proposition; it was possible both to believe in the ideals of scientific rationality and to recognize the reality of planning politics.

Starting from the practices and experiences of Chongqing’s planners and policy makers, this chapter explores the mutual constitution of science and politics in contemporary Chinese planning. Through the practice of planning, the apparent impartiality of scientific rationality enables the realization of political objectives in urban development, while political intervention produces the conditions of possibility for the continued pursuit of scientific rationality. This intersection of science and politics is mediated through the urban construction boundary, meaning that the ethical angst that Chinese planners feel about their inability to keep urbanization within the urban construction boundary is not a symptom of failure but rather is part of the normal functioning of Chinese planning. This angst was intensified by urban–rural coordination, which destabilized the fixity of the urban construction boundary and extended planners’ remit beyond its confines, undermining the continued pursuit of scientific rationality. To rescue the ethical foundations of the profession, Chongqing’s planners faced the challenge of rationalizing the unruly rurality of villages that had never before been subject to the party–state’s regime of scientific rationality. Through their efforts at rationalization, they sought to reinscribe a new form of the urban–rural dichotomy, thereby restoring the fixity and stability necessary for the practice of scientific rationality. As described in the remainder of the chapter, these strategies ultimately produced rural simulacra: villages that embodied an urban imagination of rurality and thus actually functioned as extensions of the urban fabric.

Planning Rationality and the Rationalization of Planning

The intense obsession with scientific knowledge as a key ingredient in governance can be traced to China’s military humiliation during the opium wars, which the Self-Strengthening Movement (1861–95) blamed on technological backwardness and which the New Culture Movement (1910s) blamed on traditional values (Hu 2013; Mitter 2005; Scott 2008). Reformers advocated the embrace of "Mr. Science" and "Mr. Democracy" and a turn toward technical education. This included China's first generation of internationally trained city planners (Cody 1996), many of whom studied in Europe and the United States just as modernist rationalism was gaining ground and as urban planning was establishing itself as a profession. In the first decade of the socialist regime, urban planning and policy came under the influence of the Soviet Union, which sent hundreds of technical experts to advise the Chinese on socialist urbanization (Sit 1996). Guided by a mixture of CIAM's rationalist idealism and Leninism's faith in the rational ordering of human relations (French 1995; Lu 2006), Soviet urban planning of this period used scientific rationality to produce the socialist society of the future, a key dimension of which was the rationalization of urban–rural relations (Chan and Wei 2019; Leaf 1998).[3] After the 1950s, the Sino–Soviet split brought an end to this collaboration, but scientific rationality continued to guide the practice of urban planning in China until the Cultural Revolution (1966–76), when Mao Zedong disbanded the planning profession as part of his attack on the entrenched bureaucracy (Hou 2018).

With the advent of the reform period in 1978, China's leaders made "scientism" (*kexue zhuyi* 科学主义) their guiding ideology (Hua 1995). In part this can be understood as a return to the celebration of science that had guided China for nearly a century before the Cultural Revolution. But the CCP's embrace of scientism was also aimed at limiting the excesses of charismatic leadership, including Mao's cult of personality and the extreme politicization of life that had characterized the Cultural Revolution. In the apparent objectivity and neutrality of science, a new generation of "red experts" found a salve for the collective trauma of the previous decade and a guarantee of future stability (Andreas 2009, 234–35; Hua 1995). Reform-era scientism placed bounds on political behavior, but it did not go so far as to subordinate politics to science. The "-ism" (*zhuyi* 主义) of "scientism" suggested a scientistic ideology, an aestheticization of science that required political leaders to proclaim their faith in and maintain the appearance of scientific rationality but not necessarily to practice science or follow its dictates. On the contrary,

Deng Xiaoping's maxims, such as "development is the absolute principle" (*fazhan shi ying daoli* 发展是硬道理) and "seek truth from facts" (*shi shi qiu shi* 实事求是), placed the genius of political charisma and the party's political commitment to economic growth beyond the constraints of scientifically proven knowledge, a tendency further explored in chapter 2. Meanwhile, the urban planning profession—freshly reconstituted after its liquidation during the Cultural Revolution—eagerly subscribed to the return of scientific rationality. Planners drew on both the legacy of Soviet influence and the midcentury practices of comprehensive rational planning in Europe and North America to legitimize the profession's existence (Yu 2014, 53). The CCP's formulation of scientism in response to the excesses of Mao and the Cultural Revolution set the stage for the development of a symbiotic relationship between China's political leaders and its urban planners. This symbiosis is not unique to late socialist China; rather, it represents an intensified version of technocratic planning politics widely practiced in modern democracies (Flyvbjerg 1998).

Given their deeply held beliefs about the inviolability of scientific rationality, Chongqing's planners were remarkably open about their political dependence. In one conversation, a planning professor at Chongqing University dismissed my interest in village planning standards as immaterial: "The only thing that matters is what the party secretary says. Without that, everything else is meaningless." The importance of political direction was particularly evident with changes in leadership, as represented by the commonly invoked phrase, "switch a leader, switch a plan" (*huan yige lingdao huan yige guihua* 换一个领导换一个规划). Each of Chongqing's party secretaries brought a different vision for urban development, and when Bo Xilai fell in 2012, planning practice halted for months while the municipal planning establishment waited for new direction. Gu Yin, a planner in Chongqing's municipal planning bureau, explained how disruptive these changes were for planners: "This one person can have an enormous effect on urban planning. If the thinking of leadership changes, the whole aesthetics of planning changes. What kind of lifestyle is good, and what kind of lifestyle is bad. What kind of trees are good, and what kind of trees are bad." Gu went on: "Experts might provide some ideas, but the leaders ultimately have the power to decide."

These political interventions in planning practice are by no means value neutral; rather, "power procures the knowledge which supports its purposes, while it ignores or suppresses that knowledge which does not serve it" (Flyvbjerg 1998, 226). For instance, in a discussion among urban development experts in Chongqing, one planner talked about Bo Xilai's instrumental deployment of expert knowledge, bypassing the local planning and policy establishment when he found their positions inconvenient: "Bo always made up his mind first, and only then consulted the experts. He would bring in experts from Beijing to support his view." This kind of instrumental deployment of planners' expertise constitutes a post hoc rationalization masquerading as rationality (Flyvbjerg 1998, 2, 228), an operation that both obscures and legitimates the exercise of power (Habermas 1970, 81–82; Tambiah 1990, 146–47). It is in this way that the principles of scientific rationality enacted by Chinese planners—and by other experts within the Chinese policy establishment—become constitutive of the paternalistic politics of the one-party state. Without the benefit of democratic legitimacy or the populist charisma of Mao, China's political leaders instrumentalize the apparent objectivity and impartiality of scientific rationality to advance their political agendas while preempting the possibility of political contestation.

The Magical Thinking of the Urban Construction Boundary

When used to legitimize preexisting beliefs and commitments, "science" no longer denotes the operations of the scientific method as a basis for verifying the "objective truth" of the world. Rather, it functions as an ideological system, more closely resembling the practices of ritual and magic against which scientific objectivity is conventionally contrasted (Tambiah 1990, 10). In this light, "planning [can] be thought of as a kind of social ritual, the function of which is to legitimize government activities that, if frankly described, would arouse conflict and dissent" (Peattie 1987, 19). Planners are no longer dealing in cause and effect but rather in rhetoric and persuasion (Tambiah 1990, 80), repackaging the arbitrariness of political decisions in a more socially palatable and efficacious form. The ritualism of planning is not unique to China. Regardless of context, the proper enactment of prescribed planning processes helps to legitimate planning decisions, defuse potential dissent, encourage the consensual adoption of planning outcomes, and thus ensure the social efficacy of the plan. But the ritualistic dimensions of planning become especially prominent in polities that lack robust alternatives for legitimizing political decisions, such as democratic or communicative processes. Moreover, the role of ritual resonates culturally in China, where "ritual propriety" (*li* 礼) has historically played a prominent role in guiding social decision making (Fei [1948] 1992). In this respect, it may be helpful to compare contemporary planning to the oracular tradition in Chinese history. Much of city planning in early China was based on oracle readings, which sought to foretell future events and determine the auspiciousness of sites and orientations (Flad 2008, 55; Puett 2002, 2).[4] Like scientific rationality in contemporary urban planning, early Chinese divination rituals represented a rationalization of political decision making into a formal system (Puett 2002, 6–7), which then became a source of legitimacy and authority for those in power (Flad 2008, 403). Diviners who served political elites thus had little control over the results of divination, which were highly influenced by political direction (Flad 2008). The routinization of divination rituals was also aimed at constraining upstart rulers who claimed divine powers for themselves and thus threatened the stability of the existing political system (Puett 2002, 191, 258). Just as scientific rationality was meant to inoculate the Chinese polity against the transcendent charisma of a new Mao, so was the textual authority of divination rituals meant to subordinate efforts at self-divinization during the Warring States period.[5] This parallel with oracular divination suggests that the authority of planning practice does not derive from the principles of scientific rationality per se but from the ritual propriety with which those principles are enacted. Even when viewed as a ritualistic practice, planning is still rational, but its reasonableness derives from its adherence to the principles of China's development politics rather than its fidelity to any abstract principles of science.

The ritualistic and persuasive quality of planning becomes particularly evident in the designation of the urban construction boundary (Figure 10). In 1997, the State Council turned Chongqing into China's fourth provincial-level municipality, and Chongqing's leaders felt the city was too small for its important new role as the provincial capital. In 2001, Huang Qifan arrived from Shanghai to serve as Chongqing's deputy mayor with a remit to expand the city into a growth pole that could catalyze development in the rest of the municipality. But the State Council, which has the authority to "examine and approve" (*shenpi* 审批) Chongqing's master plans, was also nervous about overheated urban growth and rising rural unrest, meaning it was reluctant to allow an expansion of the city's urban construction boundary. In order to persuade the State Council to approve a fourfold expansion of the city's built area, Huang proposed to draw the urban construction boundary along the second ring road, the plan for which the State Council had already approved as part of the municipality's previous master plan, completed in 1998 (Figures 10, 11, and 12). In 2003, work began on Chongqing's new master plan in order to expand the reach of the second ring road and ritually enact the new growth boundary under the guise of scientific rationality (Figures 8, 9, and 10). At the same time, construction on the second ring road also commenced. The persuasiveness of Huang's choice—reflected in the plan's ultimate approval in 2007—thus relied less on the rational placement of the boundary than the fact that the boundary already existed as a construction site. Like the practice of ritual or magic, which does not directly affect the external world but can influence the intentions and motivations of other actors and thus their behavior in the world (Tambiah 1990, 81), the success of the road-cum-boundary was not measured by its actual ability to limit the process of urbanization but by its efficacy in assuaging the concerns of the State Council and thus persuading them to support the city's expansion.

Once the urban construction boundary was approved, Chongqing's planners began their work from the assumption of its efficacy. Like other forms of magical practice, the designation of the urban construction boundary functioned as "ritual action that is held to be automatically effective" (Tambiah 1990, 7). This teleological approach to planning served to collapse the messy and political process of urbanization into the abstract and timeless present of the plan. On the one hand, the designation of the urban–rural boundary made possible the fiction that the plan constituted an accurate representation of a scientifically certain and soon-to-be-realized future. Unevenness and uncertainty were reduced to a frictionless abstraction, a passive container to be filled in by political fiat—and by bulldozers and backhoes flattening Chongqing's hilly topography into a uniform horizon of development potential. The transition between

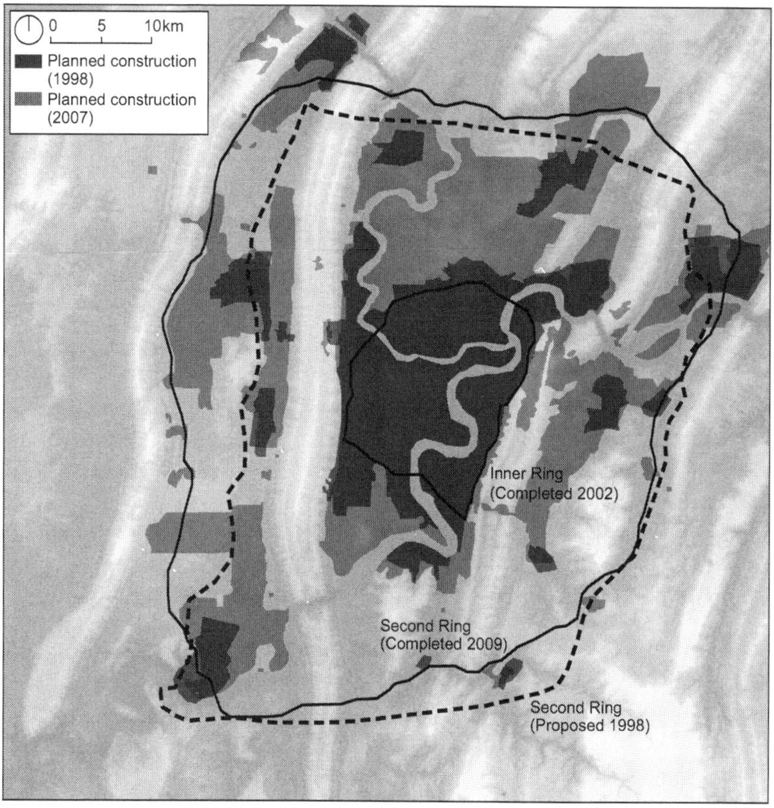

Figure 10. Chongqing's Master Planning: 1998 and 2007. This drawing provides a schematic representation of Chongqing's 1998 and 2007 master plans, along with the placement of Chongqing's two ring roads. The full extent of the planned urban construction area is shown in dark gray (1998) and light gray (2007). Two routes for the second ring road are shown; the dotted line shows the proposed route in the 1998 plan, and the outer solid line shows the final route, completed in December 2009.

the real present and the imagined future was elided into a mechanical process that had been scientifically predicted, controlled, and thus already achieved. Meanwhile, planners imagined a virtual end to historical change after the plan's realization. In describing the second ring as Chongqing's "final boundary," Duan Leishi quoted a speech Huang Qifan delivered early in the planning process for the 2007 master plan: "The Chongqing we build today will provide the city's framework and scope for a hundred years to come."

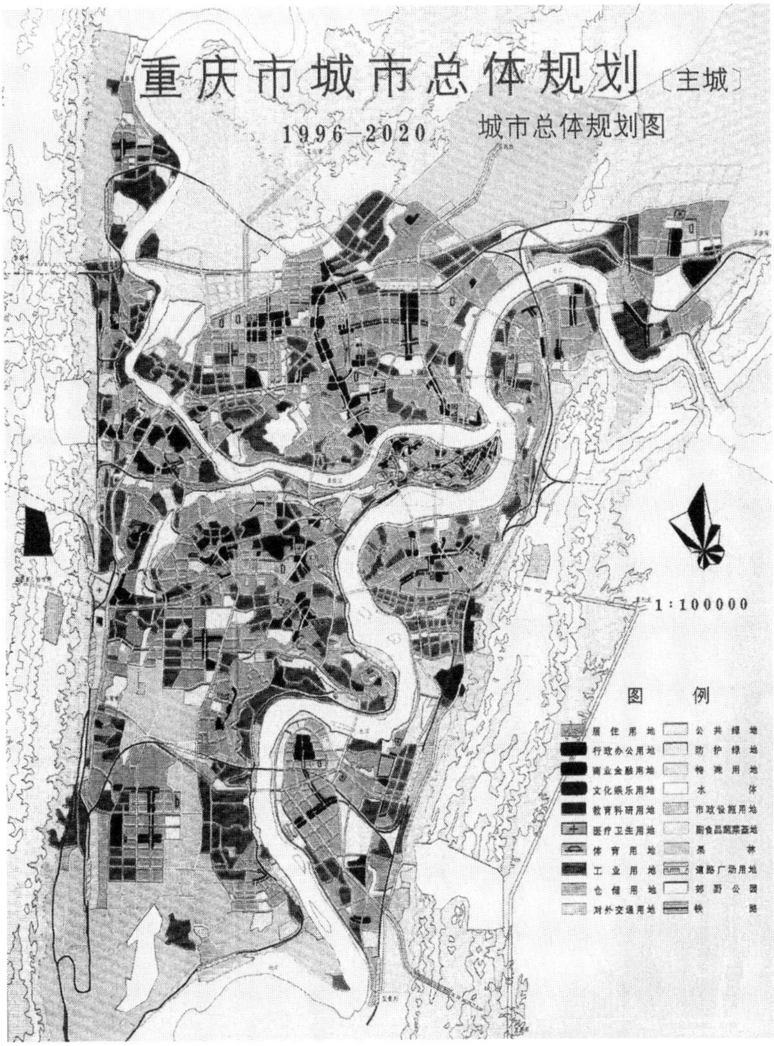

Figure 11. Chongqing's 1998 Master Plan: Main City. The land use plan for downtown Chongqing shows the planned extent of urban construction in 1998, with most development limited within the ring road and the city bounded on either side by mountain ridges. The Zhongliang Mountain tunnel and the beginning of the Cheng-Yu Expressway are shown center left. Courtesy of Chongqing's municipal planning bureau.

Figure 12. Chongqing's 1998 Master Plan: Metropolitan Ring. The land use plan for the area surrounding downtown Chongqing shows a series of distinct satellite settlements, including Baishiyi (center left), all connected by the initially planned route of the second ring road. The plan, still focused on development control in peripheral areas, does not demonstrate an orientation toward periurban expansion. Courtesy of Chongqing's municipal planning bureau.

In 2011, the urban–rural boundary still seemed indelible. Throughout our journey on the second ring, Duan kept denying the possibility that Chongqing would ever expand beyond it. He pointed to the west, past the mountains, "Now we're getting ready to build a third ring road. But the third ring doesn't have any bearing on the construction of the city. If the city were to reach the third ring, it would be humongous—6 or 7,000 square kilometers! That would be 60 to 70 million people! It would be like a country all its own." Duan continued, "The local government can't just expand and expand for hundreds of kilometers. We can't expand all the way to Chengdu!" By 2014, this impossibility had itself become the reality of the plan. China's State Council released the National Plan for New-Type Urbanization, which proposed to merge Chongqing and Chengdu into an urban megaregion with a projected population of 60 million. The ritualistic efficacy of Huang Qifan's material growth boundary had been superseded by the development vision of a higher political power legitimized through the scientific quality of its own planning process.

The Politics of the Urban Construction Boundary

The urban construction boundary works a reciprocal magic for China's planners, who rely on the boundary as a necessary precondition for the practice of planning. Without the urban construction boundary, planners would have nothing to plan, because under China's planning system, urban plans can only govern urban land. The boundary effectively allows planners to ignore the rural even as they seek to bring ever-more scientific rigor to the urban. For instance, while rural migrants provide cheap and disposable labor for China's manufacturing juggernaut (Chan 2010; Lee 2007), the household registration system allows planners to omit them from plans. There is thus no need to plan for additional schools or low-income housing, because migrants are not entitled to them (Leaf 1998; Solinger 1999). Similarly, cheap rural land enables continued urban expansion and props up municipal finances (Hsing 2010; Lin 2009), and all rural land must be expropriated by the state and then converted to urban status before it can be developed. Planners therefore can ignore informal development and sprawl in periurban areas because the potential for such development does not technically exist (Po 2008; Lin 2009, 81–82). Meanwhile, when the provision of urban infrastructure is surpassed by the demands of a growing urban population, new roads, railways, and electrical lines are built in rural areas to support the city, resulting in the displacement of rural people and the fragmentation of rural land. Urban–rural division thus provides a rural reservoir of labor, land, and resources that resolves the inevitable imbalances of scientific rationality and absorbs its inevitable externalities, stabilizing urban rationality even as the irrationality of the rural intensifies.

Despite the importance of the urban construction boundary for the continued pursuit of scientific rationality in Chinese planning, the boundary cannot itself be the product of scientific rational planning. As one of Chongqing's senior planners described, "The important things, like the scale and size of development, are all determined by local government leaders. Once they're decided, only then do you plan." As a profession that legitimizes its practice through an appeal to scientific principles, planning is incapable of justifying its own existence or determining the areas or processes that require planning, which are questions that demand recourse to ethical judgment (Rittel and Webber 1973; Schön 1983; Weber [1946] 2009). Because China's urban planners are primarily tasked with rationally guiding *urban* development, they must first be told what counts as urban (i.e., what is within the urban construction boundary). But this necessarily violates the principles of scientific rationality because it must ultimately rely on ideological assertions of value without any rational basis. The commitment to scientific rationality therefore entails an internal contradiction that can only be resolved by "decisionism" (Habermas 1973, 265). This decision is represented in the authoritative intervention of political leaders, like Huang Qifan, who "decide" the placement of the urban construction boundary that planners then use in their practice. Judged on its own terms, therefore, scientific rationality is itself a form of value-laden ideology, one that eliminates the possibility of rational choice and obscures the value judgments and political horse trading inherent in decision making (Habermas 1973, 265.).

Scientific rationality and political decisionism thus form a closed circuit of mutual legitimation that undergirds the paternalism of the Chinese party–state. Planners rely on party–state leaders to decide the object of scientific rationality, and party–state leaders depend on planners to rationalize their political agendas for development. One of the places this mutual obfuscation risks exposure is the urban construction boundary, where the arbitrary separation of urban from rural inevitably exceeds the limits of rationality. On the other side of the urban construction boundary, where it is no longer hidden by the logic of scientific rationality, urbanization emerges for what it is: intensely political and irrational. On my tour with Duan Leishi, the limits of scientific rationality were evident as we crossed the city's previous urban construction boundary, exiting off Chongqing's inner ring and into the two-kilometer tunnel that runs under Zhongliang Mountain and out toward the second ring. As we inched along, Duan again bewailed the traffic: "This tunnel is always crowded, because its designed usage has already been exceeded. It's not because of a lack of foresight, but rather because the speed of development was too fast." As in the case of magic, where failure never suffices to disprove the efficacy of ritual practice but is instead blamed on outside interference or inappropriate changes to the surrounding environment (Tambiah 1990, 21, 46), the rationality of the tunnel's planning was not to blame for its inefficacy. Instead, the tunnel was simply planned for a reality that had already been surpassed. Forty minutes later, we emerged into the light again, and Duan apologized for the delay: "If we had taken this tunnel back in the '90s it would have been easy—no traffic at all. It was only in the early 2000s that it started getting crowded." Implicit in Duan's statement was his belief that political intervention was to blame. After all, it was the early 2000s when Huang Qifan arrived in Chongqing and started pushing for urban expansion, making the 1998 plan and the tunnel (completed in 1995) obsolete. The certainty of scientific rationality only existed within the parameters defined by politics.

Urban–Rural Coordination and the Expansion of Scientific Rationality

Urban–rural coordination simultaneously threatened to destabilize the practice of scientific rationality and promised to expand it. By proposing to undo the inequalities of urban–rural difference in Chinese society, urban–rural coordination meant that the rural could no longer be so easily separated, ignored, and exploited in the pursuit of scientific rationality within urban areas. But urban–rural coordination also reconfirmed the party–state's commitment to the principles of scientific rationality as the best way to rationalize the rapid urbanization of the 1990s. To end the exploitation of rural areas in the service of urban rationalization, urban–rural coordination would ensure that both urban and rural areas were subject to the rigors of scientific rationality. This was the task of Chongqing's bureau of housing and urban–rural development, the office responsible for overseeing urban–rural coordination in the municipality. Tian Ye, a senior official in the bureau, was explicit about the rationalizing logic of urban–rural coordination: "The urban I can understand rationally. But I don't understand the rural. So we are forcing urban rationality onto rural areas." Under urban–rural coordination, the messy and irrational disorder of the rural would be made intelligible to local governments, enabling more effective regulation and control. Meanwhile, villagers' thinking would be transformed in order to facilitate their integration into urban-based markets, with the circulation of capital, labor, and goods extending from urban to rural areas. Chongqing's urban–rural coordination program thus represented a radical expansion of China's politicoscientific regime of urbanization to rural areas: "Urban–rural coordination and urbanization (*chengzhenhua* 城镇化) are not so different. If you view urban–rural coordination as an outcome, then urbanization is the only way to achieve that outcome. But," he qualified, "in truth, urban–rural coordination is also a process." What Tian elaborated was a political program to push the country asymptotically toward total urbanization. As a process, urban–rural coordination would increase China's urbanization rate from 50 percent to 70 percent and beyond.

What Tian Ye described was not so much rural development as urban expansion, in which cities would export their excess capital to passive rural areas: "It's not a mutual exchange. It's a kind of excess. The city gives the countryside what it has left over, and we coordinate that transfer." Through such transfers, urban–rural coordination would bring public services and infrastructure to rural areas and thus shrink the prosperity gap between urban and rural. But rural areas would not be given the capabilities to provide these public goods for themselves; instead, they would perpetually rely on the excess wealth of cities for their survival, reproducing and intensifying rural dependence. Most villages would only benefit indirectly, as development trickled down and as strengthened towns carried surrounding villages. Some Chongqing officials envisioned a future when most villages would cease to exist, and in 2012, Chongqing's interim party secretary, Zhang Dejiang, called for the municipality's most remote villages to be fully depopulated. This tendency toward accelerated urbanization and greater rural dependence was reflected in the municipality's plan for regional development, which called for the majority of Chongqing's population to be concentrated within a "one-hour circle" around the main city, defined by the radius of a one-hour car drive from downtown Chongqing. This included both the area within the second ring road and the nearest population centers, such as Hechuan and Jiangjin, which would grow into satellite cities. Meanwhile, Chongqing's mountainous and underdeveloped hinterland would be turned into sparsely populated zones of ecological protection and resource extraction.

Chongqing's two marquee reform programs, "household registration reform" (*hu gai* 户改) and "land reform" (*tu gai* 土改), were the primary mechanisms for facilitating this process of concentration. Under its household registration reform policy, the municipality created a path for all of the municipality's rural residents to gain urban registration by selling their rural land use rights and using the proceeds to purchase urban social welfare (Liu et al. 2016; Tian 2010). Under its land reform policy, the municipality allowed rural residents to return their allocated rural construction land to agricultural use, thereby producing a tradable asset, known as a "land note" (*dipiao* 地票), that permitted the buyer to use an equal amount of agricultural land elsewhere in the municipality for construction (X. Cai 2010; Yep and Forrest 2016; Zhang 2018). Both programs offered innovative, market-based approaches for reintegrating population and land management regimes that had long been divided along urban–rural lines, yet they also risked institutionalizing villages' and villagers' dependence on the municipal party–state. Because household registration reform required villagers to give up their land use rights, they could no longer return to farming, meaning that many were more reliant on wage labor for survival and thus were more directly exposed to the ups and downs of the labor market. Similarly, land reform involved transferring development capacity from villages to cities, mortgaging the possibility of future village-scale, grassroots development in exchange for a short-term payout made to individual households. Both reform programs also required villagers to abandon their self-built housing and relocate to a city or a town, meaning that villagers were atomized and separated from their support networks in the village. For many, this meant increasing (or, in some cases, quite sudden) reliance on the party–state for municipally subsidized public housing and welfare programs.[6]

For Tian Ye, as for many members of Chongqing's policy establishment, rural dependence was a natural aspect of China's reform era. "Development," he claimed, "is always based on difference. We can't all develop together." Tian pointed to the "ladder-step" process of reform, whereby the central government allowed coastal provinces to develop before the interior: "China has always been like this. Otherwise, there would be no Shenzhen. Shenzhen would never have developed without relying on preferential policies. . . . If Chongqing wants to develop," Tian concluded, "we also need to rely on preferential central policies." This politically driven system of development then reproduced itself within the municipality, with a majority of rural investment coming from the government.[7] Much of this money was funneled through Tian's office in the bureau of housing and urban–rural development, which directed tens of billions of renminbi in municipal subsidies to city and town governments. In addition, 100 towns classified as "central towns" by the municipal government were each allotted 200 *mu* (13 hectares) of land to increase their development capacity. And four specially designated "important towns" were given even more in financial subsidies and policy leeway. This included Baishiyi, the town in which Hailong was located. Tian anticipated claims of continuing urban–rural inequity: "Some people say public services should be equalized. I strongly object to this idea. Equalization is an ideal state. It's something you would never be able to realize. A city is a nucleus. How can it be equal with the rays that radiate from it?" Tian then described the network through which urban wealth trickled down through small cities, central towns, regular towns, and finally out to villages. "So the big city can't be equal with the villages," he continued. "Public services can't be equalized. They should be balanced." Urban–rural difference and urban superiority were thus baked into the very logic of urban–rural coordination. In its implementation, urban–rural coordination would not eliminate urban–rural difference but rather reproduce it in new ways.

The Rationalization of Village Planning

The extension of scientific rationality under urban–rural coordination included the revision and renaming of the 1989 Urban Planning Law as the Urban–Rural Planning Law in 2007, the same year Chongqing was designated as a pilot area for urban–rural coordination. While planning for urban and rural areas was still separated into distinct systems (Shi 2008), these changes brought urban and rural planning under a single, unified legal framework, consolidating government control over rural planning activities, including village plans (Bray 2013a). After 2007, responsibility for Chongqing's rural planning was moved from the bureau of housing and urban–rural development to the municipal planning bureau, thus integrating urban and rural planning within one administrative bureaucracy. As the director of the municipal planning bureau explained, the rural had always lain beyond the planner's gaze: "In the past, there was no oversight of village planning. The planning bureau only managed the urban." But under urban–rural coordination, planners would no longer be able to ignore the rural in their efforts to rationalize the urban. The director continued, "In 2007, the municipal planning bureau was suddenly responsible for the management of village planning. . . . Even now, our work on village planning is still only in its initial stages." Where the planning bureau had previously been responsible only for the main city of Chongqing and the several hundred cities and towns in the wider municipality, it now had to manage the planning of a vast hinterland of 8,660 villages scattered over 82,000 square kilometers. In other words, extending planning to rural areas meant a rescaling of planning activities, both down to the micro scale of individual villages and up to the macro scale of the entire municipal territory (Bray 2013a). In theory, this should have represented a dramatic expansion in the authority of Chongqing's planners and their discipline of scientific rationality. But the data on which planning practice relied was almost entirely limited to urban areas. In many rural areas, the necessary data did not exist; where the data did exist, they were neither comparable nor reliable. As one planner observed, "By the time accurate and reliable data could be collected from all 8,660 villages, they would already be hopelessly out of date." Beyond the urban construction boundary, the municipality was essentially blind. For the planners in the municipal planning bureau, the radical expansion of planning beyond the urban construction boundary was thus more than an opportunity; it was an existential threat that risked exposing the limits of scientific rationality.

To deal with this challenge, the planning bureau established the rural planning management division in 2009, thereby bracketing off village planning and reinscribing the administrative separation of urban and rural. The rest of the planning bureau thus continued much as before, ignoring the rural as it pursued the scientific planning of the urban. Meanwhile, the rural division, staffed with just a handful of planners, became responsible for Chongqing's portfolio of 8,660 rural villages. As one planner exclaimed, "Chongqing has 8,660 villages, and every one is different!" In late 2011, I attended a series of meetings convened by the rural division where Chongqing planners discussed the development of a village planning standard for the municipality. With a sufficiently scientific standard, it was claimed, Chongqing's villages could be treated as 8,660 data points rather than 8,660 idiosyncrasies. Site visits would no longer be necessary, providing the understaffed rural division the leverage it needed to oversee all of these villages. Moreover, by minimizing the degree of subjective judgment involved in reviewing village plans, a planning standard would ensure their scientific quality.

Discussion at these meetings focused on the effects of Chongqing's two main reform programs: household registration reform and land reform. To planners responsible for managing village planning in Chongqing, the greatest challenge to scientific clarity was population mobility. By providing a pathway for all the municipality's rural residents to acquire urban household registration, Chongqing's household registration reform program made urban services, infrastructure, and welfare formally available to millions of its residents. Most importantly, personal choice became a significant factor in determining official residential location. For the first time, planners had to account for unpredictable location preferences in planning settlements. This new "indeterminacy" (*bu queding xing* 不确定性) was the source of much anxiety among planners in the rural division: "In rural areas, population is the most difficult issue. The direction, mode, and tendency of population movement are all extremely difficult to make clear." The effort to collect village-level data offered an opportunity to eliminate this uncertainty. Planners suggested using the data to establish a "regular pattern" (*yiding guilü* 一定规律) of population movement or to predict the "static state" (*tingzhi zhuangtai* 停滞状态) of population distribution after migration slowed. As one planner claimed, if such a static state could be predicted, it might reveal a future without villages, thus negating the need for so much village planning: "Look at the developed countries. Their rural population barely changes. For instance in America, out of every fifty people, perhaps only one is rural. China might not ever be able to reach this level, but we need to think ahead. Otherwise, we'll have to keep redoing our plans over and over again." But as the difficulty of collecting this data became clearer and the possibility of scientifically determined estimates more distant, meeting attendees rationalized the existing system of politically determined population numbers: "It's not a purely technical question. It's based on the opinion of the government bureau. Of course, the planner can make a suggestion based on his experience. But ultimately it's up to the bureau to decide." In essence, Chongqing's rural planners were reproducing the logic of the urban construction boundary; they were accepting political decisionism as the only possible guarantee of scientific rationality.

Village land presented an equally worrisome challenge. To change village land use, village planners had to negotiate with officials at the land management bureau, which governed land use planning and the land quota system. In Chongqing, conflict between the planning and land management bureaus was exacerbated by mismatched land use categories. As one planner complained, the land management bureau had an overly restrictive understanding of village development, in which construction land could only be approved for housing, roads, and public infrastructure: "Nothing else counts. But in a village plan, we have many types of construction: ecological buildings, public buildings, industrial development. Even a 400-year-old historic landmark would be difficult to get approved!" This left too little room for planning discretion: "If you want to plan a village, there needs to be a gray area for some things." Chongqing's land reform policies had removed much of this gray area. Where planners had once been able to negotiate the intergovernmental trading of land use quotas across administrative boundaries, this was no longer allowed under the land note system. As the head of the rural division explained, "We can always increase the scale of urban planning and exceed the [land use] quota. But the scale of rural planning can't be made bigger; it needs to obey the quota. . . . This change in government policy has therefore had a profound impact on village planning." Where Chongqing's land reform program had actually made it easier to expand the urban construction boundary and resolve the irrationalities of urban planning, it had made it almost impossible to do so in the municipality's villages, which instead faced the possibility of dramatic reductions in the amount of village construction land.

Imposing a Rational Village Planning Typology

Boxed in by the demands of urban planning and the strictures of urban–rural coordination, the rural planning division decided that a village planning typology was the best way to rationalize the inherent irrationality of village development. After the 2007 revision of China's Urban Planning Law and the unprecedented expansion of planning to rural areas, municipal, provincial, and national planning agencies across China have developed village typologies as guidance for rural planning efforts. Villages are often distinguished on the basis of their level of economic development and type of economic activity, but these typologies have also included factors such as topography, urban propinquity, ethnicity, scale, disaster risk, settlement type, and population growth (Du 2014; Han 2013). While development of village typologies can help to avoid the universalizing and thus homogenizing tendencies of scientific rationality, the urge to taxonomize is itself an expression of rationalization, as idiosyncratic villages are disciplined into monofunctional categories defined by the intersection of scientific rationality and political expediency. Thus simplified, villages become more susceptible to the calculative and disciplinary technologies of the planning establishment (Chen, Zinda, and Yeh 2017). The search for a village planning typology in Chongqing dated back to the founding of the rural planning division in 2009, when Mo Ying and Tan Qing, two senior planners at the Chongqing Municipal Planning and Design Institute (CMPDI)—a for-profit subsidiary of the municipal planning bureau—undertook a new project, Research on the Planning of Villages in the Suburbs of Large Cities. As Mo explained after the Rural Planning Division met to discuss village planning standards, the issues at the heart of urban–rural coordination were most intense on the urban periphery. This also happened to be the area where the newly established rural planning division had the most direct responsibility. While it played only an advisory role in other parts of the municipality, it was tasked with formally approving all plans for the 871 administrative villages within the jurisdictional boundaries of the main city of Chongqing. Like the 2011 meetings in the Rural Planning Division, the 2009 report sought to bring rational order to this new challenge.

Confronted with the destabilization of urban–rural difference and the radical expansion of planning to include rural villages, Mo Ying and Tan Qing used the principles of scientific rationality to reconstitute the urban and the rural as distinct planning objects. As they argued, the urban and the rural have different "tasks" (*renwu* 任务) in the dimensions of land use, economic development, social structure, and ecological protection, which they can only fulfill if kept separate. By contrast, the report pathologized the intersection of urban and rural development in periurban areas, which were seen to produce settlements that were simultaneously both and neither. As in the 2011 meeting at the rural planning division, the unpredictability and "stochasticity" (*suijixing* 随机性) of population movements and land use changes presented a threat to rational planning, creating areas of urban–rural integration, functional diversity, and ontological contradiction. The report thus sought to delegitimize villages like Hailong, where industrial development had attracted large numbers of factories and migrants, resulting in a loss of control over land use, conflict between industrial and agricultural development, and unstable economic growth. According to the report, residents of such villages were also hampered by short-term thinking, which led them to build haphazardly and according to whim. Misled by a "blind yearning" (*mangmu xiangwang* 盲目向往) for city life, they too easily adopted urban development patterns, such as concentrated settlement types, tall buildings, and modern architecture.[8] This led to development that was messy and unplanned, with dangerous, winding roads and extensive environmental degradation.

As Mo Ying and Tan Qing concluded, in order to protect villagers from themselves, existing rural development had to be replaced by modern scientific planning guided by the insights of systems theory. As a basis for this, the report cited three rationalist planning precedents, including the "third magnet" of Ebenezer Howard's Garden City, which rationally integrated only the best of both town and country (Howard 1902); "landscape cities," an idea developed by a Chinese rocket scientist who advocated integrating pastoral qualities into the urban; and "smart growth" theory, which emphasized growth boundaries as a rational method for controlling disordered urban spread into rural areas (Duany, Speck, and Lydon 2010). Rescaling these theories to village planning, Mo and Tan advocated limiting village development through the consolidation of dispersed settlements, the implementation of village growth boundaries, and the creation of periurban green belts through municipal land banking. In fact, these arguments for growth limits constituted a post hoc rationalization of Chongqing's existing political commitment to village consolidation, as expressed in the municipality's land reform policy, which had been launched in the preceding year.[9] By sacrificing village development to enable the further growth of urban areas, such limits on village growth effectively reinforced the existing system of urban primacy.

To cleanse periurban villages of unwanted urban influences, the CMPDI report classified these villages into urban and rural types. "Urban industrial" villages were to be modeled on urban residential areas and eventually incorporated into cities and towns as urban neighborhoods. By contrast, "agricultural" and "touristic" villages were subject to strict development controls and defined in opposition to the urban. New housing, for instance, would not be allowed to exceed three stories and had to be arranged organically. The report also advocated beaux arts–inspired road layouts that framed rural landmarks and local architectural styles, as well as materials that created landscapes resembling traditional garden scroll paintings. These recommendations were supported with references to a series of international rural planning precedents that served to reify the rural as a pastoral playland, including photographs of a fake donkey, a tractor on a country road, grazing cows, autumn foliage, and an apple orchard. These representations constructed a "rural idyll," in which a fetishized pastoral landscape offered a nostalgic escape from the corrupting influences of urbanization (Bunce 2003; Williams 1973). Through these measures, Mo Ying and Tan Qing explicitly sought to preserve villages' "rural character" (*nongcun xiangtu qixi* 农村乡土气息)

and "cultural scenery" (*renwen jingguan* 人文景观), which were valued for their ability to reconnect (urban) people with nature and tradition.

As Mo Ying and Tan Qing argued in the CMPDI report, these villages were to be developed as "functional supplements" to the city, producing goods and services that satisfied the needs of urban residents and businesses. Enabled by the consolidation of farmland into industrialized farms managed by corporate agribusinesses, "agricultural villages" would satisfy the material and bodily needs of urban residents through the provision of vegetables and other fresh consumables. Meanwhile, "touristic villages" would satisfy their spiritual and psychological needs by providing opportunities for leisure and escape. This fetishization of periurban villages as the city's playground was common in Chongqing planning circles, as articulated by the director of the Chongqing municipal planning bureau: "The development of the city suburbs is in service of the city, including leisure, resorts, agritourism, and sightseeing. As a result, urban–rural coordination is easier there." The outcome of such thinking was particularly clear in the design of the Sichuan Fine Arts Institute's periurban Huxi campus, which won several design awards. Prominently displayed in the center of the campus was a small patch of agricultural land, which was tended year round by a resident agricultural household. Overlooked by a viewing platform and surrounded by art studios, the fields represented an extreme aestheticization of agricultural labor as an object of urban consumption.

Rather than articulate a typology based on villages' own development trajectories, the CMPDI report thus taxonomized villages in relation to the city and the needs of urban inhabitants. This reflected a widespread "romantic reappraisal" in China, where rising middle-class affluence has led to the idealization of rural life and the consumption of rural products and experiences as emblems of an elite lifestyle (Griffiths, Chapman, and Christiansen 2010; Kipnis 2016, 126; Schein 2001, 226). The CMPDI typology also gave expression to the dependence thesis articulated by Tian Ye, who explained that rural development and urban–rural coordination would always rely on the economic dynamism of cities. The logic of this approach was already present in the "socialist new countryside" (*shehuizhuyi xin nongcun* 社会主义新农村), a rural development campaign that relied on fiscal transfers from local governments and often resulted in "face projects" or village beautification, including agricultural tourism (Abramson and Qi 2011; Cheung 2012; Looney 2015; Rosenberg 2013; Steinmüller 2013). And it anticipated the launch of the "beautiful countryside" (*meili xiangcun* 美丽乡村), a national campaign that only intensified the aestheticization of the rural in order to protect its ecological and cultural qualities from urban influences (Wu 2018). These initiatives have often privileged the interests of the state over the aspirations of village residents (Rosenberg 2013), and they have tended to "spectralize" the rural, relegating villages into positions of economic dependence without attempting to understand their complex dynamics and trajectories (Abramson 2016, 3).

In striving to protect the rural from the urban, these efforts have ironically accelerated the urbanization of China's villages. By reifying the rural, Mo Ying and Tan Qing unwittingly produced an ersatz rurality, one that no longer reflected the reality of villages as social and political communities but that rationalized villages according to the demands of the urban. As rural idylls, villages were cleansed of the dense housing, industrial landscapes, and migrant populations that Mo and Tan so strongly criticized in villages like Hailong, but they were simultaneously infused with images and functions defined by an urban sensibility. For instance, the garden landscaping recommended in the CMPDI report is often regarded as marking "the difference between a rural and an urban built environment" in contemporary China (Bray 2013b, 2). Where the rural is typically associated with the messy, productive landscapes of agriculture and village life, manicured shrubbery distinguishes spaces of residence and consumption from spaces of production (Bray 2013b). While the expansion of village planning in China has urbanized some villages through their integration into town peripheries or the construction of high-rise housing (Rosenberg 2013), the recommendations of the CMPDI report were more subtle. In the apparent intensification of villages' rurality, Mo and Tan were rationalizing the rural into China's urban hegemony. In the words of Tian Ye, they were turning the rural into something that urban people could rationally understand and consume.

Urbanization by Other Means

Through the implementation of urban–rural coordination, Chongqing's planners and policy makers pursued a radical expansion of state-led urbanization that would include all rural territories and populations. Faced with the potential destabilization of one of their foundational assumptions, Chongqing's planners could not simply abandon the division between urban and rural. Instead, they redefined the rural as a subset or extension of the urban. For instance, when I expressed an interest in the implications of urban–rural coordination for villages, Tian Ye emphasized that the "rural" (*xiang* 乡) in "urban–rural coordination" (*chengxiang tongchou* 城乡统筹) was distinct from the "rural" (*nong* 农) of villages. In Tian's strict interpretation, urban–rural coordination only referred to the *xiang*, which included the state's administrative network of rural towns but not the collective-governed villages. Similarly, Mo Ying and Tan Qing's village planning report transformed villages from the "working rural" (*nongcun* 农村), into the "rural countryside" (*xiangcun* 乡村). Where *nong* is associated with "peasants" (*nongmin* 农民) and "farms" (*nongchang* 农场), *xiang* is associated with "native places" (*jiaxiang* 家乡) and "dreamlands" (*mengxiang* 梦乡), evoking a nostalgic imaginary that necessitates a critical and emotional distance from outside the rural—that is, from the urban. The word for "rural" in "urban–rural coordination" thus encodes an urban positionality, one where the messy and irrational lives and livelihoods of rural people are replaced with orderly and rational spaces of consumption and leisure. The rural becomes a simulacrum reimagined through the lens of the party–state's urban governance apparatus and the desires of urban elites, including the planners and policy makers who predominantly live and work in cities.

At the same time, Chongqing's planners and policy makers were also pursuing the material transformation of rural villages into functional supplements to the city. The most remote areas were designated for depopulation and transformation into ecological protection zones or resource extraction sites (cf. Chen, Zinda, and Yeh 2017). More accessible villages were aestheticized as rural playgrounds for the urban elite or industrialized as the city's agricultural breadbasket—policies that foreshadowed subsequent party–state programs for the "beautiful countryside" and the "vertical integration" of agriculture. In its implementation, therefore, urban–rural coordination ironically seemed to reify and intensify the divide between urban and rural: the urban became more urban, while the rural became more rural. In the process, however, the very nature of rurality changed. Rural villages ceased to exist as distinct sociospatial systems for ordering life and instead became extensions of urban processes that extract agricultural surpluses and ecological resources for concentration in cities (Brenner and Schmid 2015).

Together, these categorical and processual transformations amounted to what I call urbanization by other means: villages were more tightly integrated into state-dominated de jure urban systems, even as signs of de facto urban–rural interpenetration were erased. Villages might not show the conventional hallmarks of urbanization, such as land use intensification and high-rise buildings, and in fact, urban–rural coordination meant villages were even less likely to urbanize in these ways, as rural populations were increasingly resettled in towns and cities. But rural areas were being both categorically redefined and functionally reshaped as extensions of Chinese urbanization and the party–state's politico-scientific ideology of urban development. These changes thus posed an existential threat to villages' existing sociospatiality and the strategies of stability, survival, and growth explored in the following two chapters. In particular, messy, hybridized villages like Hailong were delegitimized and pushed to integrate into the expanding spatial fabric of the city. Indeed, just as Mo Ying and Tan Qing were leading research on their report, the very same team of CMPDI planners was simultaneously formulating Hailong's new village plan. Mo and Tan chose a different village in West City as their report's official case study, but, as Mo later confessed, nearby Hailong loomed large, acting as a foil for the planners' idealized proposals. As becomes clear in the following chapter, Hailong Village and its cadres offered an entirely different interpretation of urban–rural coordination that posed a direct challenge to the municipality's experimental program of reform.

CHAPTER 2

Village Growth Machine

Charismatic Authority and the Urbanization of the Party

Two hundred party cadres dressed in camouflage fatigues stood at attention in rows of five at the southern end of Hailong's central square. One by one, each row marched to the front and then turned in a pinwheel formation. Over nearly half an hour, 200 north-facing cadres became 200 east-facing cadres. Under the watchful eyes of an air force captain, the last quintet finally embarked in lockstep. As they began their pivot, the middle-aged man on the end of the row forgot to lengthen his stride, took an extra hop to catch up with the accelerating end of the arc, slipped on the smooth outdoor tiles, grasped at the next cadre's arm, and stumbled to the ground, pulling his neighbor down after him. Titters scattered through the ranks. Someone yelled out "pretty boy" (*shuai ge* 帅哥), a play on the man's surname, Shuai, and a lighthearted nickname for men who trade on their looks. Laughter spread, then broke into groans as the captain ordered them all back to their original formation to start over. Neat rows of cadres temporarily unraveled into a crowd of villagers with the day off work, wandering back to their assigned positions in chatty knots of two or three.

The marching exercise was part of the village party branch's semiannual military training, a daylong event mandatory for all party members in Hailong. The day included lectures on party doctrine and teamwork from village leaders, local military officers, and a professor at Chongqing's party school, as well as team-building exercises and military drills. As Hailong's party secretary, Yan Jing, explained that morning, the objective was to strengthen the discipline, solidarity, and teamwork of the village's party members so they could operate as a single, unified whole. The drills

Figure 13. Hailong Plaza. Facing south, this photograph of Hailong Plaza shows the statue symbolizing Hailong's development on the right, the Hailong Exhibition Hall on the left, and two six-story apartment buildings in the background, one crowned with the Hailong logo.

also served as a visible demonstration of the party's power in the village. As residents looked on from the square's shady edges, the cadres' maneuvers animated what was otherwise an empty space measuring 3,500 square meters—the largest open space in the town of Baishiyi (Figure 13). This was the physical and symbolic heart of the new village center, which Hailong built in 2007 (Figure 14). Even more than tall skyscrapers, large squares are a ubiquitous symbol of Chinese urbanity. All such plazas refer to the awe-inspiring scale of Tiananmen Square in Beijing (Hershkovitz 1993), and in Chongqing's hilly topography, large flat spaces are especially prized. Many of the place-names in the city include the character for "flat" (*ping* 平), and all Chongqing's urban centers are oriented around sprawling plazas. Hailong Square situated the village in this hierarchy of urban places, and the marching, uniformed cadres invoked the televised nationalist pageantry of the military parades in front of Tiananmen Gate (Lee 2011).

The cadres began their maneuvers underneath Hailong's giant red

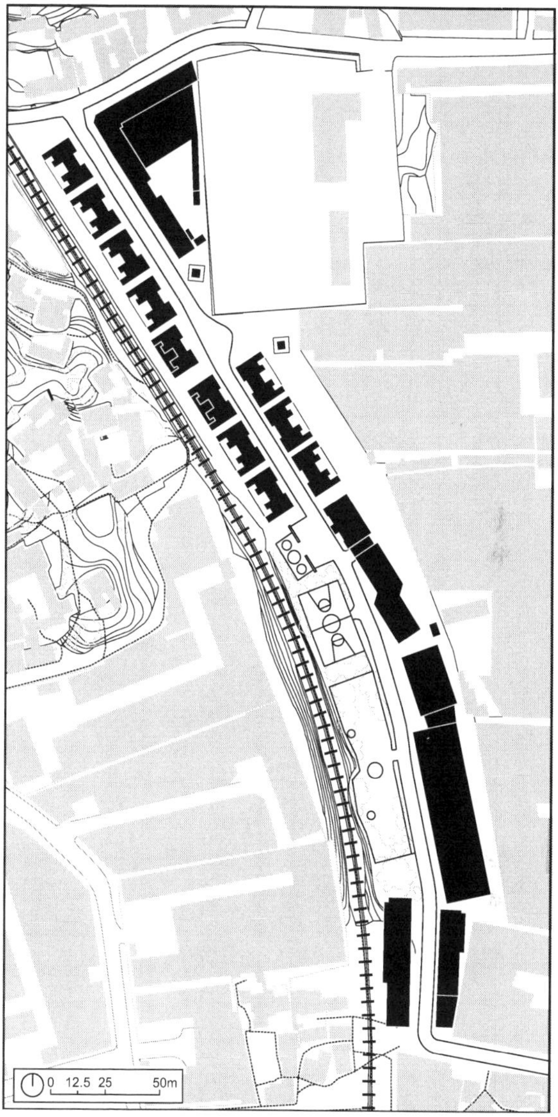

Figure 14. Easy Street. This figure–ground drawing shows Easy Street, highlighted in black, adjacent to the rail line. At the north end, a wet market and a shopping complex abutted the power substation (the large empty space to the right, which was occupied by transformers). On either side of the road were 11 three-story apartment buildings, which had commercial space on the ground floor. Farther south were the village's office buildings, the village's exhibition and meeting halls, and four larger apartment buildings. At the southern end of Easy Street was Hailong Plaza, complete with a basketball court and a fountain.

logo scrawled across the roof line of an adjacent six-story apartment building, and they pivoted in front of a steel monument symbolizing the village's progress and affluence. As each row completed the drill, they stood facing the Hailong Exhibition Hall, which celebrated the village's past accomplishments and speculated at its future glory. Next door stood a pair of midrise office buildings, one for the village committee and the other for the village development corporation. Once the cadres had mastered the pinwheel formation, they marched out of the square and down Easy Street (lit. "street of easy living," or *kangju jie* 康居街), which ran for nearly a kilometer, the entire length of the village center. The cadres filled the narrow street, squeezing between two rows of gray three-story apartment buildings (Figure 15). Onlookers poked their heads out windows and stood in the doorways of restaurants, beauty parlors, massage parlors, mahjong parlors, small grocery stores, pharmacies, cell phone shops, clothing boutiques, an internet café, a karaoke bar, and a state gambling outlet. At the end of the street, the cadres came to a halt. The air force officer called the cadres to attention in front of Yan Jing, and in unison they shouted, "Coordination is the greatest ability! Teamwork produces the greatest force!"

This pageant of party unity was a remarkable symbol of Hailong's transformation. Ten years earlier, in 2001, the village party branch had just 47 members. Less than half would show up for mandatory meetings, and those who attended only did so for the small stipend and the meal. By 2011, membership had grown to 239, a fivefold increase, and Hailong's party branch meetings drew attendees from neighboring villages. Even more extraordinary was the very existence of the square they marched in, which had cost the village 11 million RMB to build.[1] In 2001, the village owed nearly 1 million RMB in debt and was known as one of the weakest and most troubled villages in Baishiyi. By 2011, the village collective was earning more than 8 million RMB annually and owned 80 million RMB in assets. In the intervening decade, Hailong's economy had undergone a dramatic transformation. In 2001, with annual net income averaging just 1,500 RMB per capita, an estimated 70 percent of working-age villagers had migrated away from Hailong in search of work. The village was primarily agricultural, but with no one around to tend the fields, nearly 40 percent of Hailong's agricultural land lay fallow. By 2011, the village

Figure 15. Military Training. Hailong's party members engaged in periodic military training, which included marching down Easy Street. Apartment buildings built by the village are shown in the background.

economy had been almost completely industrialized, with over 150 manufacturing firms—most producing wooden furniture or machine parts for Chongqing's automotive industry—generating a gross annual product of more than 2 million RMB. Many of Hailong's sojourning villagers returned, and average incomes grew by an order of magnitude, to 12,000 RMB, a third higher than the average for villagers in Jiulongpo District. Industrialization also drove a demand for labor, with more than 13,000 migrants living alongside the registered village population of 1,954. Easy Street and Hailong Square were the physical and symbolic expressions of this economic dynamism and accumulated wealth. Hailong's exhibition hall placards portrayed the new village center as the "butterfly" that had emerged from the "larval worm" that Hailong had once been.

Hailong's meteoric rise first came to the attention of the CCP's senior leadership in 2006 when Wang Yang, then Chongqing's party secretary, visited the new village center.[2] Soon afterward, Hailong's party secretary, Yan Jing, was recognized by the municipality as an "outstanding party cadre," and in January 2009, Yan flew to Beijing to be recognized as an "Outstanding Personage of Chinese Reform." In Yan's account of the trip, he was feted by the party's most senior leaders: "Xi Jinping met me at the airport with a red carpet and a limousine. A motorcade escorted us through the city to the People's Hall, where I met with President Hu." By 2010, Vice President Xi had taken a personal interest in Hailong, which promised tantalizing answers to some of the party's most pressing rural issues. Over the preceding decade of urban–rural coordination, many of the central government's marquee rural development programs had paradoxically precipitated a sharp decline in village cadres' organizational capacity and the relevance of the CCP in villagers' daily lives (Chen 2014). By contrast, Hailong had not only escaped its debt, transformed its economy, increased villager incomes, and built a new village center, but had also made the party relevant again, growing the size of the village party branch when party membership in most villages was shrinking. Hailong thus offered a potential alternative approach to urban–rural coordination that spoke directly to national leaders' desire to strengthen the capacity of rural cadres through grassroots "party-building" initiatives (Wen 2003).

"The sky is still the same sky; the earth is still the same earth; the villagers are still the same villagers. How could Hailong Village achieve such a great leap of rapid development in so few years?" This was the question posed by a member of the Jiulongpo District Standing Committee, Ye Jianhua, in an editorial penned in 2012. Much the same question motivated then–Vice President Xi Jinping to dispatch a research team to Hailong in May 2010. Led by Zheng Keyang, a veteran party member and an expert on party building, the research team from the Policy Research Center and the Organization Department of the CCP Central Committee spent a week in Hailong preparing a report for the Central Committee Secretariat. In a brief commentary appended to the report, Xi, who would soon become president, praised the findings and recommended the report to his colleagues on the secretariat. As argued in the report, the cause of Hailong's transformation was relatively simple: Yan Jing. On the first page of the report, Zheng quoted the ecstatic praise of the villagers he had interviewed: "Without Yan Jing, there would be no Hailong." He then traced the origins of Hailong's progress to Chongqing's "capable village leader" (*nengren zhicun* 能人治村) program, under which Yan was named as party secretary. In his comments on the report, Li Yuanchao, then the director of the Central Committee's Organization Department, echoed this analysis: "A good party secretary drove a team. A team drove all the people of the village." But what does it mean to be a good and capable village leader? The report offered little in the way of specifics, stating only that capable village leaders need to be educated, accomplished, and willing to think in new ways, while good village leaders need to have a strong sense of responsibility, a willingness to serve the people, and a staunch resistance to corruption. Hailong's cadres proudly invoked the report as proof of Yan's charisma and the village's rising fortunes, but how exactly these qualities resulted in Hailong's transformation—or if in fact Yan possessed these qualities at all—was never specified by Zheng and his team. Zheng's report assumed that Yan's leadership skills caused Hailong's rapid development, in part because this confirmed the CCP's political commitment to grassroots party building. As will become clear in the following discussion, however, Yan's charisma was just as dependent on Hailong's sociospatial transformation.

What it takes to catalyze village development—and the role of village leadership in that process—has been a central question for scholars of rural China over the last 20 years.[3] There are at least three models of transformation: corporatist, entrepreneurial, and moralistic. Each model also roughly corresponds to one of three village leadership types commonly referenced in the Chinese policy literature: the "strong" (*qiangren* 强人), the "capable" (*nengren* 能人), and the "good" (*haoren* 好人) (He 2003, 256–58). Primarily reflecting village development strategies pursued in China's coastal areas during the relatively prosperous 1980s and early 1990s, "local state corporatism" describes villages (as well as townships and counties) that operate collective-owned enterprises—commonly known as township and village enterprises (TVEs)—as branches of a larger quasi-corporate organization, with the village party secretary acting as chief executive officer (Oi 1992; 1999, 97). More recently, this corporatist model has been distinguished from the rise of "entrepreneurial cadres," who use their private-sector expertise, connections, and wealth to catalyze the development of their villages (Chen 2014, 262). Finally, a moralistic model describes how villages' economic resources are (or are not) translated into public goods and argues that the moral obligations of solidary groups, such as lineage, philanthropic, or religious organizations, can compel village leaders to act (Tsai 2007, 17).

This chapter engages these models not as theoretical alternatives but as a suite of mutually complementary strategies, which Hailong's cadres deployed in response to the rural development crisis. In Hailong, this included both a crisis of political legitimacy confronting village cadres' attempts to exercise authority and a crisis of financial and organizational capacity undermining their efforts to catalyze village development. By selecting Yan Jing as party secretary and highlighting his qualities as a strong, capable, and good leader, Hailong's cadres sought to produce a charismatic aura that could convince people that the village's leaders were capable of delivering development. Under Yan's leadership, Hailong's cadres also crafted a new narrative of village development that emphasized the urgency of taking action at the newly constituted scale of the administrative village. Yan's charismatic authority and the narrative of collective action were used to reorient Hailong's villagers away from existing community networks rooted in their natural villages and toward a newly invented (administrative) village-scale community. This resulted in a path-dependent process of village urbanization through which resources were extracted from natural villages and households and concentrated at the scale of the administrative village. Hailong's cadres then deployed those resources to produce new forms of sociospatial transformation that would substantiate both Yan's charismatic authority and Hailong's existence as a village community, most notably embodied in the form of Easy Street and Hailong Square. Hailong's transformation thus revealed the emergence of a village-scale "growth machine" (Logan and Molotch 1987), in which cadres pursued development to reinforce their legitimacy and sustain the material basis for the very idea of the village.

The Cadre Legitimacy Crisis and the Promise of Charismatic Leadership

Hailong's existence only dates to the early 2000s. Before this, Hailong comprised two separate "administrative villages" (*xingzheng cun* 行政村), Hailuo and Longtai. In 2001, under Chongqing's "capable village leader" initiative, Baishiyi began combining administrative villages to destabilize existing power structures and install more capable leaders, part of a national effort to consolidate villages and costs by eliminating redundant village cadres (Chen 2014, 195). At the insistence of the Baishiyi government, Hailuo and Longtai merged in March 2002, officially forming the village of Hai-Long. These artificial beginnings underline the ambivalent position of the administrative village in Chinese governance. Drawing on administrative systems instituted by the Japanese and the Kuomintang during the first half of the twentieth century, the CCP established administrative villages in 1954 to facilitate its control of the rural population (He 2003, 47). With the move toward people's communes after 1958, production brigades replaced administrative villages, and then administrative villages were reinstated as part of de-collectivization in the early 1980s. In their contemporary incarnation, administrative villages can vary from several hundred to several thousand officially registered villagers, though the unofficial population can vary significantly with migration. Depending on local settlement patterns (Jin and Li 1992), this population may be organized into a single, unitary village or, as was the case in Hailong, divided among several "natural villages" (*zirancun* 自然村), which are socially and morphologically defined clusters of households. In Hailong, it was the natural village rather than the administrative village where inhabitants experienced the strongest feelings of attachment and solidarity, an orientation that is more fully discussed in the following chapter.

In China's south, where much of the existing scholarship on village urbanization is based, strong lineage organizations and compact village morphologies mean that administrative villages often coincide with preexisting modes of village governance and solidarity. Rooted in patriarchal forms of traditional authority (Weber [1946] 2009), the lineage organizations of southern China bind villagers into tightly integrated communities where agnatic blood relations are entwined with intergenerational ties to the land (Faure and Siu 1995; Fei [1948] 1992). Before the socialist land reforms of the 1950s, lineage organizations frequently managed extensive ancestral land trusts, giving them a corporate character where the lineage was responsible for village infrastructure and welfare provision (Baker 1979; Freedman 1971). During the post-1978 reform era, many of these organizations were reestablished and grew to fill the gaps in governance left by de-collectivization (Johnson 1993). Southern villages' relative access to economic opportunities and investment capital was also articulated through overseas lineage networks (Yeh 2000). Many southern villages therefore have highly integrated and effective leadership structures, with the same individuals running the lineage, the administrative village, and the village's collective economic organization (Huang 1998; Kan 2016). But in other parts of China, and particularly in the mountainous west, scattered settlement typologies and a lack of strong lineage organizations mean that administrative villages often combine several natural villages with relatively low levels of mutual cohesion. While the thick relationship networks in unitary, lineage-oriented villages help to produce a "society of friends" (*shuren shehui* 熟人社会) (Fei [1948] 1992), the artificiality of the administrative village can result in a "society of half-friends" (*ban shuren shehui* 半熟人社会), where the absence of common experiences and daily encounters undermines villagers' sense of mutual understanding and shared purpose (He 2003, 48–49). This was the case in Hailong, where the intensity of the Cultural Revolution in Chongqing destroyed any surviving lineage organizations. The administrative village of Hailong therefore included both a large number of loosely integrated surname groups and a large number of relatively insular natural villages, resulting in substantial social fragmentation. At the same time, the dearth of economic opportunities in the village meant that there were few economic elites who could mobilize villagers for collective action (He 2003). For Hailong, as for many of the villages in China's interior, the artificiality of the administrative village was therefore a central challenge for village development.

Formally separate from the government bureaucracy (which extends only down to the town level), administrative villages are technically run as self-governing collectives (Chen 2014; Pils 2005; Oi 1999), but this organizational inheritance of the socialist era is still only ambiguously defined in Chinese law and practice (He 2003; Ho 2001). Democratic elections ensure the formal representation of villagers' interests on village committees and representative councils (O'Brien and Li 2000), but village elections have been unevenly implemented (Manion 2006), and in most villages, democratically elected representatives are not the ultimate political authorities (Tan 2004; Wang 2003). Instead, administrative villages are run by village party branches, which respond to the directives of town leaders, who have the power to appoint village party secretaries (Chen 2014, 132, 150; Hsing 2006, 105).[4] As a result, improvements in democratic procedures do not necessarily provide villagers with real power (Kelliher 1997; O'Brien and Han 2009), and party leaders often capture or bypass democratic processes and organizations (Chen 2014; Kennedy 2002; Oi and Rozelle 2000). In many instances, this has factionalized village politics and eroded villagers' satisfaction with village leaders, who still rely on the cooperation of the village population to achieve their goals (Alpermann 2001; Guo and Bernstein 2004; He 2003, 259; Yao 2009).

This contradiction between superficial democratic procedure and substantive party power makes the question of village leadership a key issue for village development. Without clear institutional rules for accountability, these multiple claims to authority must be resolved in the person of the village party secretary, who is both a servant of two masters (requiring the support of fellow villagers and party superiors to succeed) and a mediator between two potential adversaries (balancing villagers' interests and the party–state's priorities). Local party organizations have devised different strategies to address this instability in village governance. For instance, some townships have required village party secretaries to stand for election (Guo and Bernstein 2004), while other village party secretaries draw on more traditional forms of authority, such as lineage organizations, to secure villagers' support (Manion 2006). But in many villages, the exercise of power ultimately relies on "charismatic" authority (Weber [1946] 2009), through which perceived personal qualities of the village party secretary inspire trust and devotion. In comments delivered at a meeting of Hailong villagers, a member of the Chongqing Municipality Standing Committee, Qin Qinglin, outlined this approach to village leadership: "The village committee is a self-governing organization. It is not an organization of the government. . . . We need village leaders to be faithful, resourceful, moral, and respectful so they can become leaders in whom the party and the masses can trust and upon whom they can rely. For village development, this is of the utmost importance."

Upon its creation in March 2002, Hailong's first challenge was to select a "good" and "capable" leader. The village party branch met for six consecutive days and took three votes yielding no decisive result. Relations between the party branch and the villagers were so tense—villagers would regularly swear or spit when encountering a party member—that no cadre was willing to stand for election. Villagers even held their own meeting outside the party branch election, declaring that they would not allow the current village leaders to continue in their posts. For a full week, Hailong was paralyzed. In the face of this crisis, one of the existing party secretaries made an extraordinary proposal to nominate a villager, Yan Jing, who no longer lived in the village. Despite his long absence, Yan's apparent success as a migrant entrepreneur was a recognized sign of "capable" leadership.[5] In 1991, after a decade as a farmer, Yan moved to Qingdao, where he worked in construction and eventually established his own construction team of 70 workers. Over the course of the 1990s, Yan built a reputation in Hailong as a capable and successful businessman, largely as a result of his acquisition of flashy consumer goods. He was widely known as the first villager in Longtai to own a cell phone, the first to purchase a 125cc motorbike, and the first to build a Western-style villa.

Yan Jing also demonstrated a set of capabilities characteristic of "good" leaders (He 2003, 256–58). For instance, in 2001, villagers of Longtai strongly opposed the drilling of wells for the Tianci Hot Springs, a resort and spa built on land that had once belonged to the village. Hundreds of villagers blocked construction, attacking village and town officials. As a concerned party cadre, Yan visited the site of the conflict and successfully negotiated a peaceful end to hostilities. Village cadres told similar anecdotes about the early years of his tenure as party secretary. When one villager refused to allow Hailong's first paved road to cut through her lotus pond and gathered her family members to block the bulldozer's path, Yan reportedly knelt in front of her and wept, begging her to join him in developing the village. After several minutes, the woman got up and quietly left. Three months later, the road was finished. Some claimed Yan lost face by kneeling in front of a villager. In response Yan insisted, "If I can push development forward, what does face matter? The only way I can lose face is if there's no development." This was the ultimate test of Yan's charismatic authority: Did the actions he took lead to the outcomes he promised? Without delivering results, Yan's charismatic image might fall apart (Weber [1946] 2009). Thus, Yan's commitment to village development, represented by his frequent invocation of Deng Xiaoping's maxim, "development is the absolute principle," was a matter of personal survival as much as a matter of ideology.

The Unfunded Mandate: Re-collectivizing Village Land

As Yan Jing took office in 2002, he faced the same structural contradiction plaguing village cadres across rural China: a mandate for development without the organizational or financial capacity to accomplish it. China's village cadres have seen a structural decline in their control over village resources and residents throughout the reform era, often as a result of the very policies aimed at alleviating rural poverty (Chen 2014). In the early 1980s, de-collectivization and the household responsibility system drove widespread gains in agricultural efficiency and rural prosperity (Zhu et al. 2006).[6] But these groundbreaking reforms also dramatically reduced village cadres' redistributive powers and undermined the economic basis for collective action (Chen 2014, 30–31; He 2003, 50–51). This situation was further exacerbated in 2003, when the enactment of the Rural Land Contracting Law proscribed the periodic redistribution of rural land parcels within villages, severely constraining one of the last remaining tools cadres could use to exert control over village land. In 1994, China's sweeping fiscal reform, which recentralized control over tax receipts, pushed the party–state's fiscal burden down the governmental hierarchy, as each level of government tried to extract more revenue from its subordinates and retain more revenue for itself. At the bottom of this hierarchy, townships and administrative villages were hit hardest by the fiscal crunch. Like Hailong, over 80 percent of China's administrative villages were indebted in 2001 (Chen 2014, 165–66, 177). In the early 2000s, the tax-for-fee reform (2002–4) and the abolition of agricultural taxes (2005–6) eliminated village cadres' last remaining sources of revenue and made them almost entirely dependent on fiscal transfers from townships struggling with their own budgetary problems (Chen 2014, 192–93).

Yan Jing and his team were keenly aware of this structural gap between their responsibility and their capacity. Yan's top lieutenant, Wen Jiancai, vented her frustration at the increasing number of costly goods and services that the municipal government expected the village to provide: "Sometimes I feel that upper level politics are meaningless. They give all the important things to the lower levels to do—sanitation, policing, elder care, you name it." Wen went on to lament the simultaneous withering of the village collective: "The great strength of China's villages is their unity. But when the land was divided up, all of the sudden villagers didn't feel they needed the village leaders anymore." She concluded with a sigh and a shake of her head: "Our country is getting individualized, just like the West." As this conversation suggested, Hailong's leaders traced their decline in power back to the de-collectivization of rural land, when much of their discretionary power over land use was ceded to individual households. Yan and his team needed a way to turn back the clock to a time when the village still mattered in people's lives and cadres controlled village resources.

Re-collectivization: Becoming the Huaxi of the West

Yan Jing's solution to this problem was to re-collectivize Hailong's agricultural land for industrialization. In what is often referred to as local state corporatism or new collectivism, collective-owned village land is used to develop industrial and commercial enterprises that operate as subsidiaries of the village conglomerate. The village then extracts profits through its right to the residual as the monopolistic owner of collective land (Oi 1999, 97–98; Chen 2014, 151–52; Lin 1995, 340). The classic form of this strategy, most commonly found in China's coastal provinces in the 1980s, relied on a prereform industrial base or the development of new TVEs (Hou 2013; Wong 2016). In 1992, Nanhai District in Guangdong

Province pursued a more systematic initiative to re-collectivize all agricultural land in order to enable large-scale farming; this approach, which entrusted the land to village-based shareholding cooperatives, later became prevalent across Guangdong and ultimately provided a basis for renting village land to manufacturers and real estate developers (Zhu and Guo 2015). By the time the TVE sector began to decline in the late 1990s (Chen 2014, 160; Huang 2008, 125–28), re-collectivization had already become a prominent village development strategy.

In advocating re-collectivization, Yan Jing was therefore following a national trend in village development, but for Hailong's villagers, re-collectivization went against decades of precedent under the household responsibility system. To convince the village to go along with his strategy, Yan made an affective appeal to residents' nostalgia for the lost sense of community solidarity under socialism. Emphasizing the importance of collective welfare and insisting that the only way for individual households to grow rich was for the village to grow rich, Yan proposed a return to the early 1980s, when de-collectivization had not yet fragmented the village and villagers were still united by shared economic goals (Smith 2019a). To make this case, Yan presented the village party branch and the village committee with an object lesson: a comparison between two icons of the early reform era, Xiaogang Village in Anhui Province and Huaxi Village in Jiangsu Province. In November 1978, 18 households in Xiaogang signed an agreement to end collective farming and divide agricultural land by household, violating national policy and earning national acclaim as "the first Chinese village to reform."[7] Huaxi, by contrast, never de-collectivized. Starting from a strong prereform industrial base, Huaxi became one of the first villages to pursue collective-led industrialization in the reform era, earning a reputation as "the first village under heaven" for its development and prosperity (Hou 2013). In 2002, Yan visited these two villages at his own expense and delivered detailed reports to the village party branch and the village committee in Hailong. Five years later, when Yan was pushing for another round of village development, he used some of Hailong's accumulated wealth to fly village officials to see Xiaogang and Huaxi for themselves.

Yan Jing expressed shock at Xiaogang's continued poverty and its lack of economic activity. Several years before, a manufacturer from Jiangsu had built a factory in Xiaogang, but because the village lacked collective resources, it was unable to provide the infrastructure necessary to support the factory, which subsequently closed. Xiaogang became a foil for Yan's vision of development, a cautionary tale of what could happen if the village allowed its internal divisions to prevent re-collectivization. Yan wrote, "In 1978, if they had just put aside petty differences . . . and drawn up a blueprint for the village's development, they could have become 'China's first 100 million yuan village.'" Instead, it was Huaxi that became one of the first villages to achieve an annual gross product of over 100 million RMB (Hou 2013; Zhou 2006). Amid the canals, industrial estates, and rice paddies of southern Jiangsu, Huaxi is visible for miles. Towering above the verdant landscape, far from the nearest town or city, Huaxi's 100-story skyscraper is an unmistakable monument to the village's aspirations. For 100 RMB, tourists can visit the sixty-eighth floor, which is covered in gold leaf and guarded by a golden bull that overlooks the villagers' BMWs and luxury villas below. The contrast with Xiaogang could not be starker, and Hailong's village cadres were deeply affected by their visit in 2006: "We were stunned by the comparison. We all wanted to make our village as beautiful as Huaxi. . . . The village was made of gold. It was like a mirage in the desert." Another exclaimed, "Everything is so wealthy. We have to work harder!" Huaxi showed Hailong's cadres what was possible if they followed Yan's lead and committed themselves to the re-collectivization of land by the administrative village.

In his report to the village committee, Yan Jing used this comparison to instill a sense of urgency in his fellow villagers. In response to the economic watershed of 1978, Xiaogang and Huaxi had chosen starkly different paths. Hailong, Yan argued, faced a similar turning point in the early 2000s. In 1995, the completion of the Cheng-Yu Expressway, which cuts right through Hailong's territory, suddenly connected the village with the city center via a two-kilometer-long tunnel underneath Zhongliang Mountain, reducing driving time from almost an hour to just 20 minutes. In combination with the urban expansion policies Huang Qifan initiated in 2001, the change in relative distance enabled a wave of industrialization around Hailong, as manufacturers sought cheaper rents on the edges of the city. In May 2002, just weeks after his election, Yan converted his old house into a factory space that he rented to a furniture manufacturer for

5,000 RMB a year. Shortly after that, Yan allowed the village collective to become a partner in his rental contract, giving his fellow villagers a stake in his success. But if Hailong did not act quickly to provide more space and infrastructure, Yan warned, the manufacturer might leave, as had happened in Xiaogang. Hailong's exhibition hall prominently displayed a quotation from Yan's report: "Opportunity is a thief. If you don't seize it, it will take everything from you!"

The Strength of Charisma and Extralegal Land Development

Not included in the exhibition hall was the rest of the quote from Yan Jing's report: "No matter how many complaints we receive, our determination to develop our collective economy cannot be shaken." Unlike Xiaogang, Yan claimed, Hailong would need to "subordinate factional interests to the interests of the whole, short-term interests to long-term interests, and individual interests to collective interests." Thus, while Yan cultivated his image as a "good" and "capable" leader who governed through consensus, he was also prepared to embrace the more coercive tactics of the charismatic strongman (He 2003, 256–58). This determination was reflected in his bearing (Figure 16). Yan was a short man, sturdily built with broad shoulders, close-cropped hair, and deep-set eyes. When he spoke at public events, he barked his words so that he could be heard in the back of the room, and even informal conversations felt as if Yan was issuing battle orders. He always seemed to fill the room, in part because of the space his deferential subordinates invariably gave him.

One day over a lunch of medicinal pork stew, several of Hailong's cadres referred to Yan Jing as the "big bully" (*da henren* 大狠人), a derogatory term used for people who are overbearing and arbitrary in their use of power. Egging each other on with toasts of *baijiu* (白酒), they began describing the village committee as the "bully committee" and the village election as an election for best and biggest bully. The conversation then turned to Yan's temper. One official admitted that he did not enjoy playing cards with Yan, and there were several nods around the table. Yan got angry when he lost, sometimes threatening people with a *bangbang* (棒棒), a wooden carrying pole commonly used in Chongqing. Someone claimed that he had seen Yan throw dog feces at people. Another said Yan

Figure 16. Yan Jing, Hailong's charismatic party secretary. Photograph by Sara M. Watson.

had joked to him before a card game: "If you win, I'll beat the life out of you. If you lose, you'll have nothing to worry about." All agreed that if you had to play cards with him, it was best to lose. But everyone also expressed confidence that Yan's temper was a sure sign of his strong leadership.

Strong, stable leadership has been a hallmark of China's most successful corporatist villages (Chen 2014, 152; Hoffman and Liu 1997; Hou 2013; Oi 1999, 113), and Yan Jing's ability to shift seamlessly along the spectrum of charisma, from capability and consensus to strength and coercion, was crucial in mobilizing villagers to participate in re-collectivization. Like the corporatist leaders of the 1980s, who used their political clout to win the support of higher levels of government (Oi 1999, 115), Yan's strength was equally important in providing political cover for Hailong's experimental practices. Yan's lieutenant, Wen Jiancai, compared Yan to the monkey king in *Journey to the West:* like the monkey king, Wen argued, no one in the "heavens" of China's government could control Yan Jing. Though Yan's political powers were far from supernatural, his timing was fortuitous. In the early 2000s, municipal and township leaders were eager for economic development, and land use regulations were relaxed in the area surrounding Hailong because it had not yet been formally included within the urban construction boundary. By the time municipal officials started asking questions about Hailong's land use practices, reality had caught up with the myth, and Yan's success in catalyzing development had earned him powerful political patrons within the CCP, including Chongqing's party secretary, Bo Xilai.

In 2003, under Yan Jing's leadership, Hailong began encouraging village households to rent contracted agricultural land to the village collective's newly established land management corporation, which then consolidated the parcels and leased them to manufacturers. Like Xiaogang's experiments in land contracting, this practice occupied a legal gray zone beyond the bounds of law and policy at a time when both were undergoing change. As part of urban–rural coordination, the State Council began regularizing the transfer of rural land use rights through market mechanisms (Trappel 2016), a set of reforms further discussed in chapter 5. But the conversion of agricultural land to industrial use was still strictly prohibited, and one village official admitted that the process violated the letter of the law: "It appears to have the feeling of being illegal. The land was transferred secretly, without permission." At first, just five households—all headed by party branch members—rented the use rights for 30 *mu* (two hectares) of agricultural land to the village's land management corporation. But three years later, most households were participating, and the village controlled more than 1,300 *mu* (86.67 hectares), or approximately 60 percent of Hailong's total agricultural land.[8] This initiative appealed to villagers' self-interest: households received 1,200 RMB annually per *mu* of land transferred, a sum that ensured villagers earned more by renting their land than by farming it. In some cases, however, villagers had to be persuaded or coerced to "volunteer," as with the lotus ponds sacrificed for Hailong's first paved road. In part this was because the land management corporation then leased the parcels to manufacturers for an annual rental fee of 2,400 RMB per *mu* for unimproved land, while factory buildings could go for as much as 4,000 or 5,000 RMB per *mu*.[9] As Assistant Party Secretary Wen Jiancai noted, many villagers were upset at the large rent gap, but nobody had submitted a formal petition of complaint. In the party–state's cadre evaluation system, such petitions function as demerits, and Chongqing's municipal leaders praised Hailong's leadership for carrying out land collectivization without one villager petitioning higher levels of government in protest.

Sowing the Seeds of Urbanization: Turning Agriculture into Industry

As Yan Jing argued in his report on Xiaogang and Huaxi, it was not enough to rely solely on land for the village's development. Hailong needed to partner with capital, using the village's physical, financial, and human resources to produce an environment attractive to investment. But in 2002, with Hailong's weak financial health and its crippling debt, Chongqing's banks refused to grant the village a loan. Instead, the village's leaders established the land management company as a shareholding corporation. In April 2003, just as they began the land rental program, they also appealed to villagers to invest their hard-earned savings in the corporation at 10,000 RMB per share—a significant sum in a village where per capita annual net income was just 1,500 RMB. Again, Yan appealed to residents' self-interest, offering a 100 percent return in five years and a 10,000 RMB annual dividend thereafter. To inspire people to contribute, Yan put up the first chunk of money, investing several tens of thousands of renminbi in the new enterprise. Together, Hailong's 47 existing party branch members contributed more than two thirds of the 1.3 million RMB raised by the village, thus giving village cadres a significant financial stake in Hailong's future success.[10] The remainder of the financing was raised from local elites and party members from beyond the village, including members of local criminal organizations who were willing to take a chance on a risky investment.

Armed with land and money, the land management corporation got to work building the infrastructure for industrialization. Yan Jing organized a village construction team modeled on the contracting outfit he had run in Qingdao. Their first task was to build a new factory for the village's one existing manufacturer occupying Yan's former house. Hailong then started construction on its first paved road, connecting the village's interior to Chongqing's larger road network and (via the infrastructure installed underneath the pavement) to municipal electric, water, and gas systems. In total, the collective built three main roads in the village, stretching 7.7 kilometers and making the majority of the village's flatter western half accessible to car and truck traffic (Figure 17). As we drove down one of these narrow, winding (but paved) roads, a village party member proudly told me, "We made these roads ourselves. We laid them out and paid for

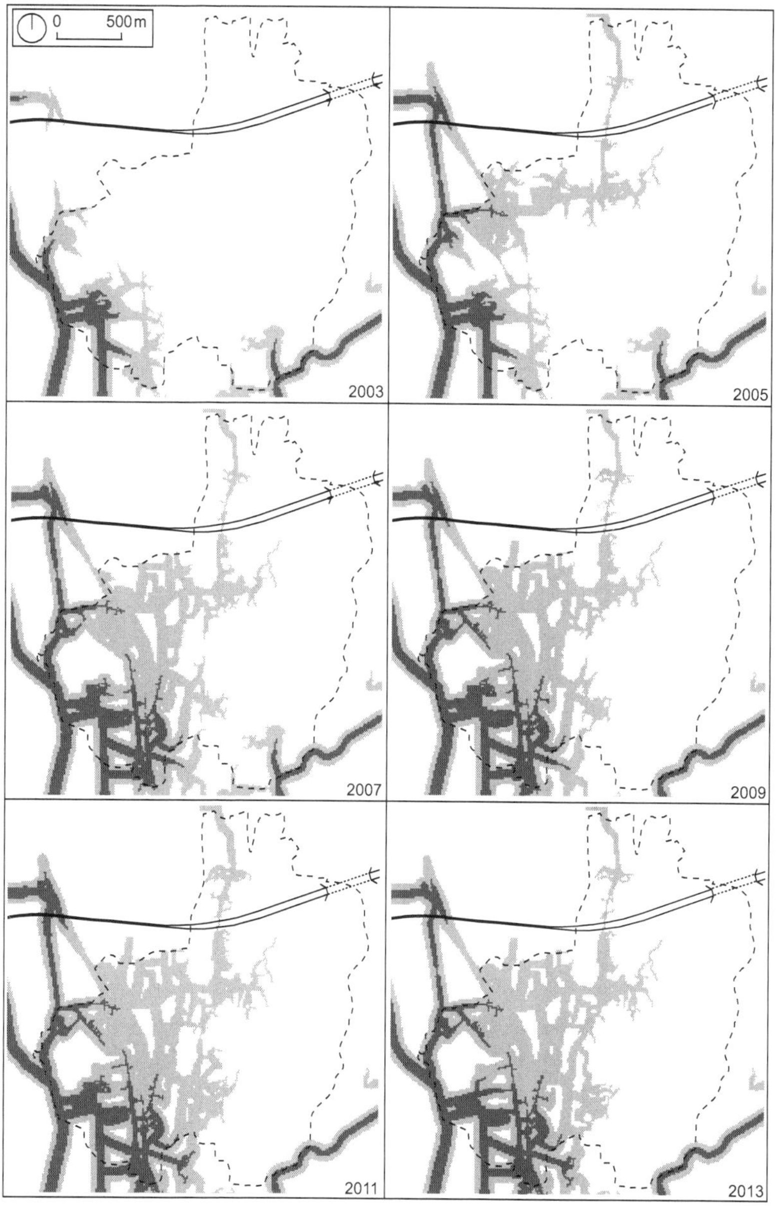

Figure 17. Car Accessibility. As Hailong expanded the village's road network, vehicular accessibility rapidly increased, making most of Hailong's flatter western third a 5- to 10-minute drive from the village entrance.

them." But as Assistant Party Secretary Wen Jiancai admitted, they had no knowledge of planning when they began: "None of us were qualified. At that time, we didn't have this idea of 'planning' (*guihua* 规划)." If they had taken the time to plan, Wen continued, "Hailong Village would simply not exist. Planning just three *mu* of land could take you a year or longer! Yan Jing wanted to use a thousand *mu*. He could turn into a mummy and still be at it!"

In 2003, just as Hailong was servicing its first batch of re-collectivized land parcels, Chongqing instituted a policy of "industrial peripheralization" (*tui er jin san* 退二进三), forcing manufacturers out of the city center to make way for the tertiary sector. Many manufacturers were suddenly in need of new factories, and Hailong offered both cheap rents and easy access to the city. By the end of 2003, the village had attracted 13 manufacturers with a total annual output of 6.2 million RMB. One of Hailong's first factories even produced components destined for orbit in China's human space flight program. Thousands of migrant laborers crowded into the village. Villagers' homes began expanding with extra rooms, additions, and three-story dormitories to accommodate them. Restaurants, convenience stores, hair salons, and gambling dens sprang up alongside rice paddies and vegetable plots. Staccato machine tools clattered over hen chirps, and acrid paint fumes wafted over lotus ponds. In the course of a year, Hailong went from sleepy agricultural backwater to crowded industrial estate (Figures 18 and 19).

Village Urbanization and the Demand for Development

Industrialization brought newfound prosperity. Within a year, villagers' annual per capita net income had tripled to an average of 4,800 RMB, and the village collective had paid off its debts. By 2006, the land management corporation was pulling in 2 million RMB in annual gross earnings, and Hailong's cadres suddenly faced a more welcome challenge: what to do with the village's wealth. The introduction of village elections in the 1990s was partly intended to improve public goods provision in China's villages by combating corruption and incentivizing the redistribution of collective resources to villagers (Brandt and Turner 2007; Luo et al. 2007; Wang 2003). But evidence from two decades of village elections suggests that democratic accountability may actually decrease with an

Figure 18. Village Industrialization. This west-facing view from Hailong's second ridge shows residences in the foreground, factories and dormitories in the middle ground, and West City in the distance.

increase in village wealth, as the economic leverage afforded by leaders' discretionary control over resource redistribution outweighs villagers' political demands for public goods (He 2003, 248–54; Wang 2003). Some scholars have therefore emphasized the role of village social networks and moral obligations in guiding the redistributive behavior of village leaders (He 2003; Tsai 2007, 12–13). This moralistic model of village leadership argues that thick village relationship networks and strong traditions of mutual aid can push village cadres toward actions that prioritize villagers' interests (He 2003, 17–18, 23–25). In particular, the social norms and moral obligations embedded in lineage organizations, religious societies, philanthropic associations, and other solidary groups can hold village leaders accountable for providing public goods (Tsai 2007, 4–5). As long as these groups coincide with the jurisdiction of the administrative village, the moral authority and social standing they offer can indirectly incentivize leaders to act in the interests of all villagers (Tsai 2007, 17).[11] These mechanisms rely on sources of "traditional" authority to balance "charismatic" leadership, and they also appeal to the desire for social status that

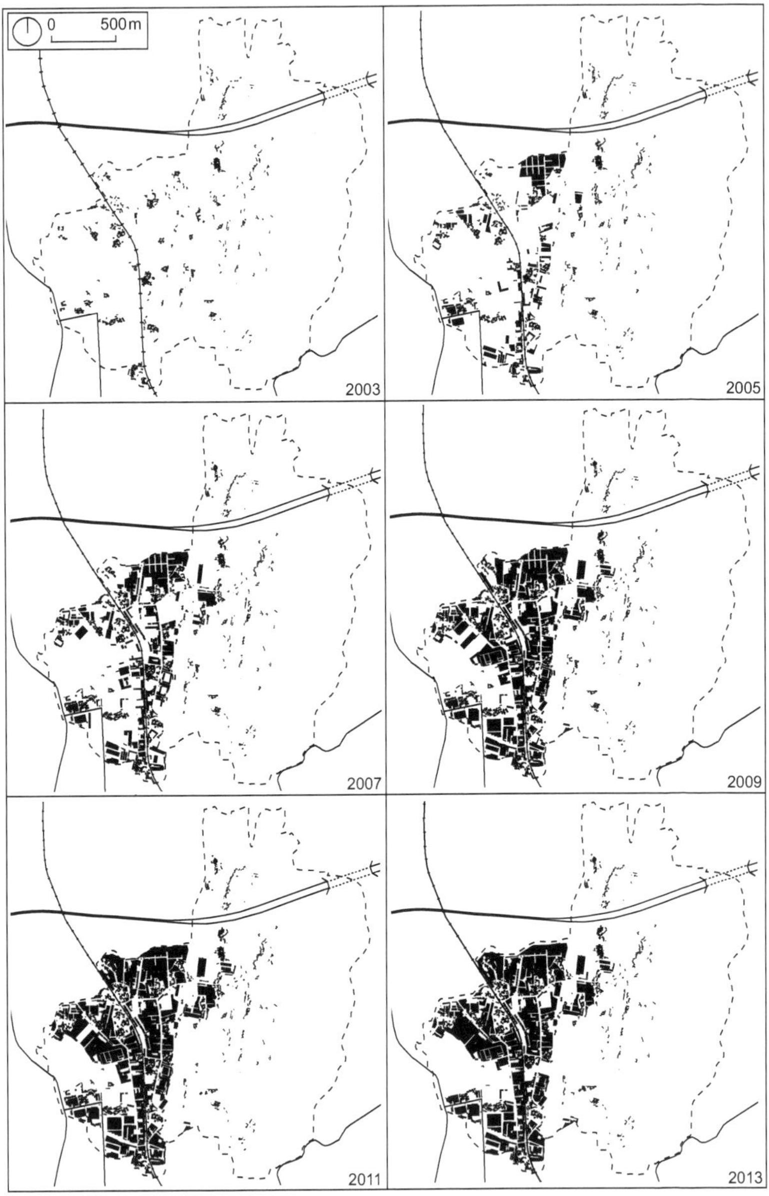

Figure 19. Village Transformation. This series of figure–ground drawings shows the rapid intensification of land use during the 2000s, as Hailong transformed from a sleepy agricultural backwater into a thriving industrial estate. The bulk of construction was concentrated in Hailong's flatter and more accessible west.

motivates "good" and "capable" village leaders (He 2003; Weber [1946] 2009). The strength of such traditional ties can even overcome national policies seen as unfair or exploitative, such as in the early 1980s, when villages like Xiaogang redistributed collective land to village households in violation of national laws. But as previously discussed, Hailong lacked such village-wide solidary groups. Its lineage organizations had been destroyed during the Cultural Revolution, and villagers' social ties were rooted in their natural villages rather than the administrative village.

In the absence of democratic or moral accountability, many scholars argue that the use of village resources will not reflect villagers' interests. Without countervailing pressure from below, the top-down power of the party–state is left unchecked, meaning that many village cadres use village resources to deliver on township priorities or secure their standing in the party (Edin 2003). Village leaders' substantial discretion over the disposition of collective resources also makes it possible for "evil" cadres to appropriate those resources for their own gain (Cai 2003; He 2003, 256–58; Wang 2003). Hailong villagers readily accused their leaders of such misdeeds, though the evidence for official malfeasance was mostly circumstantial. For instance, Ma Chuifeng, a fiery-tempered, middle-aged villager, claimed that Yan Jing had used village resources to help him get noticed by his superiors and attain promotion: "He's taken all of the money and used it on surface appearance. . . . He didn't use one cent to help us villagers. He hasn't used any of the money for anything real. It's to make other people think everything is great. But in reality, nothing is any good. It's all a superficial phenomenon." From Ma's perspective, Hailong's transformation was designed to impress delegations of senior party officials, who were given scripted tours of the most attractive pieces of the village, including the carefully curated exhibition hall.[12] Others referred to Yan Jing as a "corrupt official" who engaged in "personal behavior" (*geren xingwei* 个人行为), a euphemism for the self-interested exercise of power. As reported in the Hailong newspaper, one villager walked into a meeting and yelled, "Village officials the world over are all crows—they're all black! Collectivization just means taking everyone's money and putting it in your wallets!" As proof, villagers pointed to Yan's Mercedes-Benz and BMW, as well as his multiple properties, including a luxury villa in Hainan, China's resort island. But Yan professed his innocence. According to his defenders, he was guilty only of success, not corruption.

The accountability vacuum in village leadership can also attract criminal elements, who form alliances with village cadres or who seize outright control of village assets (O'Brien and Han 2009; Wang 2003, 45–46), and indeed there were indications of criminal activity in Hailong. Wang Ye, referred to as Brother Wang by village officials, was a gregarious and popular party cadre. He vaguely introduced himself as an entrepreneur who did "a little of this and a little of that." Officially, Wang ran a trucking and construction management business responsible for much of the earth moving in Hailong. He also was involved in construction projects throughout Chongqing, and his trucking business periodically took him on long trips to distant provinces. Wang was well connected, with a wide network of local officials, and his lavish fortieth birthday celebration included dignitaries from the district government and many of the neighboring towns. One night, Wang invited me out for karaoke in Baishiyi. In one room, I sang "red songs" with a group of Hailong cadres and Yan Jing's relatives.[13] In the next room, women from Wang's prostitution ring entertained officials from Xipeng, where Wang was in the process of bidding for a construction contract. Wang held no formal position in the village bureaucracy, but he was widely recognized as the village fixer. For example, when the power cut out at the construction site for the new village center, Wang knew where to send the cash-stuffed envelope to get things going again. He was often in meetings at the land management corporation offices, and he referred to their work with the pronoun "we," even though he was not treated as an employee. On the day of the village party branch's military training, Wang was the only cadre not in uniform. During the speeches and lectures, he sat in the back of the room looking at his phone, and while his fellow cadres marched, he jeered them on from the sidelines. Later that day, as we sat outside a restaurant on Easy Street, he called Yan Jing over to join us. It was the only time I ever saw anyone speak so familiarly to Hailong's all-powerful party secretary. I then watched Wang publicly shame Yan into drinking a glass of beer, even though Yan was known to be a teetotaler. As Wang gave me a ride back to the bus stop in his fully equipped BMW, I wondered who really called the shots. At the very least, Wang and the other investors in the land management corporation demanded repayment of their investments in the village, to the tune of 1.3 million RMB a year.

Wang Ye was also a member of Hailong's village party branch, which dramatically expanded its membership from 47 in 2001 to 207 in 2009. The village party branch played a central role in leading Hailong's transformation, and village development was simultaneously conceived as a way to strengthen the party organization. Assistant Party Secretary Wen Jiancai claimed that they were trying to "make the party relevant to people again" by providing economic leadership, and red banners filled with such slogans hung from the village's newly installed streetlights. The village also published *Hailong Party Building,* a magazine dedicated to celebrating the village's progress and the leadership of the party. Party membership came to be seen as an established pathway to wealth and power within Hailong. Party members owned the majority of Hailong's small businesses, and the high dividends paid to the land management corporation's original investors created a significant concentration of wealth within the party membership. For those who wanted to participate in guiding Hailong's development, and for those who just wanted a job working for the village, party membership was a necessity. All village officials were either party members or party applicants, and many staff members held concurrent positions in the party organization, the village collective, and the village enterprises. In the absence of a village-wide solidary group, Yan essentially created one from whole cloth, expanding the reach of the village party organization throughout Hailong's scattered neighborhoods and concentrating the village's power and wealth in the hands of party members as well as instilling military-style discipline and solidarity. This also established Yan atop a network of clients who made up 10 percent of the village population and whose loyalty he ensured through the distribution of favors and perquisites. Like China's other patronage networks (Hillman 2014), this strategy required a process of expansion and reproduction, in which the activities of the network continued to produce a surplus that could be redistributed to its members.

These various constituencies—Yan Jing's superiors, local creditors, and party members—all converged on the newly invented administrative village and the narrative of development Yan had promised. In their own ways, each group demanded that Yan deliver on that narrative and the promise of his charisma: his superiors demanded visible signs of progress, his investors demanded repayment (and new opportunities for graft), and his cadres demanded patronage. For the first few years of Hailong's development, land consolidation and industrialization were enough to satisfy these demands, but soon the village began running out of land, and between 2006 and 2009, the land management corporation added only 270 *mu* (18 hectares) to its existing total of 1,330 *mu* (88.7 hectares). To resolve this new crisis, Hailong turned toward a more intensive form of property development expressed in the apartment buildings and commercial spaces that lined Easy Street. By shifting out of manufacturing and into real estate, Hailong pursued a spatial fix to the declining returns of industrial development.[14] The greater density and higher rate of return would allow Hailong to earn enough income to satisfy its various constituencies, even as the village ran out of land. Thus, in the absence of democratic and moral accountability, it was in part the existence of corruption, criminality, and patronage politics that incentivized Hailong's cadres to build a new village center that would serve the Hailong community.

Village Urbanization and the Politics of Spectacle

The development of Easy Street and Hailong Square also reflected Yan Jing's need to burnish his charismatic reputation through the politics of spectacle. The great weakness of charismatic leadership is one's mercurial followers. If their perception of the leader's charismatic image falters, then the leader's authority evaporates (Weber [1946] 2009). One way that charismatic leaders combat this possibility is by extracting a surplus from society and then investing that surplus in symbolically weighted urban spectacles that reinforce their charisma. This can be seen in the geomantic design of China's imperial capitals, which used topographical features, axiality, and numerology to reinforce the leader's position as the link between heaven and earth (Wheatley 1971). A similar tendency can be seen in the design of Tiananmen Square and Chang'an Boulevard, which reoriented Beijing's axis and produced a monumental expression of Mao Zedong's charismatic connection with the masses (Hershkovitz 1993). Likewise, in Hailong, Yan's production of Easy Street and Hailong Square offered material proof of the strength and wisdom of his leadership, most powerfully expressed in the semiannual ritual of the party branch's military training. In this respect, Hailong's development was not only intended for the consumption of his superiors, as villager Ma Chuifeng had claimed; it was also aimed at villagers. Even if they objected to how Hailong's resources were redistributed, it was hard to argue with Yan's success in amassing and mobilizing those resources in the first place.

At the same time, Hailong's investment in Easy Street and Hailong Square also reflected an effort to institutionalize the administrative village as something more than just a bureaucratic invention held together by Yan Jing's charisma. Located adjacent to both the village's main pedestrian corridor (the rail line) and the village's most important social space (the area next to the rail crossing), the choice of site for the new village center was symbolically important (Figure 14). Here, Hailong began using its accumulated resources to build an alternative social space that would transcend the parochial networks of the natural villages. Instead of running their errands in nearby Baishiyi, residents could shop for groceries at the wet market or purchase medicines at the village pharmacy. Families could host weddings and other important events in the village meeting hall rather than renting a restaurant in town. A basketball court, Ping-Pong tables, and exercise equipment supported outdoor recreational activities. A kindergarten provided childcare for both villager and migrant families, though elementary and high school students still commuted to Baishiyi. This collection of buildings and services soon came to embody the idea of Hailong, not just as an administrative entity but as a community. Though they lived within the jurisdictional boundaries of the administrative village, Hailong's residents almost uniformly referred to Hailong as "over there," pointing toward Easy Street and Hailong Square.

On Friday and Saturday nights, the village police force carted a giant sound system out onto Hailong Square for night dancing (lit. "dancing on the flat," or *babawu* 坝坝舞). Under the glare of the square's stadium lights, hundreds of residents gathered to take their places in lines of dancing silhouettes, to gawk and gossip from the sidelines, or to spill into raucous Easy Street, where restaurants served beer, *baijiu,* and barbecue. In an echo of the lines of marching cadres, this noisy pageant of community togetherness signaled the constitution of Hailong as something more than mere administrative artifice. In Chongqing's urban centers, where high-rise apartment buildings and regimented workdays make it difficult to maintain dense social networks like those in Hailong's natural villages, night dancing is where community relationships beyond the family are fostered and reinforced.

While many of these functions existed in parallel with the social infrastructure of Hailong's natural villages, cadres framed other activities as direct substitutes. Just as the land management corporation embarked on building the new village center, the village collective also spent 200,000 RMB to purchase instruments and hire a conductor for the Hailong ladies' marching band, which practiced every Tuesday and Thursday in the village meeting hall next to Hailong Square. In a misogynistic twist on *The Music Man,* Yan Jing established the band to get women away from the village's mahjong tables. There, he claimed, women developed bad habits like gambling and gossip, which they might pass on to their husbands and children. But, as discussed in the following chapter, Hailong's mahjong parlors also provided an important venue for relationship building within and across village neighborhoods (and they catered to all members of the village population, including both men and women). By seeking to replace mahjong with band practice, Hailong's leaders were thus weakening neighborhood-based relationship networks in favor of a social experience organized by the administrative village. More than 50 villagers initially joined the group, including many of Hailong's wealthiest elites and most senior cadres, as well as members of Yan's own family.

Finally, the new village center, with its office buildings full of cadres, parking lots full of official vehicles, and signboards full of party propaganda, also supported the growth of Hailong's party branch. Easy Street and Hailong Square provided a space in which the members of this new community interacted and formed a corporate identity separate from their individual identities as residents of their respective neighborhoods. And, of course, the new village center offered the venue for the pageantry of military training, during which the teamwork and unity of the village party branch were put on display for the benefit of the entire village. Far from passive recipients of the redistributive largesse meted out by the municipal party–state through urban–rural coordination, Yan Jing and his fellow cadres were turning themselves into the protagonists of Hailong's transformation, catalyzing an urban future that would soon come into conflict with municipal visions of village development under urban–rural coordination.

Village Growth Machine

From a poverty-stricken village overwhelmed by China's rural development crisis, Hailong transformed itself into a vibrant industrial estate with an impressive village center in the span of just a few years. Yan Jing used a variety of approaches to build support for his bootstrapping initiative, essentially redefining the foundational category of rural life as the administrative village rather than the household or the natural village. Through the process of re-collectivization, village cadres extracted resources from Hailong's scattered households and natural villages to support the intensification of land use at the scale of the administrative village. This resulted in a path-dependent process of village transformation, with the construction of a new village center that would satisfy the demands of the invented community's various constituencies and substantiate Yan's claims of charismatic authority. Most importantly, the development of Easy Street and Hailong Square materially embodied the abstract category of the administrative village, providing an urban spectacle that residents identified as "Hailong" and a suite of activities and services that increasingly oriented residents toward the village as a meaningful category of belonging. This included providing a site for the continued growth of the village party branch, which became the main protagonist of village development and exercised primary control over the resources concentrated by the administrative village.

Hailong's strategy for escaping China's rural development crisis might be characterized as a "village growth machine." In the original formulation of the "growth machine" in the United States, private landowners maximize the value of their parcels by attracting development to the area, enlarging the population, and intensifying land use—in short, by producing growth (Molotch 1976; Logan and Molotch 1987). Scholars of Chinese urbanization have also used the growth machine to characterize China's cities, though in the Chinese context, the state's ownership of urban land gives the municipal government a dominant role in any growth coalition (He and Wu 2005; Wu, Xu, and Yeh 2007, 109–10). This leads to a specifically Chinese form of state-led growth machine, in which municipal governments, "as market players and regulators, have more complicated ultimate goals than 'growth'" (Wu, Xu, and Yeh 2007, 109; Xu and Yeh 2005, 302). Much the same phenomenon can be seen in Hailong, though collective land ownership and the village party branch took the place of state land ownership and the municipal government. In Hailong, the party branch's successful pursuit of village development quickly resulted in a path-dependent commitment to continued growth. Like the "urbanization of the local state," where China's municipal governments have become increasingly reliant on urban development to reinforce their legitimacy (Hsing 2010), the political and economic fortunes of Hailong's cadres came to rely on the ever-increasing extraction and concentration of resources by the administrative village. Similar growth-oriented tendencies were therefore driving both Chongqing's expansionist interpretation of urban–rural coordination and Hailong's efforts to catalyze village development. As Chongqing's development program continued to expand and Hailong's transformation continued to intensify, these competing visions put the municipality and the village on a collision course.

CHAPTER 3
Living on the Edge
Residents' Urban-Rural Strategies of Survival

By 2003, when village cadres were just beginning the process of recollectivization and industrialization, Hailong's villagers had already spent the first 25 years of the reform era struggling to make ends meet. While the 1980s were a decade of relative prosperity for rural villages along China's coast, economic liberalization brought little benefit to villages like Hailong, located in China's mountainous western interior. One villager recalled her childhood in the 1980s: "When my brother and I were young, there was never enough food to eat. . . . When I was little, noodles, bread, and dumplings were all luxuries. And when I was in high school, I dreamed of buying a cake. I wanted to eat cake so badly." In the summer, her father would wake her up at three in the morning and send her down to the bottom of the well to collect what little water had accumulated overnight. As the new millennium began, Hailong was still mired in poverty. Crime was common, corruption was rampant, and villagers frequently petitioned upper levels of government with their grievances. The village still lacked basic infrastructure like running water and cooking gas. Eighty percent of families lived in the same mud-and-timber houses they had inhabited during the war (Figure 20). As one elderly villager put it, "The road was dirt, and our houses were dirt. On sunny days you were covered with dust. On rainy days you were covered in mud."

A decade later, the conditions in Hailong had improved significantly, but villagers were still quick to blame their troubles on China's urban–rural binary and the party–state's exploitation of rural areas. Like Xu Jianguo's substitution of "urban–rural equal pay" for "urban–rural coordination," many villagers responded with derision when I asked about the party–state's

Figure 20. Mud-and-Timber Housing. Village houses from before the reform era were made of timber frames and earthen walls. Many of these houses were still inhabited in 2011, even as villagers built larger houses made of brick.

efforts to reduce urban–rural inequality. One villager retorted: "There is no coordination, only difference." Like other Hailong residents, he was upset that Chongqing's urban residents enjoyed much higher levels of welfare, with retirement benefits as much as 10 times greater than those received by rural residents. Another villager explained that "being rural means being forgotten," arguing that rural people and their needs are always deemphasized by the party–state in its pursuit of rapid urbanization. One villager's away message on social media summed up a common village sentiment: "To be a rural villager in China is pitiable, lamentable, detestable." Hailong residents acknowledged the many benefits that the village's decade of development had made possible, like access to electricity, running water, and cooking gas. But in their eyes, even development was a form of exploitation. Some people always benefited more, especially urban people and village cadres. Rural villagers always seemed to come last, and the material benefits of development had not changed the fundamental inequality of urban–rural difference.

Despite their frustrations at the exploitative nature of urban–rural difference, Hailong residents also prized their rural status. Whenever I mentioned Chongqing's household registration reform program, which offered all rural people in the municipality a pathway to become formally recognized urbanites (Tian 2010), Hailong residents would vociferously reject the idea of converting to urban registration status. Even sojourning migrants from remote villages with few prospects for near-term development would answer with a firm no.[1] The topic came up at lunch one day with a group of villagers and migrants eating together at the house of a village family, the Wangs. As a migrant entrepreneur from one of Chongqing's most remote and mountainous corners, Hu Hao already had been targeted by the municipality's new reform policy. But he flatly rejected the idea of converting to urban registration and instead rhapsodized about the flexibility of village life: "The rural is a wide paradise. You can run or walk anywhere. . . . Rural life is free and self-reliant." Picking up another morsel of fried cabbage with his chopsticks, he continued, "In the city, all you can do is eat what the state gives you." Villager Li Xiaowei echoed the sentiment: "There's too much pressure in the city; you always have to be producing. You can never get ahead." In contrast to the welfare paternalism of the party–state and the discipline of wage labor, they praised the "relaxed" and "simple" environment of the village, which offered the freedom to choose one's own path. Our host, Wang Dai, explained their objections with a common saying: "If you have your family" (he used his chopsticks to gesture at the people around the table), "your health" (he pointed his chopsticks at his heart), "and meat to eat" (he popped a piece of sausage in his mouth, grinning and smacking his lips), "then everything is good!" The phrase encapsulated three pillars of village life that Hailong residents were so reluctant to give up: the stability of family and community, embodied strategies of economic survival, and the conviviality of the shared meal.

Why were Hailong residents so ambivalent about urban–rural difference? If their shared identity as rural was such an important factor in their continued exploitation, then what could explain their desire to cling to that identity at all costs? In existing scholarship, rural residents' resistance to losing their rural status is often viewed as a function of the value attached to rural land use rights (He et al. 2009; Guo 2001; Yep

2013; Zhao and Webster 2011). In one version of this argument, rural residents are profit maximizers seeking a greater cut of the land rent increment captured by the local government through land sales (Yep 2013; Zhao and Webster 2011). From another perspective, residents are seen as welfare maximizers seeking enough compensation to ensure their continued survival after they lose access to their most basic guarantee of subsistence, their land (He et al. 2009; Guo 2001). Land was also an important consideration for Hailong residents, who would have to give up their rural land use rights to claim urban registration under Chongqing's reform program. Hailong residents were concerned with the maximization of both profit and welfare; however, as indicated by the conversation over lunch at the Wangs, there was something more going on than a mere desire for compensation. The rationalist language of utility maximization and monetary compensation obscures the inherent violence of displacement, in which rural people's affective ties to community and place are permanently disrupted (Chuang 2014; Sargeson 2013). As will become clear through the course of this chapter, considerations of profit and welfare cannot be separated from the social, spatial, and moral fabric of village life.

To understand why Hailong residents would reject household registration reform, it is necessary to see rural land use rights as more than merely rights to use land. Land use rights were also the guarantees of a way of life built up over decades of exploitation and neglect, through which Hailong residents ensured their stability and survival. Left to their own devices by China's bifurcated urban–rural system of administration, Hailong residents turned to time-honored principles of filiality and reciprocity enacted through the affective practice of "human feeling" (*renqing* 人情). Through the exchange of *renqing,* residents entangled diverse actors into assemblages that spanned the urban–rural spectrum, constructing a distributed model of agency that subverted the hierarchical discipline of the party–state's dominant urban and rural categories. Within families and neighborhoods, they built networks of mutual support that served as informal social insurance. And within their households, they built networks of economic diversification, pursuing riskier profit-making endeavors like entrepreneurship and migration that connected them to far-flung urban processes. Households stitched these strategies together through the only resource that was truly theirs: their land use rights. The use of housing construction land for self-built housing materially embodied networks that might otherwise seem ephemeral or intangible. The house and its proximity to neighborhood social spaces provided a physical connection to mutual support networks within the village. At the same time, it also offered a shared space through which to consolidate the gains of economic diversification and to which distant members of the household could return when risky ventures failed. Hailong's residents thus relied on the very system of urban–rural difference that perpetuated their exploitation, even as they challenged the hierarchical relations of urban dominance and rural dependence. By bringing an end to the village as a distinctive way of life, urban–rural coordination and household registration reform threatened to disrupt these adaptive strategies and force Hailong residents into newly uncertain modes of urban life.

A Moral Vacuum: Risk and Reliability in China's Social Insurance Systems

After decades left navigating poverty on their own, many residents felt abandoned by both the state and the village, whom they believed had failed in their moral duty to ensure residents' subsistence. In particular, China's state-sponsored social insurance programs, riddled with corruption and inefficiency and increasingly exposed to marketization, were often seen as unreliable and extortive (Chang 1993; Cook 2002; Liu 2007; Lora-Wainwright 2011). For instance, Chongqing's new rural health insurance scheme addressed small ailments and accidents relatively well, covering 80 percent of costs incurred at the local clinic, but as one moved up the hierarchy of hospitals, costs rose rapidly and coverage declined. When Lin Yi's elderly father ended up in a level 3 hospital with a serious stomach ulcer, his insurance only covered 30 percent of his costs, and Lin expected to pay almost 20,000 RMB out of pocket. Again and again, health insurance abandoned people precisely when they needed it most, and many faced crippling debt when their insurance ran out. Elderly villagers receiving chemotherapy racked up hundreds of thousands of renminbi in debt that their children would never pay off, others stopped treatment for terminal illnesses because they ran out of money, and some parents had to choose between monthly medication and tuition for their children to go to a better school. Like villagers in nearby Sichuan (Lora-Wainwright 2011, 119), many Hailong residents viewed health insurance as a state-sponsored swindle. Even among those rural residents in Chongqing who chose to convert to urban registration, a large proportion elected not to sign up for social insurance, excluding themselves from the very programs considered to be at the heart of urban privilege.

Criticisms of the government and the village and the failures of their support systems were often expressed through comparisons to advanced welfare states. For instance, in a conversation about life in the United States, villager Mi Antian maintained that American citizens did not have to work or pay for food. Her neighbor, Lei Hushi, expressed incredulity: "Now, that's not possible. Who's going to feed you? If no one is working, who's going to feed everyone?" In response, Mi replied, "Robots feed you. You command them, and they feed you." Neither woman imagined the state playing any role in this technocommunist paradise. For Lei, welfare always entailed a reliance on other people, and the only way Mi could imagine escaping such a necessity was to invent an army of robot servants. Another villager, Ren Ting, criticized those who relied on state welfare instead of mutual support. For Ren, migrants who left their children behind to be cared for by the state were failing in their moral duty. As Ren put it, "All you're doing is increasing the state's burden." She compared this to her daughters, who sent her money every month: "Why would we need the state for this? Some people want to take advantage of the situation. They say, 'I'll just leave my parents in the village, and then the state will have to take care of them.' This is just plain wrong." Like Mi Antian's imagined robot utopia, Ren's critique was remarkable for the omission of any moral responsibility on the part of the state, which should be turned to only as a last resort.

Residents' critiques of the government and the village instead pointed to an alternative system for ensuring stability and survival in the context of urban–rural difference and rural exploitation. As China's reform period has led to the retreat of entitlements and the marketization of state welfare institutions, community-based systems of mutual support have become increasingly important as mechanisms of informal social insurance.[2] In many villages, these networks are strongest at the level of the natural village or production team, where generations of colocation and shared responsibility have produced tight-knit relationships of trust (Chan, Madsen, and Unger 2009, 322–23, 365–66).[3] On the basis of shared values of filiality and reciprocity, and rooted in the sociospatial fabric of Hailong's natural villages, these grassroots systems of rural social welfare possessed precisely the moral accountability and reliability that residents felt China's formal welfare systems lacked.

Networks of Mutual Support and the Practice of *Renqing*

"Have you eaten?" The phrase is a stock greeting in China, a polite inquiry between friends and acquaintances passing on the street. During my first visits to China, I learned to respond in the affirmative, even when I was starving. To do otherwise was to embark on a parody of politesse—dueling invitations, refusals, reiterations, and deferrals. Once I arrived in Hailong, it took me some time to get used to the idea that people in the village actually meant it when they asked. Rather than using it as a pleasantry, village residents often used it as a bona fide invitation to eat. Contrary to my experience on the streets of downtown Chongqing, to say that I had already eaten was to rudely shut down the possibility of a meal together. And as I became a more familiar face in Hailong—as I graduated from formal honorifics, like "teacher," to familial ones, like "uncle"—the invitations became more insistent, sometimes culminating in brief, good-natured scuffles as my soon-to-be-host struggled for a firm grip on my arm. Slowly, I realized that these invitations were far more than a superficial social protocol. They were an effort to integrate me—and my knowledge, relationships, and resources—into the community. I learned to arrive in Hailong with an empty stomach.

So even at 10 o'clock in the morning, as I sidled past the Wangs' dog, whose loyalty (or whose grudging indifference) I had won only recently, and peered through the open doorway of the dimly lit mud-brick living room, I was unfazed by Shi Chunliang's shouted greeting—not the familiar question I was ready for, but the imperative: "Come eat!" It was one of Chongqing's rare crisp fall days, and I was soon installed on the Wangs' doorstep with a bag of peanuts and a bowl of green oranges, while Shi and her father-in-law, Wang Anshi, began preparing the midday meal. As I started to protest, Shi shushed me: "We always have people over to eat—family, neighbors, friends. Everyone knows that they can come eat with us. There's no need to tell us you're coming. Just show up and we'll have food to eat." The Wangs were one of the poorest families in the village, but what Shi said was true; it seemed there were always at least one or two people gathering at their house for a meal. At lunch that day, nearly a dozen people crowded into the main room around the Wangs' table, including Wang Anshi's two sons, Wang Bo and Wang Dai, as well as their families; Hu Hao, a migrant entrepreneur; Shi Yuzhen, a villager who worked in one of Hailong's factories; Li Xiaowei, who was born in Hailong, worked most of her life for a state-owned enterprise in another province, and had recently returned to live in the village; and, of course, a researcher from the United States. The Wangs' lunch table represented the full spectrum of village society, and each person seated at the table in turn connected us to an even wider network of personal relationships and resources. Through our shared meal, we wove the filaments of a network that spanned Hailong, Chongqing, China, and beyond.

Like the many meals being enjoyed across Hailong at the same time, the Wangs' lunch table was a site for the active production of *renqing*, a word used for the everyday exchange of favors or gifts, the long-term building of relationships, and the larger moral landscape of the village. One villager described *renqing* as the opposite of the moral vacuum left by state and village welfare systems: "Between people you need reciprocity—mutual reliance, mutual concern, mutual help. . . . For everyone to benefit, you have to sacrifice a little of your own." Scholarship on *renqing* often conceptualizes these practices in relation to Chinese "relationship networks" (*guanxi* 关系), where *guanxi* is described as the more instrumentalized—and urban—form of the affective ties constituted through traditional, rural practices of *renqing* (Yang 1994, 68–71).[4] But like the distinction between urban and rural, the distinction between *guanxi* and *renqing* is not clear-cut (Wilson 2002), and the two practices can best be conceived as different articulations of a single "total social phenomenon" that encompasses both the economic and the affective dimensions of social life (Kipnis 1997; Mauss [1950] 2000). In this system of ethical action, the formation of personal relationships is both means and ends. The cultivation of *renqing* expresses the current shared emotional experience of human attachment and anticipates a future time when that connection may serve a more instrumental purpose (Kipnis 1997, 11).

The principle of reciprocity that undergirds *renqing* is most clearly manifested in the exchange of gifts, which pervaded everyday life in Hailong, just as it does in much of China. To refuse a gift was to reject a relationship with the giver, whereas to accept a gift was to take on a responsibility to reciprocate at some point in the future (Yang 1994, 142). *Renqing* is thus constituted through relationships of mutual obligation, reinforced over multiple rounds of exchange that demonstrate both the loyalty and the reliability of the actors (Kipnis 1997, 31; Wilson 2002, 7; Yang 1994, 68, 145). This store of *renqing* ensures one's ability to gain access to community resources through the request of a favor or mutual aid, which in turn entails an obligation to reciprocate (Wilson 2002, 7; Yang 1994, 68–69).[5] These obligations are sometimes settled monetarily, and the rise of the money economy during the reform era has made the exchange of cash *renqing* gifts commonplace (Wilson 2002), but outside of weddings and holidays, cash was frowned on as overtly instrumental and therefore insufficiently endowed with *renqing*. For instance, when my lunch host, Wang Dai, asked a wealthy nearby villager and distant cousin, Wang Yangfei, for a loan of 10,000 RMB, Yangfei demurred. Even in the form of a loan, the exchange of so much money violated the principles of *renqing*. It would be years before Dai could repay the loan, and because it was a *renqing* gift, Yangfei would not be able to collect interest. Finally, they arrived at a compromise: Yangfei would use his business contacts (thereby incurring a new debt of *renqing*) to get Dai a fake job at a nearby construction site. All Dai had to do was show up, and the construction company would pay him enough money to cover his expenses. This would avoid the embarrassment and inconvenience of a monetary debt, thereby keeping the exchange of mutual obligation entirely within the *renqing* circuit.

By far the most common mechanism for reciprocating a gift and building *renqing* was the shared meal (Kipnis 1997, 14; Steinmüller 2013, 172). This was an important reason why Li Xiaowei often came by the Wangs to chat but only occasionally ate at their house, complaining euphemistically that it took her days to recover from the "heavy" food. As a wealthier villager, eating too often at her neighbors' houses meant burdening herself with *renqing* debts that demanded repayment. Conversely, this was also why there was always a big meal on at the Wangs' house despite (or rather because of) their relative poverty. They relied on the generosity of others to piece together odd jobs, doctors' visits, and childcare, and an invitation to lunch was one of the few ways to balance the ledger. Seated at the Wangs' lunch table, I was not only witnessing the enactment of *renqing* networks, I was also entangling myself in them, one morsel of food at a time. This much became clear as Wang Anshi gathered the dishes and Wang Dai pulled me aside to offer me a cigarette and ask for a favor. Both his children suffered from congenital health issues, and he did not trust the medicine dispensed by the hospital. Could I fill their prescriptions in the United States the next time I went home? I was the only non-Chinese person he knew and the only person in his network who could help make sure his children received reliable medicine: "We're friends, right? I would owe you big time."

The prominent role of food in *renqing* and the frequent use of consumables (such as liquor, fruit, candy, and cigarettes) as *renqing* gifts was no coincidence. Whether it be a bowlful of rice or a puff of smoke, their literal absorption into the body materially enacts the mutual entanglement of the desired social relationship. The reciprocal obligation of *renqing* means that a gift is never fully alienated from the giver or fully possessed by the receiver: "Donor, gift, and recipient share a common symbolic substance, a linkage made possible through the medium of the gift" (Yang 1994, 191–202). The personal substance of the giver is attached to the gift and thereby attached to the receiver, breaking down the barrier of otherness and transforming the other into the familiar (Yang 1994). This means that people are not self-contained individuals independent of the exchange of *renqing* (Fei [1948] 1992). The gift and the relationship it embodies instead constitute the self as a fluid collection of social relationships (Kipnis 1997, 8). Thus, while it is possible to talk about "possessing" one's own *renqing* network, each person also functions as a node in the wider shared network that unevenly interconnects the whole of the social world. The "human feeling" of *renqing* is therefore not an internal psychological state but a shared social experience, where the exchange of gifts gathers and materially manifests the relationships tying the participants together (Kipnis 1997, 28, 48). In this respect, the exchange of gifts can be understood as the circulation of affect, the intersubjective articulation of emotions and attachments through which subjects are formed and their relationships constituted (Massumi 2002; Thrift 2004). As an affective practice, *renqing* serves as a means of constituting the socially distributed self through the entanglement of diverse actors, resources, and networks, all of which can be called upon in the future.

As I will show in the following pages, this social constitution of the self also extends to the nonhuman world, as actors share food, exchange mahjong tiles, build and inhabit houses and courtyards, and migrate to distant cities. Through the practice of *renqing,* village residents were therefore also engaged in the production of assemblages, emergent and unbounded phenomena in which social agency is distributed across rhizomatic, nonhierarchical networks of internal relationships that include nonhuman (but nevertheless social) actors (Farías 2012; McFarlane 2011; cf. Latour 2005). To understand village society and its reliance on *renqing,* it is thus necessary to examine both the material fabric of village space and the spatial practices of its inhabitants.

Turning the Outside In: Village Courtyards and Social Heat

Perched on the threshold as I waited for lunch at the Wangs, I was paradoxically seated at the very center of their house. As I peeled an orange and tried to stay out of the way, Wang Anshi lit the fire of an outdoor stove, where he began frying a head of cabbage that was too large to cook on the stove inside. Nearby, an earthen pit awaited sausages that village families smoked for the New Year. The hearth is the symbolic center of the Chinese household and the site of the Kitchen God (*zao jun* 灶君), the most important of the Chinese domestic gods that protect the family (Simoons 1990). By keeping a second hearth outside the walls of the house, the Wangs made a symbolic claim on this outdoor space even though they did not hold legal title to the land. It was a claim of inclusion rather than exclusion, blurring the lines between the space of the family and the surrounding community. As Wang cooked the cabbage, people walked by on a neighborhood path. Some lingered and chatted, and by the time lunch was ready, there was a small knot of people outside the Wangs' home gossiping, snacking, smoking, and tending to the growing flock of scampering children.

The open space outside the Wangs' house was one of countless "courtyards" (*yuanzi* 院子) that served as important nodes in Hailong's *renqing*

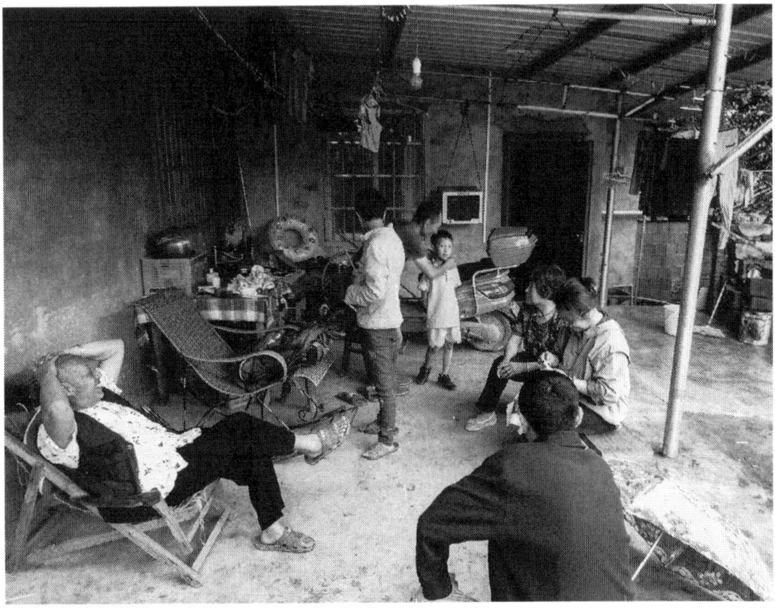

Figure 21. A Village Courtyard. The threshold of a village house served as the extended family's most active social space and a meeting place for people from the neighborhood.

networks (Figure 21). The classic form of the courtyard is a walled and gated space exclusive to the household, but the term can also refer to a semienclosed or loosely delineated space, such as an area of pavement or shade adjacent to the house. This was especially true both in Chongqing, where a mild climate meant residents treated indoor and outdoor spaces as an integrated whole, and also in Hailong, where the original enclosed courtyards of the old landlords had been divided up among multiple families during socialist land reform. In Hailong's neighborhoods, every interstitial piece of flat land counted as a courtyard, functioning as an outdoor extension of the neighboring houses.[6] Used for playing badminton, smoking meats, sharing gossip, or just watching the day go by, courtyards provided spaces of social intersection, where the household's private world became entangled with the village's public sphere (Figure 22). These activities turned courtyards into sites of "social heat" (*renao* 热闹), where people came together and connected with each other.[7] What makes social heat hot is the friction of social encounter, as the conventional divisions between inside (private) and outside (public) are broken down.[8]

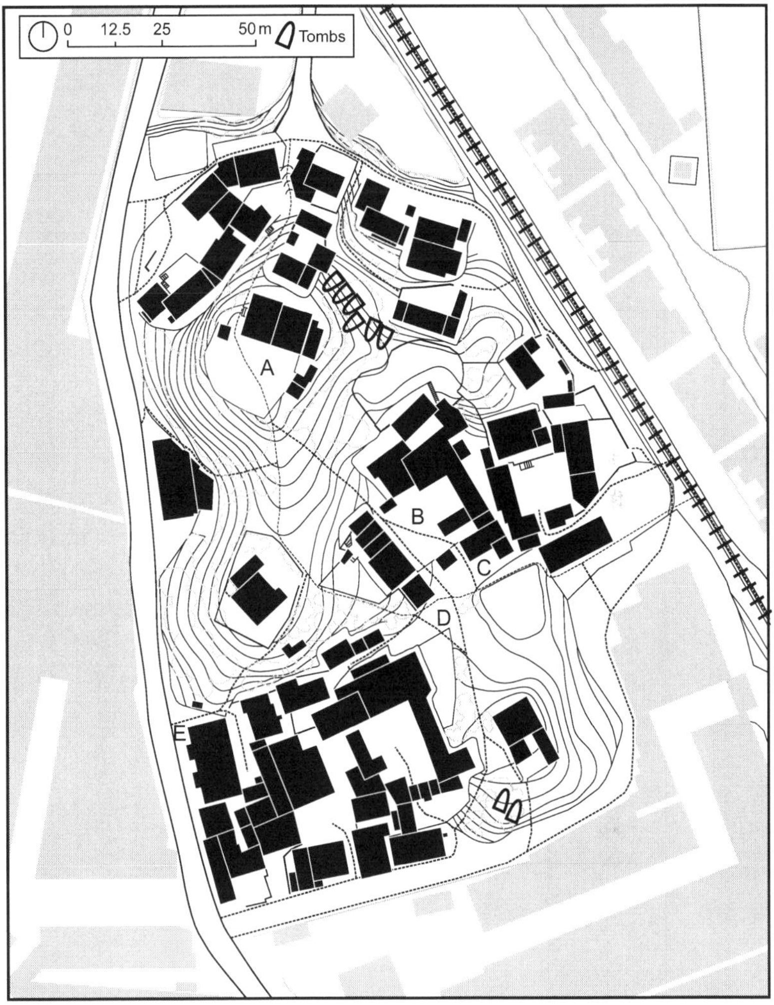

Figure 22. Community Two. This figure–ground drawing depicts one of Hailong's many natural villages, which was surrounded by factory buildings. Villagers' self-built housing and migrant dormitories were interspersed with tombs, agricultural plots, and interstitial social spaces. Active social spaces are labeled on the map: (A) an extension of a villager's house and a neighborhood thoroughfare; (B) a courtyard often used for badminton and other outdoor games; (C) an extension of a villager's house and a popular congregating spot; (D) the site of an outdoor smoking pit; and (E) a mahjong parlor and convenience store.

The same relationship underlies *renqing*, which "is expressed in the attempt to transform the other into the familiar, to bridge the gap between the outside and the inside" (Yang 1994, 193). Part of the overwhelming attraction of social heat in Chinese culture is thus the desire to sublimate the self into the social, thereby strengthening the socially constituted self through the extension of *renqing*.

The attraction of social heat made Hailong's courtyards privileged sites for the practice of "visiting" (lit. "stringing together doors," *chuanmen* 串门). Residents would often pull up a stool just outside their houses, engaging friends and neighbors as they passed. Doors were typically left open, making the entrance rooms to people's houses publicly accessible, and acquaintances would wander in after calling out to make their presence known. By stopping by for a quick chat or a longer visit, friends and neighbors metonymically reproduced the mutuality of *renqing* (Kipnis 1997, 13), and by providing opportunities for gossip, visiting allowed them to gather information that could guide future *renqing* acts (Farrer 2002, 8). Lin Yi expressed the importance of visiting when he explained why he was comfortable leaving his son and his parents behind in Hailong for months at a time while he and his wife ran a factory in Chengdu. He was confident in the knowledge that if anything happened, their neighbors and friends were "just outside the door" and ready to lend a hand. By contrast, he feared the anomie of high-rise living: "In the city, it's like this: your door's across from your neighbor's, but you don't know each other. When you walk in the door, it's a security gate. It's an iron grille shut against the world."

Households' courtyards were part of a wider network of such spaces that spanned the village, with more active courtyards located near the intersections of paths and roads, where there was plenty of social heat. The two most important of these courtyards functioned as the spatial centers of Hailong's social networks and were located where the village's access roads met the rail line that bisected the village and served as its main pedestrian thoroughfare. Tucked under a large tree at the southern end of the village lay the courtyard where I encountered Xu Jianguo and his poetic reformulation of "urban–rural coordination" into "urban–rural equal pay." The other—a shady collection of stone blocks and wooden stools that overlooked the village's main rail crossing—primarily served northern Hailong. Around three o'clock in the afternoon, residents would gather in the lengthening shade, trading gossip and watching the melee of factory trucks, luxury sedans, and three-wheeled tuk-tuks. As individual residents made their rounds, moving from one courtyard to the next, their circulating bodies connected these spaces together, sharing bits of gossip from one household or neighborhood with another and allowing even the most isolated residents to participate in the village's *renqing* networks.

Hailong's courtyards thus provided the spatial infrastructure necessary for the everyday encounters through which residents strengthened and extended their *renqing* networks. Much of the existing literature on *renqing* practices has focused on periodic celebrations. In particular, weddings present prime opportunities for extending *renqing,* as new kin groups are welcomed into the village and distant relatives return to celebrate (Bradnstädter 2003; Kipnis 1997; Steinmüller 2013). Celebratory events like weddings, birthdays, and festivals also punctuated social life in Hailong, and they served as important opportunities for building *renqing,* especially for those who no longer resided in the village. Like the village's lunches, these events involved shared meals, and they often included heavy, ritualistic drinking, through which individual attendees both affirmed their mutual regard and broke down the inhibitions that might prevent the affective outpouring of *renqing.* In the social lives of Hailong residents, however, the village's courtyards and the everyday encounters they facilitated were far more important. The ethical principles that structured more formalized gatherings were also inscribed into the everyday sociospatial fabric of the village, thereby producing repeated opportunities for building *renqing* that occasional visitors could not easily access. The practice of *renqing* and thus the village's networks of mutual support and reciprocity intimately relied on the sociospatial infrastructure of Hailong's courtyards.

Mahjong Parlors and Gambling

Hailong residents also built their *renqing* networks through gambling. One of the most common spaces in Hailong was the "mahjong parlor" (*majiang guan* 麻将馆), which could be found hidden in storefronts, covered courtyards, and back rooms. Here, residents played mahjong or "landlord" (*dou dizhu* 斗地主), a three-player card game. Though some residents had serious gambling problems, most played for a symbolic one-*kuai* ante, and a clear distinction was made between the valorized act of playing (*wan* 玩) and the ostracized act of gambling (*du* 赌) (Steinmüller 2013, 182). In this context, gambling losses could even be considered a kind of "prestation" (Mauss [1950] 2000), in which the loser gains prestige through a lack of self-regard (Oxfeld 1993). Players may also lose on purpose as a means of informal gift giving (Steinmüller 2013, 185), thereby ensuring the winner's continued participation in the game, because refusing a subsequent round after winning would demonstrate a miserly disregard for *renqing* (Festa 2007, 94). On summer afternoons, Hailong's mahjong parlors were full of players and onlookers escaping the heat of the sun for the social heat of the game. Over time, circles of friends gravitated toward one parlor or another, and there were weekly games that even nonresidents regularly attended. Variations in the ante created some socioeconomic segregation, but few games were played for more than five *kuai* a point. Overall, the mahjong parlors were remarkably egalitarian spaces, where social differentiations of wealth, class, occupation, and household registration were temporarily set aside (Festa 2007, 111; Oxfeld 1993, 16). The need for three players in landlord and four players in mahjong meant that strangers or distant acquaintances played together nearly as much as close friends, and when players had to leave, an onlooker would take their seat. Like courtyards, mahjong parlors also hummed with gossip, which both displayed social closeness and provided information necessary for the navigation and mobilization of *renqing* networks. Even for those without the money for gambling, mahjong parlors were thus key sites of social heat, and onlookers often outnumbered the players.

In different ways, the games of mahjong and landlord produced spaces in which people could transcend their otherness and recognize their mutuality. The tactile nature of mahjong creates a synchronized rhythm between the players, inducing a near-hypnotic state where everything but the movement of hands and clicking of tiles recedes into the background. While there may be winners and losers, in mahjong, you play both against the other people at the table and with them. Together, the four players are agonistically engaged in a common battle with each other and with luck. The "spell-binding sensuosity" of mahjong denaturalizes the borders between self and other, as the psychological sovereignty of the self is sublimated into the shared embodiment of play (Festa 2007, 103, 111). The self-effacing quality of mahjong can be understood as a medium for the players' experience of their shared *renqing.* In Hailong's mahjong parlors, my lack of experience made me an undesirable fourth, not because I often lost—that much made me an easy mark—but because I was often caught overthinking my next move, betraying an excessive self-regard and disrupting the rhythm of the social encounter.

In the game of landlord, the construction of sociality is symbolic rather than haptic. After the deal, the three players bid on the basis of the strength of their cards. The high bidder becomes the landlord, playing alone against the other two players, who become a team—the peasants. Rather than transcending the social divisions of the real world, as in mahjong, landlord essentializes them, emphasizing differences in wealth and power and calling attention to the social atomization of rural life. Landlord reflects the social world back on itself, crystallizing players' fears of social isolation and creating a context within which they can playfully fight back against those fears. The two peasants are codependent, but, as in the game of bridge, they cannot coordinate their play. Instead, they must overcome their separation by reading each other's intentions through the cards they play. If they win, the strength of their *renqing* is confirmed, and the landlord must pay them both. If they lose, it might be blamed on the cards or, the spell now broken, the ineptitude of one's partner. Playing landlord therefore both symbolically expresses the shared desire for connection (and the shared fear of losing it) and materially strengthens the *renqing* between the two players. As with the *renqing* gift, the act of playing is both means and ends.

Kinship Networks and House Building

By destabilizing the presumed opposition between outside and inside, *renqing* networks effectively extend principles of kinship, such as mutual obligation and responsibility, beyond the family to the wider social sphere (Bradnstädter 2003, 437; Kipnis 1997, 17; Yang 1994, 305). It is little surprise, therefore, that Hailong residents facing problems often turned to close kin before their networks of neighbors and friends. And just as access to community *renqing* networks relied on the sociospatial infrastructure of courtyards and mahjong parlors, so too did maintenance of kinship networks depend on relatives' colocation. As in many Chinese villages, Hailong villagers achieved this through innovative approaches to self-built housing, which they continually adapted and redesigned to accommodate the changing needs of their extended families, thereby keeping their kinship networks intact and ready to respond to the dangers of living in China's urban–rural interstices. In the context of urban–rural difference and rural exploitation, villagers' self-built housing provided spaces within which to advance their own systems of meaning making and social solidarity. China's rural houses represent "a centring of moral choices and a centre of moral judgement" that is committed to the continuation of the family and its reciprocal exchanges with the community (Steinmüller 2013, 93)—precisely the ethic of *renqing* that structures village life.

In building their own houses, villagers bypassed formal design and construction practices in favor of "self-design" (*ziji sheji* 自己设计) and the labor of informal workers and friends (Figure 23). Ma Chuifeng, who built his two-story house in 1997 for 25,000 RMB, described the process: "In my mind, I thought about how to do it. I started from how we would use it. . . . I designed it myself." Shi Nuo, who built his two-story house in 1995 for about 10,000 RMB, similarly rejected professional design services as an unnecessary extravagance: "You don't need design. Just think with your head and you'll know how to build it. . . . Those designers all want a lot of money to prepare drawings. Here we just use our heads and build it. Why would you need a drawing?" In both cases, design emerged from anticipated family needs and a shared understanding of functionally determined housing typologies. These self-designed construction projects relied on villagers' access to "housing construction land" (*zhaijidi* 宅基地), which was provided to each registered household for building activities. In the flatter western section of Hailong, village households also expanded beyond their designated land allotments to build on "wasteland" (*huangdi* 荒地), a residual category including all rural land not formally designated for other uses. Though villagers could not secure use rights to this land, building on wasteland was generally allowed, and the practice offered cash-strapped villagers a way to expand their housing without paying the extra cost of building higher.[9]

Figure 23. Building a Mahjong Parlor. Three workers built an extension to a village household's self-built housing, aided by the household's patriarch.

To see the importance of self-designed housing for villagers' mutual support strategies, it is only necessary to return to the Wangs, who often needed extra help with childcare. Lacking substantial financial resources, the Wangs constructed their housing incrementally and adaptively, periodically redesigning their housing to accommodate the arrival of new family members (Figures 24 and 25). To the east of the original mud-and-timber building, Wang Anshi's older son, Wang Bo, built a two-story house with a separate entrance for himself and his wife. To the west, Wang Anshi's younger son, Wang Dai, built a two-room addition, including a living room, a bedroom, and a bathroom. This addition had both its own entrance and a door communicating with Wang Dai's old bedroom in the original house, affording Dai's family their own living space while allowing them to share the kitchen and living rooms in the original house. Dai and Chunliang acted as primary caregivers for their children, and the semidetached housing allowed Wang Anshi and Wang Bo's wife to fill in as needed. When Dai and Chunliang both took on new jobs, Chunliang's mother moved in to provide more regular childcare. With this change, the Wang family added another bed and bath suite to the front of Wang Dai's wing and installed an awning over the

Figure 24. Exterior of the Wangs' House. The exterior of the Wangs' house in 2011 shows the adaptive use of courtyard space for agricultural activities. Wang Bo's addition is to the left and Wang Dai's to the right. The original mud-and-timber house is shown in the center.

house's unenclosed courtyard to expand its living space. When Wang Anshi compared their self-built housing to the possibility of moving into high-rise relocation housing, he described the house as "wide" (*kuan* 宽): "Those apartments aren't as wide as our house. Why would we want to move?" While "wide" is often used to indicate size, the Wangs' relocation housing actually would be larger than their current house when measured in total square meters.[10] When I pointed this out to him, Wang Anshi emphasized the term's connotations of relaxation and flexibility. His use of "wide" in this context was intended to communicate a concern not just with the absolute size of the housing but also with the degree to which it fit (or could be made to fit) with their lives. Villagers' self-built housing could be endlessly adapted, supplemented, and rebuilt to accommodate new family arrangements. By contrast, high-rise units came in a limited number of configurations, thus forcing families to adapt to their housing rather than vice versa. In the case of the Wangs, they would have to divide their relocation housing between two separate apartments, further challenging their mutual support strategies.

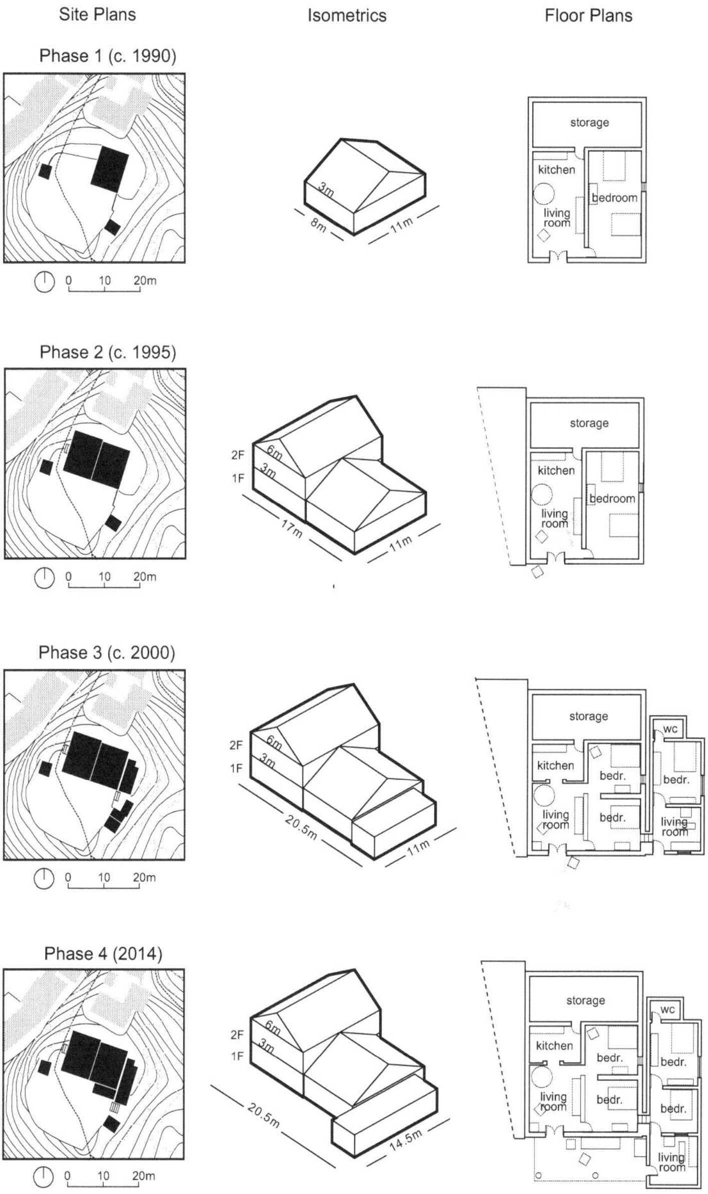

Figure 25. Adaptation of the Wangs' House. From 1990 to 2015, the Wang family went through three main phases of construction. First Wang Bo added a two-story addition with a separate entrance; then Wang Dai added a two-room annex; and most recently an extra bedroom was added to the annex to accommodate Wang Dai's mother-in-law. In the most recent adaptation, a corrugated metal awning was added to the front of the house, reflecting the tight sociospatial integration between the living room and the house's exterior.

Figure 26. Exterior of the Lis' House. This exterior shot of the Lis' house shows the three-story house, with a covered roof and an enclosed courtyard.

Just down the hill from the Wangs, Li Xiaowei and her two siblings banded together to care for their mother, who had been paralyzed and bedridden for years. One of Li Xiaowei's brothers, Li Huangyu, and his wife, Ren Ting, who had little in the way of income, provided daily care,

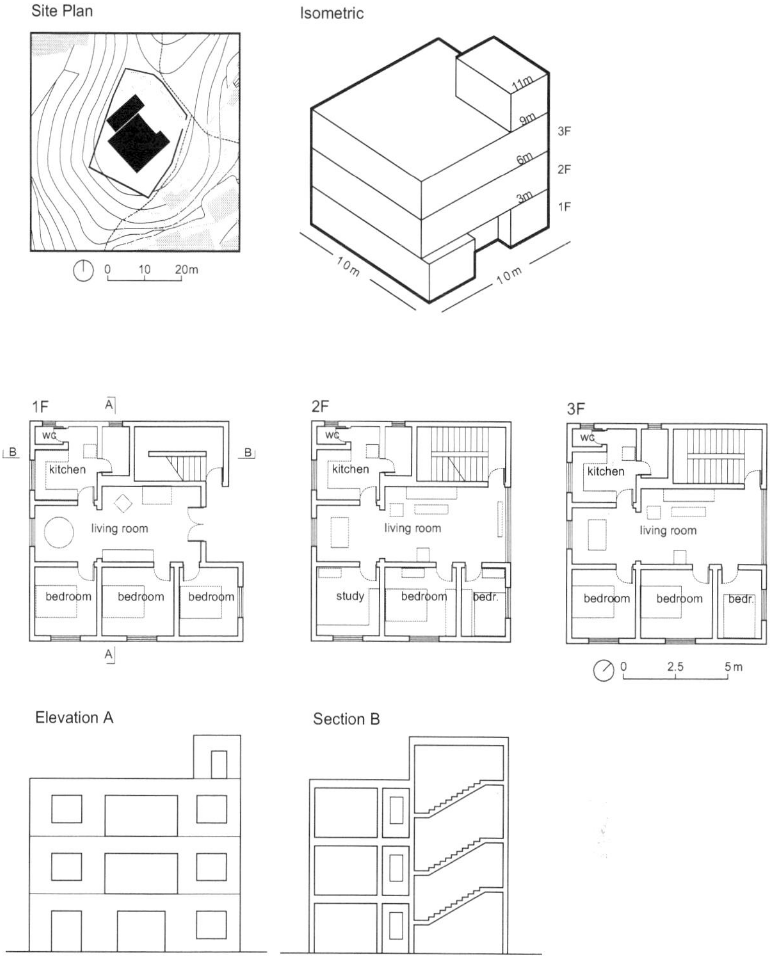

Figure 27. Structure of the Lis' House. The Lis' house was composed of three main floors, each of which was home to a separate branch of the Li family. An attached staircase with an exterior entrance allowed convenient access. The Lis' ailing mother lived in the expanded bedroom at the front of the first floor. A private garden occupied the rear of the site, allowing the Li family to grow their own vegetables.

while the other two siblings contributed toward monthly expenses. Like the Wangs, this family effort was rooted in their self-built housing, but where the Wangs built their housing piece by piece, the Li siblings pooled their money to build a three-story house on their family's housing construction land (Figures 26 and 27). The house was built with an attached staircase accessible from the front courtyard, meaning that the three floors could function as separate housing units. This allowed each branch of the family to occupy a separate floor, preserving their social and economic independence as distinct households while also enabling their cohabitation and the pooling of resources and care provision. The building also included an additional room on the ground floor to accommodate their ailing mother and facilitate home care. All three branches of the Li family pointed to the importance of their cohabitation in enabling mutual support, but some members of the extended household chafed against their forced participation in the family's performance of filial harmony. For instance, Ren Ting proudly described how living together in one house meant that they all had to trust each other and work together, but she also complained that most of the caregiving burden ultimately fell on her shoulders. The material integration of *renqing* principles into the very architecture of village housing, combined with her lack of independent resources, meant that she felt trapped by her filial duties, unable to escape the Li house even to visit her own grandchildren. Sometimes as we sat in her courtyard, Ren would erupt in frustration that she alone was responsible for feeding and bathing her mother-in-law: "Every day until she dies, I have to take care of her. In my heart, I cry every day until I go to bed." Ren was not alone in feeling exploited, and her predicament underlines the systematic inequities of informal welfare in rural China, where the burden of care provision and the cultivation of *renqing* often falls on the women who marry into village households.[11] Thus, while *renqing* might be valorized as a means to escape and subvert the domination and exclusion of rural populations by the party–state's system of urban–rural difference, it cannot be celebrated as a liberatory panacea.[12] The reliance on kinship for mutual support and the material inscription of *renqing* relationships into the male-dominated household property structure tends to reinforce rather than challenge the patriarchal social structure that has long characterized village life.

Economic Diversification and Urban–Rural Entanglement

In Hailong, the guarantee of subsistence provided by the village's *renqing* networks also enabled households to pursue risky profit-making ventures that they might otherwise have avoided. These practices of economic diversification in turn enabled mutual support and informal social insurance, providing the resources that households used to purchase good standing in the village's *renqing* networks and that other households drew upon when in need of support.[13] Just as with mutual support networks, economic diversification was rooted in the household and the kinship-derived practices of *renqing*. The same principles that drove *inter*-household collaboration—such as those described in the Wang and Li families—also guided the organization of *intra*-household diversification. Here, the affective ties between husband and wife or between parent and child provided the basis for economic codependence, in which household members expressed their mutual attachment through contributions to household finances. The reciprocity of these relationships produced a kind of diversified portfolio strategy, combining multiple independent sources of income and social insurance so that the loss of any one source would not prove disastrous, a tactic also known as "income smoothing" (Morduch and Sharma 2002, 581). Like the *renqing* networks that constituted the village's mutual support system by entangling diverse community members, households maximized income by entangling diverse opportunities and resources, including through migration and entrepreneurship. These strategies inevitably extended beyond Hailong's territorial bounds and the rural status assigned to its residents, producing hybrid positionalities that exceeded China's urban and rural categories.

Migration and Geographic Diversification

In China, rural villagers often pursue economic diversification through migration, enabling some household members to pursue new sources of income while others stay home to ensure the productivity of stable land assets (Fan 2008, 12; Fan and Wang 2008; Zhao 2003; Zhu 2007). This often takes the form of the "split-household" strategy, which is based on the gendered division of labor and the practice of circular migration, allowing the household "to obtain the best of the origin and the destination" and to accrue capital for a future life after migration (Fan 2008, 3, 10; cf. Guldin 2001, 135). These strategies transpose the inside/outside opposition to the scale of the village, connecting opportunities for work and entrepreneurship outside the village with the sources of subsistence inside the village (Fan 2008, 11). These resources were integrated through residents' self-built housing—often funded through migration remittances—which both symbolically and materially united far-flung members of the household and anticipated their eventual reunification. This can be seen in the Lin family, who used remittances from Lin Yi to rebuild their house from a one-story brick building into a two-story brick-and-concrete structure (Figure 28). While the new house included a significant amount of unused space, it was built to accommodate a range of unforeseen uses. For instance, family members occasionally used the additional bedrooms while providing eldercare, and an empty room at the front of the house was intended to serve as a place of business when Lin Yi returned from working in Chengdu. More importantly, the house was built in anticipation of the family's eventual reunification, with three generations living together under one roof, an arrangement that the family symbolically enacted when Lin Yi and his wife returned to Hailong to celebrate the Chinese New Year.

In the literature on Chinese migration and village urbanization, registered villagers and migrant laborers are often represented as irreducibly different (Chan, Madsen, and Unger 2009; Guldin 2001; Siu 2007; Wang 2010; Webster and Zhao 2010, 66). This results in part from the scholarly emphasis on south China, where migrants from inland provinces are often socially and culturally distinct from local villagers (Guldin 2001, 226, 244–45). Scholars have also pointed to the disparities in social and economic resources that turn registered villagers into a rentier class that owns its own housing and enjoys access to local welfare and services, while migrants serve as industrial labor and must rent housing and pay for services (He et al. 2009; Zhang 2001). Similar advantages benefited Hailong villagers: many village families grew rich by building small factories and dormitories on their housing construction land, resident villagers were able to live in their own self-built housing, and some benefited from the dividends paid by the land management corporation. But the windfalls in Hailong were not evenly distributed. The village leadership's re-collectivization initiative limited opportunities for land development, only investors earned shareholding dividends, and many villagers lacked the capital to build dormitories or factories. Moreover, the constant threat of expropriation and demolition undermined the expected value of Hailong's land use rights. In contrast, although migrants could not pursue land development in Hailong, they could be confident that their

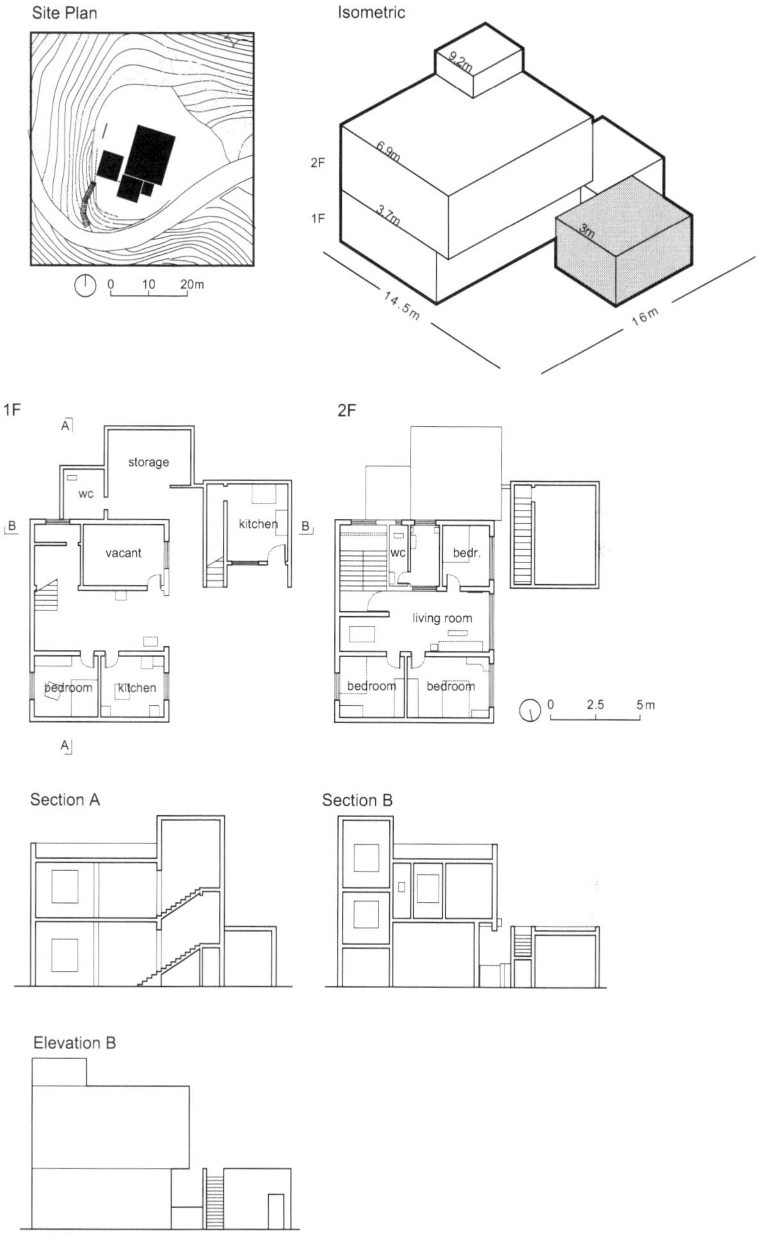

Figure 28. Structure of the Lins' House. The Lins' house comprised two floors with attached outbuildings, including a shed, a washroom, and a preexisting brick structure (shaded) that served as a kitchen. The main living area was on the second floor, with a dayroom and a kitchen on the first floor. One room on the first floor was kept vacant in anticipation of a future sideline business, and an extra bedroom on the second floor accommodated visiting family members.

villages would still be standing when they returned. Far from representing a dominant and unified rentier class, Hailong villagers were highly differentiated in terms of wealth, and many villagers were economically no better off than their migrant neighbors.

Rather than opposed classes, villagers and migrants in Hailong found a common identity in their shared experience of migration. Almost all of Hailong's registered adult villagers had migrated at some point in their lives, and many, like Lin Yi, were still at it. Other villagers had returned to Hailong only to take up jobs alongside migrants in Hailong's factories. This was the case for Lin Yi's mother, who worked on an automotive assembly line in the village. Meanwhile, some migrants owned the factories that villagers worked in, and some of the village's longest-tenured residents held household registration outside Hailong. Because most migrants in Hailong came from other parts of Chongqing and Sichuan, villagers and migrants also shared a common geography, cuisine, culture, and dialect. Migrants in Hailong even referred to themselves as "locals" (*bendi ren* 本地人) rather than "outsiders" (*waidi ren* 外地人), a common marker of migrant alterity.[14] The dormitories migrants lived in were often adjacent to villagers' self-built housing, and migrant families sometimes rented rooms or entire floors in villagers' homes (Figure 29). As a result, migrants were fully integrated into the village's *renqing* networks, which did not discriminate between villagers and migrants. Members of the two groups shared meals and played mahjong together, and when newly arrived migrants did not participate in the village's social networks, they were noted as misanthropes.

The inclusiveness of these social networks was on display at the lunch hosted by the Wangs, which included a range of villagers, migrants, and people who fit neither category. For instance, their relatively wealthy neighbor, Li Xiaowei, was born in the village but later acquired urban *hukou* as a worker in a state-owned enterprise. She owned several properties in and around Chongqing, and her daughter worked for a state-owned enterprise in the city. Also attending were two friends of the family: Shi Yuzhen, a villager who worked on the line in one of Hailong's factories, and Hu Hao, a migrant from southwestern Chongqing who owned a small machine shop at the bottom of the hill. Except for the children, all the people at the table had been migrants at one time or another, and only half were registered residents of Hailong. Even Shi Chunliang, Wang Dai's

Figure 29. Resident Land Use. A photographic cross section of land use in the village shows two migrant dormitories (left and center), a villager's self-built house (background), agricultural fields (center foreground), and a factory (right foreground), all in close proximity.

wife and our host, was registered in another Chongqing village; she had met Dai a decade ago as a migrant worker in one of Hailong's newly built factories. The table stitched together a diversity of worlds and bridged common social distinctions—between urban and rural, rich and poor, migrant and villager, entrepreneur and laborer. The Wangs' lunch table was a microcosm of Hailong society, a collection of fluid sociospatial subjectivities that were not defined by household registration but by their mutual relationships. Together, out-migration and in-migration exploded the village community far beyond Hailong's territorial boundaries, entangling geographies, resources, and opportunities throughout China's territory and beyond.

Entrepreneurship and the Politics of Quality

For many Hailong residents, one of the primary goals of migration was to build up enough financial and human capital to start a business. Villagers used their housing construction land to build dormitories to rent to migrant laborers, factories to rent to small-scale manufacturers, and storefronts for the operation of commercial sidelines. Both villagers and migrants rented these spaces to open small stores, gambling parlors, restaurants, and machine shops (Figure 30). For instance, when Wang Dai and Shi Chunliang wanted to supplement their income to purchase larger relocation housing, they opened a gambling parlor down the road from their house. Hailong's residents valued entrepreneurship for the sense of control and independence it provided. Migrant Gu Peng complained about his factory job: "When you work for someone else, you have no freedom. If you take their money, you have to do what they say. You have to serve them." By contrast, for Lin Yi, who ran a shoe factory in Chengdu, every day at work was "like a holiday." Wang Yangfei expressed a similar sentiment as he gave a younger cousin some career advice: "You don't want to work for a big company and have some boss tell you what to do. You want to work for yourself, have control over your own life."

These strategies of entrepreneurship both reinforced and challenged dominant norms of "quality" (*suzhi* 素质), a floating signifier that indexes the inherited and acquired traits of individual persons and collective populations. Quality includes questions of class, education, upbringing, ethnicity, and household registration (Anagnost 2004; Kipnis 2007; Sun 2009), with the label of "low quality" justifying exploitation, derogation, and dehumanization of marginalized populations, including rural residents (Anagnost 2004; Sigley 2009). On the other hand, entrepreneurialism, creativity, autonomy, and risk taking have all been identified as "high quality" characteristics (Anagnost 2004; Kipnis 2007; Lin 2011), leading some scholars to describe quality as the expression of "the self's value in the market economy" (Yan 2003, 494). By pursuing entrepreneurship, Hailong residents reinforced the culturally dominant valorization of quality, but they did so without subscribing to its urban associations. As discussed over lunch at the Wangs, the freedom, self-reliance, and flexibility of entrepreneurship were associated with rural life, whereas in the city, one was always dependent on the state and could never get ahead. Some Hailong residents even flipped the dominant logic of quality on its head, telling horror stories about the "uncivilized" and "low-quality" avarice exhibited by urban people. In relating a story about his trip to Beijing, Wang Anshi complained that their tour guide had led them to shops

Figure 30. Migrant Business. A typical migrant-run machine shop performed piecework for nearby factories.

and vendors where he and his fellow villagers were repeatedly fleeced. According to him, urban people had no *renqing;* they were just out to make an extra buck at the expense of others. He poignantly concluded: "They don't have any quality." For Hailong residents, quality was not measured by one's ability to make money but by one's ability to contribute back to the household and the village's wider *renqing* networks.

Together, the combination of migration, entrepreneurship, and *renqing* subverted the party–state's interpellation of rural residents as atomistic individuals whose quality is defined by their relation to the urban. For instance, the party–state distinguishes between periurban villagers, whom it portrays as undergoing "passive urbanization" (*bei shiminhua* 被市民化) in the process of urban expansion and expropriation, and rural–urban migrants, who are thought to seek the benefits of urban status voluntarily. China's premier, Li Keqiang, has referred to such people as "half-urbanized" (2012), a term that assumes the desirability and superiority of the urban as the telos of all rural striving. This view, which is based on a teleological model of permanent rather than circular migration (Fan 2008, 3, 10), sees migration as the expression of a desire to become urban (Ge 2006). Urban–rural hybridity is thus treated as a temporary, and undesirable, stage in the urbanization process. Those who persist in bridging urban and rural categories are pathologized and dehumanized as "blind" (*mangmu* 盲目) or "amphibious" (*shui lu liangyong* 水陆两用).[15] Any resistance to full urbanization is ascribed to their low quality. For instance, a lack of education means rural residents might have difficulty understanding the benefits of urban citizenship (Cheng 2003; Zheng 2005). Informal solutions for market failure, such as cooperation and subsistence bartering, have also been labeled as low quality (Yan 2003; Zukosky 2012). Such alternative sources of stability and survival threaten China's efforts to build a hegemonic state-directed system of market production (Yan 2003). The politics of quality are ultimately concerned with the creation of subjects who will conform to the state's vision of a socialist market economy, remaining complacent and obedient state subjects (Tomba 2009). In this context, household registration and state welfare can be reinterpreted as mechanisms for the pacification of potentially restive populations (Solinger 2011).

Hailong residents' practices relied on the party–state's administrative imposition of urban–rural difference but rejected any sense of urban–rural hierarchy or teleology. Rather than treating these categories as mutually exclusive, they hybridized the urban and the rural and navigated the interstices of the state's hegemonic urban–rural system. This dynamic tension reflects the politics of *renqing*, which cuts across and subverts the hierarchical ordering of the party–state but never directly confronts it (Yang 1994). *Renqing* networks poach the resources distributed by the market and the party–state, then redistribute those resources according to their own logic, thereby destabilizing the disciplinary effects of state structures while still leaving those structures in place (Yang 1994, 204–6, 306–9). For instance, by sending some members out to engage in migration and entrepreneurship while other members stayed in the village, households could take advantage of urban opportunities without giving up their access to rural land use rights and village support networks. The subtlety of this move was revealed by Lin Yi, who was simultaneously a villager, a migrant, and an entrepreneur. Lin lauded Hailong's networks of mutual support and care provision as the basis of a truly "harmonious society" (*hemu shehui* 和睦社会). The term Lin used echoed the party–state's rhetoric of the "harmonious society" (*hexie shehui* 和谐社会), but Lin used a slightly different word for "harmony," and his delivery placed special emphasis on the altered syllable.[16] This slight difference in language suggested a subversion of the state without explicitly rejecting its authority. The residents of Hailong still supported social harmony, just one based on different principles.

Living on the Edge

Launched in August 2010, Chongqing's household registration reform program initially seemed like a great success. During its first 16 months, over three million people traded in rural registration to become officially urban. But this strong initial interest reflected pent-up demand from prior years, when limits on household registration conversion were more stringent. The number of applications subsequently dropped precipitously, to just 400,000 in 2012 (Zhuma 2013). Widespread resistance to the program called into question Chongqing's ambitious 2020 goal of 10 million new urban residents, and by extension the success of China's national urbanization project, which aimed for 100 million new urban residents nationwide.[17] Chinese policy analysts explained the program's struggles by portraying rural residents as profit maximizers weighing the relative value of two packages of goods: urban registration versus rural registration (Gu 2011; Liao 2011). According to this logic, the low participation rate meant that municipal policy makers had underestimated the value rural residents attached to their land use rights. Policy analysts argued that if Chongqing could offer more monetary compensation or improve the expected value of urban social welfare, more people would be willing to convert to urban registration and the municipal reform program could be saved.

Hailong residents' resistance to household registration reform was grounded in a set of ethical claims and commitments that were inscribed into the very sociospatial fabric of the village and that could not be so easily replaced with an increase in compensation (Smith 2014b). Monetary calculations that focused on lost physical assets or increased welfare payments left out what really mattered to residents: the relationships that constituted the village. Moreover, the survival strategies residents enacted were dependent on the very system of urban–rural difference that caused their exclusion and exploitation. Mutual support between kin and neighbors relied on the de jure separation of collective-owned rural land from state-owned urban land and the allocation of rural land use rights to individual households, who could then build and adapt their housing in ways that enabled their continued participation in village social networks. At the same time, households' economic diversification only existed by virtue of China's de facto urban–rural interconnections, through which residents could become migrants, entrepreneurs, or investors. By separating village residents from their rural way of life and disciplining them into one-dimensional urban roles as wage laborers and renters, household registration reform undermined these strategies. As will become clear in the following chapters, the village-scale urbanization pursued by Hailong's cadres posed a similar threat to residents' survival strategies. Even though the cadres' plans were meant to avoid the necessity of Chongqing's household registration reform, the radical transformation of the village's sociospatial fabric would nevertheless force residents to disconnect from their mutual support networks and find new ways of ensuring their survival. The resistance to both Chongqing's and Hailong's approaches to urban–rural coordination can only be understood as a result of the existential challenge these programs posed to the village and its ethical principles.[18] By uprooting Hailong's village-scale institutions, urban–rural coordination entailed fundamental changes to the organization of rural life, leaving Hailong residents confronting an increasingly uncertain urban future.

Hailong residents' *renqing* practices pointed to an alternative approach to urbanization and urban–rural coordination, one that intersected with and appropriated the resources and practices of both the party–state and the market but that operated on its own ethical principles of reciprocity. Scholars of urbanization have commonly argued that principles of reciprocity cannot sustain urbanism, which requires hierarchical ordering or capitalist organization to concentrate and redistribute resources; at best, reciprocity might function residually at the edges of such processes (Harvey 1973, 226–27). But the rejection of reciprocity-based urbanism derives from a naively spatial understanding of urbanization, in which the urban inevitably constitutes a center hierarchically distinguished from a nonurban periphery. Alternatively, urbanization can be understood as an intensification in the circulation of affect across assemblages of human and nonhuman actors defined by their mutual interactions rather than by their relation to a territorial or scalar hierarchy. Through the lens of *renqing,* it therefore becomes possible to see urbanization as the rearrangement and entanglement of resources and not just as their concentration in a single center. Thus, urbanization need not entail teleological transcendence of the rural or movement toward a predefined urban center. Instead, it could comprise the interpenetration and interconnection of multiple centers of inhabitation and action. This emergent possibility was concretized in the building and networking practices of Hailong's residents, whose ethical principles of *renqing* were simultaneously centripetal—oriented toward the centering of social life—and centrifugal—oriented toward the interconnection of inside and outside. On the one hand, residents' survival strategies relied on the party–state's system of urban–rural difference and their rural land use rights, which they used to concentrate and redistribute resources within the household and the village community. On the other, residents' strategies of migration and entrepreneurship also exploded China's hegemonic system of urban–rural difference, entangling people, networks, and resources that reached far beyond Hailong's borders. In the interstices of the urban and the rural, Hailong's residents found new ways of surviving and thriving that simultaneously reified and rejected urban–rural difference.

CHAPTER 4

Coordinative Planning

Property, Politics, and Uncertainty at the Urban-Rural Edge

During the October 2011 discussion of village planning standards in the Chongqing municipal planning bureau's rural planning division, an argument broke out over the status of Hailong Village. The division head, Cai Libo, outlined the importance of land use planning and pointed to Hailong as an example: "It took us more than a year to do its plan precisely because of the lack of clarity around land use. We had to go through endless negotiations—it's a model village, so we had to be very cautious." Laughing, Cai explained how after many rounds of negotiation, they used "fuzzy science" (*mohu kexue* 模糊科学) to arrive at a compromise. Rather than referring to principles of uncertainty or approximation, he used "fuzzy science" as a euphemism for political compromise, exposing the tensions Chongqing's village planners felt as they navigated the competing demands of political expediency and scientific rationality. The result was a unique plan that Cai believed might require its own category in the village planning standard: "It's really a special case. It's half urban and half rural!" Tan Qing, who led the formulation of Hailong's plan, interjected: "You really can't call Hailong a model village." After more than a year of working on Hailong's plan, Tan had only just learned what was really happening. The land management bureau was still refusing to approve the plan, and the only way they would ever agree to do so was if the central government designated Hailong as a model village. As far as the land management bureau was concerned, Hailong was a "village-in-the-city" and should be treated as such: Its land should be expropriated and the village liquidated. Hailong would never become a model village, Tan explained, because it would not even be a village.

Chinese planners use the term "village-in-the-city" (*chengzhongcun* 城中村) to pathologize villages that succeed in urbanizing. Like Hailong, these urbanized villages also occupy liminal positions in China's binary urban–rural system. Surrounded by government-led urban development but occupying collective-owned construction land, they have experienced rapid land use intensification and population growth despite their rural status (Guldin 1996; Wang, Wang, and Wu 2009). Labeled as "dirty, messy, and inferior" (*zang luan cha* 脏乱差), they are portrayed by local governments and planners as sites of congestion, waste, danger, and criminality (Lai et al. 2014; Po 2012; Shen and Zhong 2007; J. Zheng 1997). These "malignant tumors" in the city's organic body adversely influence the city's healthy development (Yang 1996). To solve the problems posed by villages-in-the-city, planners have drawn on the precedents of mid-twentieth-century urban renewal in Europe and the United States. Planners prescribe urban surgery to "remake" and "renew" these cancerous nodes and transform their "perverse" urbanization into the "true urbanization" (*zhenzheng chengshihua* 真正城市化) of the city (Shen and Zhong 2007). These prescriptions follow the tenets of scientific rational planning described in chapter 1: the urbanized village is replanned, razed, and turned into an undifferentiated part of the urban fabric. This was the fate Tan Qing recommended for Hailong.

Contrary to Tan Qing's prediction, Hailong did not just disappear. It was not swallowed up by the city or rationalized according to principles of scientific rationality. Instead, it became a battleground for Chongqing's fraught periurban politics, as party–state leaders, municipal planners, and residents continually negotiated the relationship between the urban and the rural. The outcome was a Solomonic compromise, in which village cadres and municipal planners agreed to split the village in two, running the urban construction boundary through the middle of the village. To the east of the boundary, Hailong would remain rural and would be governed by a statutory village plan, while to the west of the boundary, the village would become urban and would be integrated into the municipal plan for the expanding "High Tech Zone" (*gaoxinqu* 高新区), a rapidly growing industrial zone. There was no way to rationalize this contradictory outcome as scientific, and Tan's frustration with the fuzzy science that determined Hailong's planning had motivated the village planning report that he prepared with Mo Ying in 2010.

To understand this process of political contestation and the practice of fuzzy science, it is necessary to move beyond the ideology of scientific rationality explored in chapter 1 to investigate how Chinese planning intersects with the growth machine politics outlined in chapter 2. Like Hailong's cadres, who sought to overcome their budget shortfalls by developing the village's collective-owned land, Chongqing's municipal government was also incentivized to promote growth on state-owned land (He and Wu 2005; Wu, Xu, and Yeh 2007, 109–10). The centralization of tax receipts and the devolution of responsibility for public goods and services in the mid-1990s left municipal governments with sizable funding gaps. To raise additional revenue, municipal governments began charging taxes and fees for the use of urban land, which they typically control as the primary agents of party–state ownership. The result has been the "fiscalization" of land, in which "land values accrue directly to the state for revenue purposes" (Rithmire 2015, 34). This system also incentivizes periurban expansion because the municipal government can expropriate rural land and convert it to urban construction land, thereby capturing the land rent increment (Brandt et al. 2002; Sargeson 2004; Lin 2009). The municipal government of Chongqing and the village cadres of Hailong thus faced similar and competing growth-oriented incentives. Both of these local party–state actors wanted to control Hailong's valuable periurban land in order to extract revenue from its development.

The resulting conflict between the municipal government and the administrative village ultimately played out through the statutory planning process, with both the municipality and the village competing to exercise planning powers. Contestation over planning processes can become particularly intense at the urban construction boundary because urban plans organized by the municipal government only govern formally designated, state-owned urban land. Municipalities also use urban plans to help justify the expansion of the urban construction boundary and the expropriation of collective-owned periurban land. State ownership of urban land means that rather than acting as an external constraint on land ownership, planning powers and land ownership are mutually entangled. Realizing the full value of the land depends on the exercise of planning powers, and conversely, the exercise of planning powers is conditioned by the effort to realize land value. As I argue below, China's distinctive urban political economy means that planning powers thus function as residual control rights that derive from the party–state's ownership of land. Like other property rights (Knight 1992; North 1990), planning powers depend on both the economic incentives and the political power of those who claim—and ultimately wield—them. In many cases, the overweening power of the municipal government means that villages have little opportunity to contest urban planning processes. Where village cadres have sufficient political clout within the party–state apparatus, as they did in Hailong, urban planning and the placement of the urban construction boundary can become a political battlefield. In these contexts, planning serves as a process of coordination through which the competing interests of different party–state actors are negotiated and resolved, sometimes resulting in the sharing or trading of planning powers between rival claimants to the land.

This chapter explores how the politics of coordinative planning unfolded in the formulation of Hailong's statutory village plan. The village's economic success had attracted the attention of higher-level party leaders, including Chongqing's party secretary, Bo Xilai, and China's future president, Xi Jinping, who praised the CCP Central Committee's 2010 report on Hailong. With Xi's imprimatur, the party secretaries of both Chongqing and Jiulongpo rushed to claim Hailong as their own, offering political support for the village's leaders and calling for the formulation of a new village plan that would ensure Hailong's success as a model of village development—a village relaunch. But as this process unfolded, the municipality's High Tech Zone was also preparing to expand its territory to encompass Hailong. The zone's expansion had been outlined in the 2011 revision of Chongqing's master plan, constituting part of the city's westward expansion proposed by Huang Qifan, Chongqing's mayor and vice party secretary. Hailong was thus subject to two competing development plans prepared by two different party–state actors, each of whom enjoyed high-level political clout within the CCP and had a top-down mandate for growth. The negotiated compromise between the village collective and the municipality effectively split Hailong in two: half urban and half rural. Hailong's formal land rights were left intact, but planning powers were divided between the village collective and the High Tech Zone. Ultimately, two statutory plans were prepared for the village: the development zone organized a plan for the village's western third, and the village collective organized a plan for the remainder of Hailong. This outcome thus underlined both the artificiality and the power of China's urban–rural divisions, as well as the political contingency of any effort to implement urban–rural coordination.

Competing Rationales for Planning: Countdown to Relaunch

By the time I arrived in Hailong in August 2011, the inevitability of redevelopment hung over the village. Hailong's leaders heralded this new phase of development as Hailong's "relaunch" (lit. "second start," or *erci chuangye* 二次创业), the next chapter in their narrative of progress. Chongqing's planners talked about it as an opportunity to integrate the rogue village into the municipality's planning regime. Residents nervously discussed the threat of mass demolition and resettlement. The impetus for Hailong's relaunch came from the highest levels of the party–state. The attention of Xi Jinping and other central party leaders brought increased scrutiny from local government. Both the municipal and district governments commissioned their own reports calling for Hailong to be turned into a national model for village development and directing the various organs of local government to provide whatever support was necessary. The district report included a five-page itemized list of tasks and duties for its subordinate departments to carry out. This initiative was aimed at accelerating Hailong's development and doubling villagers' incomes within five years, to 20,000 RMB in 2015. It also called for the improvement of Hailong's living environment through the construction of a new residential district with a built area of 200,000 square meters.

Yan Jing and his colleagues celebrated this as a new opportunity to be seized, echoing the logic they had used to legitimize Hailong's first round of development. In an open letter to Hailong villagers, Yan exhorted them to support the relaunch. Invoking a common Chinese saying that "wealth never lasts longer than three generations" (*fu buguo san dai* 富不过三代), Yan insisted on the folly of self-satisfaction: "Without the relaunch, the village will inevitably decline." Addressing the village's increasing concerns with the inequitable distribution of development windfalls, he railed against those who would oppose Hailong's development just to protect the profits they had already made. Only by first making the cake bigger, he claimed, would it be possible to ensure that everyone got his or her fair share.[1] But the Hailong relaunch was not just continuing the status quo ante. According to the directives of the district government, the key to transforming Hailong into a model village was standardization. In an editorial written for Hailong's newspaper, the Jiulongpo District party secretary, Ye Jianhua, argued, "If Hailong wants to be advanced, it needs to be first; if it wants to be a model, it needs to be standardized." Ye continued, "Before, Hailong's development was fast. Now it can't be fast. It has to be good. Only with a good foundation can development accelerate again." Drawing on principles of scientific rationality used to criticize villages-in-the-city, this rhetoric of standardization derogated Hailong's existing development as messy, low-quality, and inefficient, and it advocated the supervision and control of local government authorities to guide Hailong's future. In their delegation of responsibilities to subordinate departments, Jiulongpo's leaders emphasized the role of the district's planning organs, including the urban planning department, land management department, and development and reform committee. These departments were tasked with improving the quality and efficiency of the village's development and rationalizing its spatial composition through the formulation of new plans for urban construction, land use, and economic and social development.

Hailong's leaders embraced the rhetoric of standardization, but far from relinquishing control to higher-level regulatory authorities within the municipal and submunicipal governments, Hailong's leaders portrayed planning as a means to consolidate their own control over village development. First, planning could be used to constrain the construction activities of village households. Assistant Party Secretary Wen Jiancai expressed this in terms of the paternalism of Chinese state planning: "People in rural areas can be like children. They don't know what to do. If you don't plan the land, the villagers will develop it anyway." Second, planning would ensure coordination with other local actors, like the town, district, and municipal governments. No longer would Hailong be subject to their developmental whims, which could force the collective to abandon or rebuild much of its property. A plan would ensure a secure and permanent future for the village.

When district and village officials talked about village planning, they meant the statutory village plan prepared under the auspices of China's Urban–Rural Planning Law. But there were actually many plans being prepared for the village, including a social and economic development plan, a real estate development plan, and an urban design plan. This list does not even mention the social and economic development plans, land use plans, master plans, and regulatory control plans being prepared by other party–state actors with claims to control portions of Hailong's territory, including the municipality, the district, the town, and the newly expanded High Tech Zone, as well as the military, the land management bureau, and the China Railway Corporation. In theory, these plans should have been formulated in series, with plans at higher levels preceding those at lower levels and more general plans preceding the more detailed ones.[2] But in Hailong, and in many other instances across China, several of these plans were formulated in parallel, often with competing and contradictory outcomes. With so many plans, which plan actually determined how the village developed? And with so many local state actors involved, who actually controlled the planning process?

Dueling Development Plans: Rival Claims to Village Land

As Hailong's relaunch got underway, there were two main claims to control the village's planning. The first came from the leadership of the administrative village, building on the strength of Hailong's past economic success and the subsequent support of central, municipal, and district leaders. The second came from the leadership of the High Tech Zone, which was in the process of expanding its territory to include Hailong. As part of a package of preferential policies designed to accelerate the zone's development, the power to organize the planning of this area had been delegated from Chongqing's municipal government to the zone's management committee. This entity simultaneously acted as a for-profit state-owned enterprise and a local territorial government subordinate to Jiulongpo District. Neither of these actors technically held the power to organize Hailong's statutory plan, a responsibility legally assigned to the supervising town, Baishiyi.[3] The town government retained this statutory power, using it to exact concessions from other party–state actors, but it lacked both the resources and the incentives to compete for effective control over the planning process. Instead, the leaders of

Hailong and the High Tech Zone jockeyed to define the parameters of the statutory village plan. These competing visions were articulated through two separate economic and social "development plans" (*fazhan guihua* 发展规划) formulated as part of China's twelfth five-year plan.[4]

Hailong's development plan was jointly prepared by the Jiulongpo branch of the National Development and Reform Commission (NDRC) and the Zhejiang University China Academy of West Region Development. The NDRC is the contemporary iteration of the state ministry that once conducted economic planning for the socialist economy, and it is still responsible for China's five-year development plans. Of the various departments that comprise local territorial governments, such as municipalities and districts, the NDRC is most directly connected to the central government and least responsive to local influence. Based in Hangzhou, the China Academy of West Region Development is a consulting and research agency established by the NDRC and Zhejiang University and is even more insulated from local government control. Responding to the enthusiasm and support of central state leaders, these two organizations formulated a plan to accelerate and intensify Hailong's existing development path. While seeking to normalize Hailong's development according to legal and regulatory guidelines, the plan essentially reflected the ambitions of the village's leaders, unconstrained by either the availability of resources or the existence of competition. By 2015, the plan called for doubling economic output, to 6 billion RMB, and average villager income, to 24,000 RMB. It also called for increasing collective assets to 1 billion RMB, collective annual income to 50 million RMB, and outside investment to 8 billion RMB. In addition to financial targets, the development plan supported Hailong's existing effort to urbanize its population, calling for 90 percent of the village population to achieve urban living standards and enjoy urban welfare levels (though without converting to urban registration). To achieve all of this, the plan recommended shifting the village's sectoral balance, upgrading existing industry, attracting higher-value manufacturers, and introducing agritourism and service activities.

In addition to a new high-rise residential area, the plan proposed three main development projects: a commercial center with a pedestrian commercial street, an industrial park with a built area of 200,000 square meters, and an agritourism park occupying 1,000 *mu* (66.7 hectares), for a total investment of 1.5 billion RMB. To populate these projects, the village would need to attract a new grocery store, a hotel, between one and three manufacturers with an annual output of at least 1 billion RMB, and between 5 and 10 manufacturers with an annual output of at least 100 million RMB. The plan also called for upgrading Hailong's existing development, including improvements to infrastructure and public facilities, a rebuilt market, and an increase in the efficiency and value of industry. Particular emphasis was placed on this last point, pushing Hailong to transition away from the industrial economy of its past and toward structural upgrading, including low-carbon products like notebook computers and designer furniture. But like most economic and social development plans, Hailong's development plan lacked spatial specificity. For instance, in discussing possible locations for the new residential area, the plan included Hailong's existing village center, where an adjacent rail line and a transformer station would have made expansion nearly impossible. The development plan called for more and better planning, including specialty plans for construction and land use, which would investigate how to concretely realize the abstract objectives defined by the development plan.

The Hailong development plan was clear about the village's territory, which it defined to encompass as much land as possible. This included areas where land had been converted to industrial uses without going through the formal legal process of state expropriation and conversion. Instead of requiring that the land be expropriated by the state, the plan simply called for the regularization of Hailong's existing land use. The plan even included areas that had already been expropriated, such as the Tianci Hot Spring development. Most profoundly, the plan called for Hailong's territorial expansion, defining what it called "Greater Hailong" (*da hailong* 大海龙), which included neighboring villages, as well as Dahe Village, a poor village elsewhere in Baishiyi where Hailong's leaders had been helping to guide development. According to the plan, incorporating this territory into Hailong would enable these villages to benefit from the managerial and developmental expertise of Hailong's leaders, and it would provide Hailong with additional development capacity.[5]

Chongqing's municipal government approved Hailong's development plan in April 2011, a month after approving the expansion of the High Tech Zone to include the village. Chongqing's High Tech Zone was first established in 1991, in China's first group of five national development zones. The expansion of the zone was proposed in the 2011 revision of Chongqing's master plan, which called for the zone's population to double, from 210,000 to 440,000 people, and for its territory to expand by 50.72 square kilometers, all the way to the western edge of Zhongliang Mountain, precisely where Hailong was located. The High Tech Zone referred to this expansion as the zone's "relaunch" (*erci chuangye* 二次创业), the same term used for Hailong's redevelopment. But the zone's relaunch and Hailong's relaunch were mutually exclusive. Along with the 23 other villages covered by the zone's expansion, Hailong's inclusion in the High Tech Zone would have meant the end of the village, as its land would have been expropriated, its population relocated, and its collective institutions liquidated or transformed into organs of the town government. The development plans for Hailong and the High Tech Zone therefore represented competing claims on the village's territory. Yet the two plans were both approved by the municipal government. This was due in part to the nature of economic and social development plans, which seek to maximize development rather than balance competing claims for resources. By contrast, urban planning, which must designate limited land resources for competing development projects, is inherently coordinative. Where the despatialized nature of development planning enables planners to disregard the necessity of coordinating with other state actors, the spatiality of urban planning makes it a privileged venue for such coordination.

Fragmentation and Coordination within the Party-State

The intersection of these rival development plans unfolded within a broader system of negotiation and coordination that comprises the intramural politics of the Chinese party–state. Chinese politics has been described as a process of pragmatic bargaining between political elites who represent the interests of their organizational units—a system of "fragmented authoritarianism" (Lampton 1987; Lieberthal and Oksenberg 1988). A legacy of socialism, this bargaining economy derives from elites' efforts to secure scarce resources that can be obtained only from other party–state units (Lieberthal and Oksenberg 1988). To do so, bureaucrats navigate dense relationship networks that intersect with and facilitate the smooth functioning of the formal structure of authority. Policy formulation and implementation therefore require the active cooperation of many party–state actors, who are nested in distinct spheres of authority and embedded in extensive bargaining relationships (Lieberthal and Oksenberg 1988, 22, 406). During the post-1978 reform period, this bargaining process has tended to transform party–state resources and powers into de facto property rights.[6] Exclusive control over goods and services allowed bureaucrats to demand more in negotiations with other state units, and over time, "lower level officials began to acquire a proprietary attitude toward the resources they had received" (Lieberthal and Oksenberg 1988, 405–6). This phenomenon is particularly evident in the control over land. Urban land is owned by the state and rural land is owned by collectives, but a variety of different local actors claim to exercise these ownership rights on behalf of the distant central state or the ambiguously defined collective (Cai 2003; Ho 2001; Hsing 2010, 34–42; Lee 1993).[7] These de facto rights can also include a range of less tangible authorities and powers delegated by the central state (Pryor 1973, 2), such as planning powers. Such rights might not be alienable, but they still hold economic value, entailing asymmetric power relations whereby the rights holder can make others do something for his or her benefit (Pryor 1973, 7–8, 279–80).[8]

As de facto property rights, the resources and powers controlled by party–state actors are not limited by statutory definitions or their recognition in a court of law (Cole and Grossman 2002; Mertha 2009; Pils 2005; Upham 2009). Thinking extralegally is particularly important in China, where laws are only inconsistently enforced and informal practices vary dramatically (Pils 2005, 284–85; Shi and Zhuo 2009; Upham 2009, 619). If instead we consider property rights as "socially recognized rights of action" (Alchian and Demsetz 1973, 17; cf. North 1990), then other political institutions can play important roles in the constitution of property rights. As a site of social and political conflict, property rights inevitably reflect the relative bargaining strength of potential property claimants as they negotiate outcomes (Knight 1992; North 1981, 62; North 1990, 68). In particular, two situations can precipitate changes in property rights: first, changes in relative prices incentivize actors to renegotiate the distribution of property (Demsetz 1967; North 1981, 29–30); and second, if property rights do not reflect the distribution of political power, or if the balance of power changes, more powerful actors will seek to change them (North 1990, 85–86; North, Wallis, and Weingast 2009, 155).[9]

Located at the bottom of China's political hierarchy, most villages can do little to resist municipal expropriation. True bargaining is only likely to occur between elites of close rank with similar access to resources who are unable to compel each other to act (Lampton 1987). But the political contingency of the bargaining economy also means that low-ranked but well-connected cadres, such as village party secretaries, can sometimes overcome the odds in conflicts with municipal agencies. By navigating the party's political patronage networks, it is possible to bypass the formal distribution of authority within the party–state hierarchy, particularly because resolving conflicts depends on the intervention of higher-level party leaders with the political clout to discipline all the competing actors (Lampton 1987; Lieberthal and Oksenberg 1988; Shirk 1992). This was the case in Hailong, where Village Party Secretary Yan Jing drew on the political endorsement of central leaders, including the support of Municipal Party Secretary Bo Xilai. He also exercised effective control over Hailong's land, without which the High Tech Zone could not achieve its expansion. Pointing to the economic value of the village's recent industrialization, Yan insisted on a high price for any proposed land expropriation. Meanwhile, the High Tech Zone called on the support of Chongqing's mayor and vice party secretary, Huang Qifan, who had touted the area as a new industrial district for the city. With the powers delegated to it by the municipality and through its relationships with the municipal planning bureau, the zone also exerted significant influence over urban planning in the area. Both Hailong and the High Tech Zone thus enjoyed similar levels of political clout, and both possessed resources that the other needed to achieve its developmental goals, a situation that precipitated a process of negotiation under China's political system of fragmented authoritarianism.

Negotiating the Urban Construction Boundary and the Power to Plan

As work on Hailong's statutory village plan and the High Tech Zone's master plan moved forward, the contradictions between the two development programs quickly emerged. The preface to the High Tech Zone's master plan, formulated by the western division of the China Academy of Urban Planning and Design, diplomatically noted that land uses and land rights are complicated in periurban areas, making coordination difficult. Taking the originally designated expansion area as their starting point, planners adjusted the new boundary of the zone to account for land suitability, territorial powers, and the distribution of functions. The resulting area was slightly larger than the original, at 50.93 square kilometers instead of 50.72. The zone's master plan referred to this adjustment as "fine tuning" (*wei tiao* 微调), as if it were just part of the normal process of making the plan more scientific and rational (Figure 31). But where it affected Hailong, the adjustment was fraught with political infighting. Over multiple meals in the spring and summer of 2012, Gu Yin—one of the planners who worked on the High Tech Zone's master plan—described the subsequent negotiation process, which had taken place behind closed doors in the municipal planning bureau. As Gu related, "The management committee of the High Tech Zone ultimately decided that the costs outweighed the benefits and it wouldn't be worth integrating the entire village into the zone's plan." Instead, they reduced the amount of land they were requesting, allowing the village to retain a portion for its own use.

Hailong's leaders were reluctant to part with any land at all. The area the High Tech Zone proposed to annex comprised the most valuable land in the village. It was in the flattest area, closest to major roads and other urban infrastructure, and the site of the majority of Hailong's existing industrial development. A large number of village households also held use rights to housing construction land there, meaning that the price for state expropriation would be prohibitive. The leaders of the High Tech Zone offered a new compromise. Only those portions of Hailong needed for urban infrastructure, such as roads, rail lines, and power lines, would be expropriated. In the western third of the village, the land would be incorporated into the urban planning area of the High Tech Zone, but it would not be immediately expropriated. Meanwhile, the power to organize the planning for the remainder of the village's land (except for protected natural resources, such as the village's national forest area) would be transferred to Hailong. The Baishiyi town government would still officially organize the statutory village plan, but real control over the process would be shifted from town authorities to Hailong's cadres. In exchange,

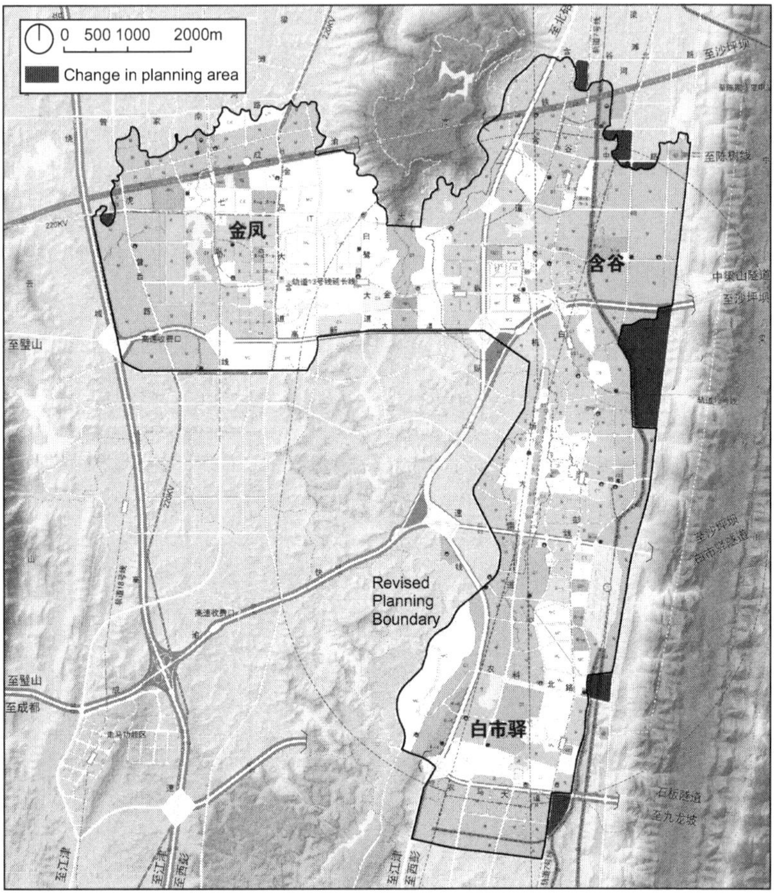

Figure 31. The High Tech Zone's Master Plan. A draft of the master plan for the High Tech Zone (dated August 2011) included parts of Hailong (center right). The plan reflected the revised urban construction boundary negotiated in 2011 (solid outline) but did not change the planned land use for the village, which remained entirely industrial. The discrepancy reveals the High Tech Zone's original intent to include all of Hailong's developable land within the urban construction boundary. Courtesy of Chongqing's municipal planning bureau.

part of Hailong's land would be used to build a water treatment plant for the town. As Gu Yin explained, "There was a very strange phenomenon. In Hailong, about one-third of the village became part of the urban planning area planned by the High Tech Zone. And two-thirds is still part of the original area, with no relation to the first third" (Figures 32 and 33).

The resulting division in Hailong's territory posed a paradox in China's

Figure 32. Hailong's Statutory Village Plan. The land use plan for Hailong reflected the final location of the urban construction boundary and the division between the urban planning area (shaded dark) and the village planning area (bordered with a dashed line). Land use categories are shown in Figure 33. Courtesy of Jiulongpo District Planning Department.

system of urban–rural administration. To the west of the urban construction boundary, Hailong's land would remain formally rural, owned and operated by the village collective, but this land would be integrated into the municipality's urban planning area and development would be managed according to urban construction regulations. Yet under China's Urban–Rural Planning Law, the urban planning area could only include land that was actually urban, and rural land should be planned according to statutory village plans. According to Gu Yin, the hybrid arrangement in Hailong represented the municipality's intention to expropriate the land at some point in the future. Over dinner, Gu explained that while

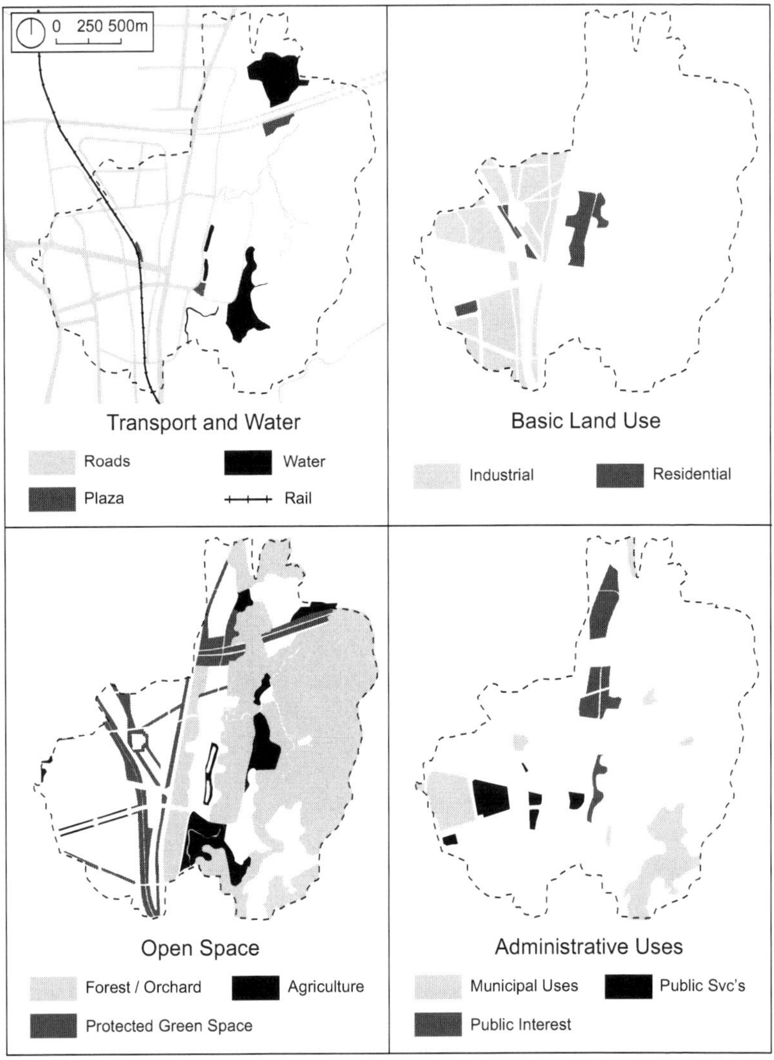

Figure 33. Hailong's Statutory Village Plan: Land Use. These drawings show the various types of land use extracted from Hailong's statutory plan (Figure 32). The site for Hailong's newly planned residential area is shown in dark gray at top right. Protected green space is largely dedicated to municipal infrastructure corridors, such as roadways and high-power lines. Municipal facilities include the agricultural college and the Longju cemetery. "Public interest" land is collective-owned, nonresidential rural construction land. This includes land designated for Hailong's high-rise industrial park (see chapter 5).

the "ownership" (*suoyou quan* 所有权) and "use rights" (*shiyong quan* 使用权) for Hailong's western third were still held by Hailong, the "planning rights" (*guihua quan* 规划权) belonged to the High Tech Zone. The land might be planned a certain way, but if the High Tech Zone actually wanted to build anything, it would first need to expropriate the land and convert it into urban land: "They can decide the character of the land, how it will be arranged in the future. They can decide whether there should be a road or a park. . . . But only after it has been expropriated can they actually build the road." However, Gu added, the government might decide not to implement the plan at all. If the cost of expropriation proved too high and the resale value too low, they might choose not to pursue it.

The Importance of Planning Powers: Internalizing Transaction Costs

If Hailong's land was not subject to immediate expropriation, then why did it matter who controlled planning in the village? Urban planning serves an important role in the operation of the Chinese growth machine, sometimes referred to as "planning for growth" (Wu 2015, 204). For instance, municipal governments often use the ideology of scientific rational planning to legitimize their claims to exercise state land ownership (Hsing 2006). Chinese planning also takes on a more direct economic instrumentalism, enhancing the municipality's overall competitiveness through economic restructuring, image enhancement, and place branding (Wu 2007; Xu and Yeh 2005; Zhu 2004b). In the case of Hailong, the battle to control the planning process revealed a more directly pecuniary function of Chinese planning. In order to maximize their land-related revenue and minimize the land-related costs produced by urban development, municipal governments (and other local party–state actors) use planning to produce specific kinds of growth on specific kinds of land parcels: those over which they exercise ownership. Urban planning does this by constraining the choices of independent land users in favor of land uses that enhance the fiscal value of the municipality's landholdings.

Because China lacks a robust property tax system, land revenue comes in two main forms, each of which also entails costs. First, the sale of land use rights earns one-time payments and fees from developers (Wu

2002; Wu, Xu, and Yeh 2007, 115; Zhang 2000). This revenue is greater for residential land, but residential development also incurs long-term costs, as land use intensification increases congestion and demand for services (Zhao 2013; Zhao, Liu, and Zhuang 2009). Second, a long-term revenue stream is earned through the return of tax receipts from the central government to local government, including value-added tax and income tax (Wang, Li, and Tian 2012; Wu 2018). This revenue is greater for manufacturing and services, but industrial development also requires up-front costs, as corporations demand infrastructure, services, and incentives before relocating (Wang, Li, and Tian 2012).[10] When residential and industrial development are in balance, they can form a virtuous cycle (Zhao 2013): the one-time revenue from residential land subsidizes industrial land (Wang, Li, and Tian 2012), which pays for the long-term costs of residential intensification (Zhao, Liu, and Zhuang 2009). But this balance can be difficult to strike, and the temporal interdependency exposes local party–state actors to risk as other factors disrupt the cycle. Symptoms of such disruption include China's growing municipal debt crisis, the overbuilding of infrastructure in underpopulated areas, and the underprovision of services in population centers (Li and Lin 2011; Zhang 2000).

While the party–state owns all urban land, it is not always clear which local agents of the party–state are authorized to exercise that ownership on the party–state's behalf. In areas where multiple party–state actors claim land ownership or where ownership is contested, the revenue-optimizing functions of urban planning are more likely to be disrupted, as different party–state actors with different ownership interests seek different arrangements of land use.[11] Specifically, the municipal government abhors residential and commercial development on land that is within its jurisdiction but that it does not own. Such development represents pure cost for the municipality, as it increases demand for expensive infrastructure and services but does not bring the municipality any revenue. In Hailong's case, as long as village land was owned by the collective (and not by the municipality), the municipal government had an interest in minimizing the amount of land used for residential and commercial development, both of which were prominent features of the village development plan. This was compounded by the pragmatic compromise proposed by the High Tech Zone—to delay the expropriation of Hailong's western third until a later date—which meant that the village could inflate the eventual price of municipal expropriation by increasing the intensity of development in the near term. For their part, Hailong's village cadres were concerned that the municipality would plan their village relaunch out of existence by imposing excessive development restrictions or running large pieces of infrastructure through the center of the village, both strategies reflected in the master plan for the High Tech Zone. If the municipality approved a plan that eliminated residential and commercial development from Hailong's land, the village would lose its main near-term revenue stream and would have no way to pay for the rest of its development.

In short, Hailong and the High Tech Zone faced a transaction cost problem. Transaction costs, which include information costs, bargaining costs, and enforcement costs, arise when valuable attributes of an economic exchange are left in the public domain or when one actor is able to influence the value of attributes held by another (Coase 1960; Dahlman 1979; North 1990, 63). The existence of these costs increases uncertainty and decreases the expected value of the asset. There are three principal strategies for dealing with transaction costs: regulation, firms, and property rights. Most economic accounts of planning focus on regulation, using Pigovian economics to argue for state intervention as a means to correct market failure (Klosterman 1985; Pigou 1920). Drawing on Ronald Coase's characterization of governments as so-called superfirms, Coasian planning scholars instead compare government planning to the planning activities of private-sector firms, which remove high-cost transactions from the marketplace and replace them with hierarchical coordination (Alexander 1992; Coase 1937, 1960; Lai 1997; Webster and Lai 2003). A third, less common approach argues that zoning and land use regulation constitute collective property rights that protect residents or landowners from the potential costs of unknown future land uses (Deng, Gordon, and Richardson 2007; Fischel 1987; Nelson 1977). By assigning ownership over high-cost attributes of a transaction, property rights provide incentives for economic exchanges that internalize costs into market prices (Coase 1960), as represented, for instance, by the negotiation of zoning variances between planning authorities and developers (Fischel 1987, 73–78).

Using this third approach, Chinese planning powers can be understood to function as residual control rights possessed by whatever local actor exercises land ownership on behalf of the party–state. These control rights serve to protect the local agent's income rights amid the fragmentation and marketization of use rights (Smith 2018).[12] As control rights, planning powers are part of the "bundle of rights" that constitutes party–state land ownership, alongside other rights such as income, use, and disposition (Demsetz 1967). But as Gu Yin emphasized, planning powers are not fully alienable in the same way as use rights: While use rights can be sold on the market, planning rights cannot. This is partly because planning powers are assigned to local governments by the central party–state, which retains the power to revoke or reclaim those powers if supervising levels of government find that plans have been improperly organized. However, the party–state *can* use its planning powers as the basis for negotiations with other land users, offering favorable planning variances in exchange for higher payments or in-kind "planning gain," such as the construction of urban infrastructure (Zhu 1999, 2004b). Further, as was the case in Hailong, planning powers can be traded between different party–state actors with land ownership claims.[13]

In Hailong, planning powers served to secure the future value of land ownership. The power to organize the planning of the village's western third was traded to the municipality and the High Tech Zone as a means of preventing residential and commercial development and an excessive increase in the cost of future expropriation, while the power to organize planning for the rest of the village was traded to Hailong's leaders as a way of maximizing the future value of their little remaining land. To compensate Hailong for the transfer of planning powers for the western third of the village to the High Tech Zone, the municipality and the High Tech Zone had to make a series of concessions and in-kind payments. First, the High Tech Zone agreed to pay for portions of village development located within the zone's planning area, including the village access road and some of the relocation housing for displaced villagers. Second, the municipal planning bureau committed to moving several high-power lines in the interior of the village to accommodate Hailong's planned residential development. Third, elements of the village's original plan were incorporated into the zone's master plan, including commercial areas along the village access road. Finally, the municipal planning bureau tacitly legitimized Hailong's existing industrial development, and the village was allowed to continue to manage and operate its industrial land until it was expropriated. Like the water treatment plant built for the town of Baishiyi, these concessions exemplified the types of negotiations China's local governments often undertake with large real estate developers. In these exchanges, local governments grant developers planning powers in exchange for planning gain (Zhu 2004a). For instance, a developer might be given broad planning discretion over a large section of the city if it agrees to plan and pay for basic public services and infrastructure. The Hailong case demonstrated that this was the rule, not the exception. Planning powers are just another resource traded in the process of coordination and negotiation between actors in the party–state's bargaining economy.

The most important concession granted to Hailong's cadres was the de facto power to plan the remaining portion of the village, the value of which became immediately apparent. The High Tech Zone had originally planned a freight highway that would have cut right through Hailong's new residential area. In April 2011, early in negotiations over the village's planning, Hailong's leaders insisted that the highway be moved. Six months later, after the negotiated agreement to split the village in two, Gu Yin and his team produced an amendment to the High Tech Zone's master plan that rerouted the highway to avoid Hailong's new residential area (Figure 34). Gu emphasized the extraordinary feat that this represented. In China's top-down planning system, higher-level plans determine the conditions of possibility for lower-level plans, not vice versa. As Gu put it, "If I tell you to move, you move." Without the necessary capability, knowledge, and power, most town and village leaders lack the ability to resist, but Hailong's leaders were able to use their political resources to redirect the course of a six-lane highway, demonstrating the extent of their control over the planning of the village's interior. Gu guffawed, "They think they are pretty awesome. They think that they are on the national team."

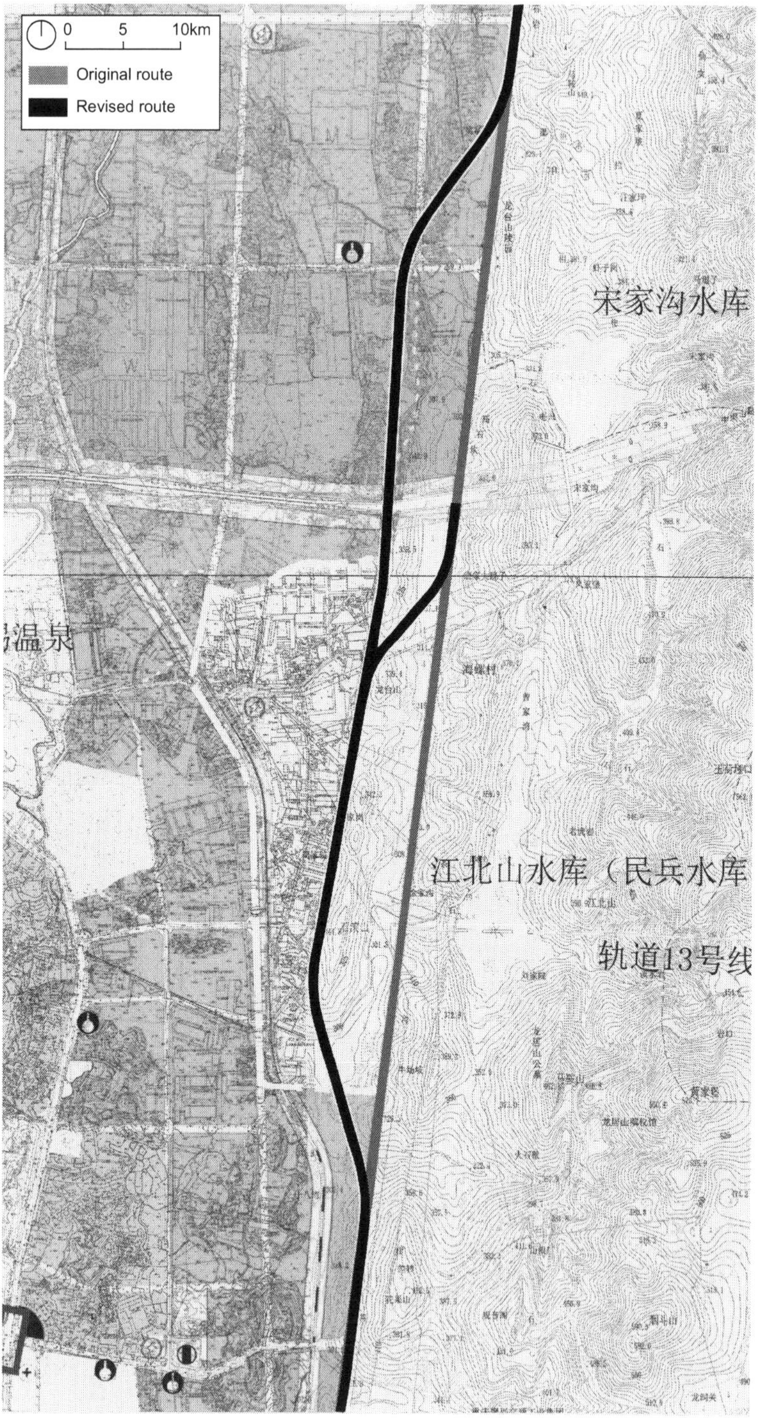

0 5 10km
Original route
Revised route
宋家沟水库
温泉
江北山水库（民兵水库
轨道13号线

Moving the Urban Construction Boundary: The Political Contingency of Planning

On February 6, 2012—eighteen months after the Jiulongpo District report on Hailong's development, and nearly a year after initial plans had been drafted and submitted for review—a black sedan sped silently past Hailong, fleeing along the Cheng-Yu Expressway that cut through the village on its way to Chengdu. Inside was Wang Lijun, until recently Chongqing's vice mayor and head of its public security apparatus. Then a phalanx of police cars full of armed officers raced out of the Zhongliang tunnel, the blare of their sirens echoing through Hailong's valleys. Wang was headed to the American consulate in Chengdu, where he offered details of elite politics and corruption in exchange for asylum. Rebuffed by the Americans, Wang was later convicted of treason by a Chinese court. But his actions rapidly accelerated what was likely an ongoing corruption inquiry into Bo Xilai and his wife, Gu Kailai. Within weeks, Bo, once a rising star in Chinese politics and a candidate for a seat on the ruling Politburo Standing Committee, had been relieved of his duties. Months later, Gu was convicted of murdering a British national and received a commuted death sentence. Bo was summarily drummed out of the party and eventually convicted of corruption and abuse of power.

Bo Xilai's precipitous fall from the firmament of the CCP left a crater in the nation's political landscape. It briefly exposed the sordid infighting and excesses of China's elite politics, and it signaled the beginning of Xi Jinping's efforts to consolidate power as he prepared to assume the mantle of China's presidency the following year. Like many of his predecessors—and ironically like Bo himself—Xi used anticorruption investigations to marginalize his opponents and rivals. In Chongqing, Bo's sudden departure produced a political vacuum. In March 2012, Zhang Dejiang, a vice

Figure 34. Freight Highway, Revised. This plan drawing shows the process of revision for the freight highway. The urban–rural construction boundary separates the light gray shading on the left from the unshaded area on the right. Alternative paths for the highway are represented in dark gray. The originally proposed path of the highway can be seen in lighter gray. Where the revised path diverted to the west, the original path continued straight, colinear with the High Tech Zone's originally proposed urban construction boundary and straight through the valley designated for Hailong's new residential area. Courtesy of Chongqing's municipal planning bureau.

premier on China's State Council, took over as Chongqing's party secretary. Zhang was tasked with rooting out corruption and cleaning up the political mess that Bo had left behind, serving as a municipal caretaker until Sun Zhengcai was appointed party secretary in November 2012 as part of the regularly scheduled national leadership shuffle. Without clear and consistent political leadership, urban planning in Chongqing ground to a halt. Even once Sun assumed control, little planning was conducted during the first year of his tenure while he pursued a comprehensive review of municipal policy.

The impact on Hailong was incalculably greater. The experimental nature of Hailong's approach to development and the ringing endorsement from Bo Xilai suddenly turned the village into a political hot potato. Without Bo's political patronage, Hailong's leaders were vulnerable to attack from officials who opposed the village's aggressive development practices. In particular, it was rumored that Huang Qifan, Chongqing's mayor and second in command, disliked Yan Jing and deplored the municipal government's lack of control over Hailong's development. In the six months after Bo's downfall, one of Hailong's cadres, Lin Qunjie, reported that fewer and fewer leaders were visiting the village. According to Lin, none of China's leaders were willing to "declare where they stood" (*biaotai* 表态), leaving Hailong in political limbo. As a result, the process of negotiating the approval of Hailong's master plan dragged out. As I prepared to leave Hailong in August 2012, I was advised not to say good-bye to Yan Jing. Village officials whispered that he was in a foul mood, and his temper was even shorter than usual. Several days earlier, he and his closest deputy attended a meeting at the municipal planning bureau, and there was no resolution to the impasse. Higher-level leaders and departments were still refusing to approve the Hailong plan. Many of Hailong's cadres attributed the delay to Huang Qifan, who was reportedly blocking any movement on the issue.

The change in the balance of political power also had a concrete impact on Hailong's village plan and the location of the urban construction boundary (Figure 35). The High Tech Zone's original proposal encompassed almost the entirety of Hailong's flat and accessible land, drawing the boundary along the lower slopes of Zhongliang Mountain. In the summer of 2011, with the benefit of Bo Xilai's support, Hailong's cadres succeeded in moving the boundary back, reducing the area of potential expropria-

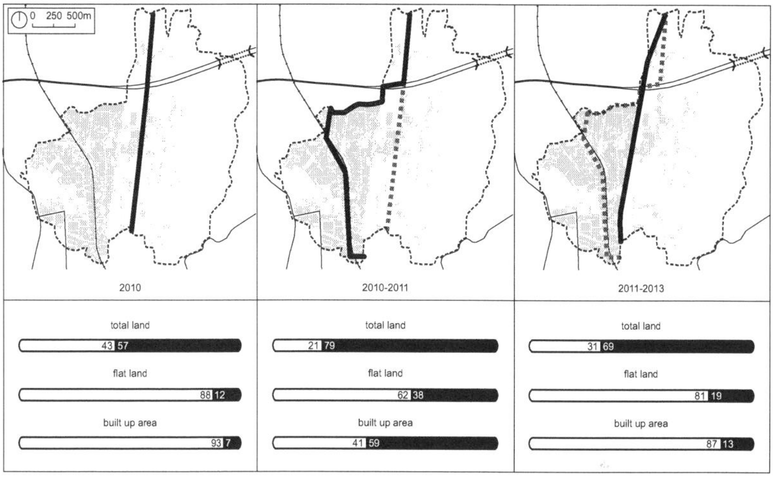

Figure 35. Negotiating the Urban Construction Boundary. The urban construction boundary was used to divide the urban planning area (to the west) from the village planning area (to the east). The boundary originally proposed by the High Tech Zone ran along the foothills of Zhongliang Mountain and would have entailed the expropriation of nearly all of Hailong's collective-owned land. In 2011, in the middle of the negotiation process, Hailong succeeded in revising the boundary to follow the rail line. The final boundary, reflected in the village's approved statutory plan of 2013, ran along the western edge of Silong Mountain, the small ridge separating western Hailong from the village interior. The majority of Hailong's existing development and most of its flat land were located on the urban side of the boundary. The changing percentages of total land, flat land, and built-up area are represented at the bottom, with the urban portion represented in white and the village portion represented in black.

tion by nearly two thirds. Revised versions of both the High Tech Zone's master plan and the village's statutory plan showed the boundary following the existing rail line. But with Bo's downfall, the urban construction boundary was once again up for negotiation. In September 2012, Huang Qifan granted his conditional support for the redevelopment of the village, but only if the urban construction boundary was expanded to include the freight highway that Hailong's cadres had once forced the municipality to relocate. The highway's new location, combined with the transformation of the adjacent rail line into a high-speed rail, increased the amount of land requiring expropriation and provided a rationale for redrawing the urban construction boundary. In the village plan that was finally approved in December 2013, this revised boundary expanded the High Tech Zone's planning area by 50 hectares (to a total of 129 hectares) and cut the territory under Hailong's planning control by more than half. Sandwiched between the development zone and the national forest, Hailong was left with only 30 hectares to plan—approximately 10 percent of its original 277.45 hectares of collective-owned land.

Managing the Uncertainty of Planning: Blowing Up Silong Mountain

For all the bargaining, negotiation, and compromise that led to the plan's approval, would the statutory village plan have any real impact on Hailong's actual development? When I first arrived in Hailong in the summer of 2011, I tried to visit the proposed site for the new village center, but I struggled to find it. The development was planned for one of Hailong's back valleys, and each road I walked down to get there led to a dead end or a mountain track winding up through the brush and vegetable fields that clung to the steep slopes of Silong Mountain. The ridge divided Hailong in two. Where I was, on the western side, relatively flat land accommodated most of the village's existing development; beyond Silong Mountain, to the east, the land began to ripple, forming two narrow valleys before it ascended into the massive Zhongliang Mountain ridge separating Hailong from the main city. Finally I stumbled onto a one-lane dirt track that snaked off the paved road. I had walked by it more than once, missing the narrow opening between the blind brick wall of an industrial compound and the gray facade of a migrant dormitory. A hundred meters up the narrow lane, the brick wall petered out, the path jogged to the right, and the land rose a bit. The clanking of machine parts and the honking of trucks faded behind me, muffled by the wet earth. But instead of climbing up the face of Silong Mountain, I stumbled into a void. A gaping trench the size of a football field had been cut through the ridge, its striated innards laid bare, towering above me on either side (Figure 36). To the south, the remains of a farmhouse clung precariously to an eroding lip of earth. To the north, an electric transmission tower threatened to teeter into the void. Below them, a teenager taught his girlfriend how to ride a bike, helping her along as she shakily picked her way through the boulders.

Just after the 2011 Chinese New Year, still in the early days of negotiating the village plan, dynamite and backhoes blasted and clawed their way through the mountain. Residents described how the demolition crew

Figure 36. The Silong Mountain Gap. In February 2011, Hailong blew a hole in Silong Mountain to connect the village's west with the proposed residential development in the east.

blew right through the ridge with onomatopoetic sounds of destruction: *"Paopaopao, gaogaogao."* As one villager put it, "The more they work on that road, the messier it gets. It's enough to drive you crazy!" Others marveled at its width and depth, marking it as a measure of Hailong's future urbanity. The gap in the mountain would accommodate a four-lane access road from Bai-Peng Road in the west to the village's inner valley—a grand entrance to Hailong's new residential area, which Hailong cadres had insisted on including in the village plan. Hailong's leaders had wasted no time. Even before a preliminary draft of the village's master plan had been completed, they took action to begin its implementation. By breaking ground, they were staking a claim on Hailong's future and securing leverage in the ensuing negotiation process. As they continued to fight to keep control of the village's western third, the hole in the mountain was a material guarantee of the village's eastward expansion and the eventual construction of a new village center. Blasting a hole in Silong Mountain was a form of insurance against the kind of process uncertainty that ended up delaying the approval of Hailong's plan for three years. Their assertiveness did not stop there. Soon after the demolition of Silong Mountain, half a dozen houses at its base were razed, including Xu Jianguo's. As Hailong continued to wait for the approval of its statutory plan, the rubble remained, a monument to the uncertain politics of Chinese planning.

Coordinative Planning

According to the ideology of scientific rationality discussed in chapter 1, the village leadership's material preemption of the plan would have counted as a prime example of regulatory failure. In this view, planning and development are two separate processes mediated through the artifact of the plan, which constitutes both the telos of planning and the instrument of development control. Regulatory failure arises from the interpenetration of planning and development and the consequent politicization of the plan. The preceding discussion of planning in Hailong shows that such politicization and negotiation—for good and ill—are constitutive of the planning process, not deviations from it. This coordinative approach to planning has deep historical roots. In the early days of the socialist era, urban planning and economic planning—the coordinating activity at the heart of the planned economy—were not formally distinguished but constituted one integrated function of the state (Shi 2005). Urban planning was thus premised on the social ownership of the means of production, including land, and the need for the coordination of the various state actors engaged in that production (Shi 2004; Xie and Costa 1993). While urban planning was subsequently established as a separate practice, it continued to be subordinated to economic planning as directed by the state (Shi 2004; Wu, Xu, and Yeh 2007; Yeh and Wu 1999). Though reform-era liberalization has led to the waning of centralized economic planning, the links between urban planning and economic planning are still robust (Leaf 1998; Shi 2004; Wu 1998). In part, this has meant the devolution of coordination from the central planning apparatus to the municipal or county level, a trend that has paralleled the wider decentralization of the Chinese state. The need for such coordination at a local level was particularly stark in the aftermath of the socialist period, when the administrative allocation of land to state work units had resulted in a high level of sociospatial fragmentation (Bray 2005; Hsing 2006; Yeh and Wu 1999). The reestablishment of urban planning in the

1980s thus provided a venue for coordinating the development of local party–state actors that had previously answered only to their independent ministerial hierarchies. Over time, however, planning has become co-constituted with state land ownership, as locally dominant party–state actors—particularly municipal governments—consolidated coordination within their territorial domains. This has meant a decline in the interest-balancing function of planning and its emergence as a de facto property right of local governments, which wield their planning powers to eliminate or capture (rather than coordinate with) development projects that might compete with the local growth machine.

By using their political clout to challenge the municipal government's land monopoly, Hailong's cadres destabilized this consolidation of planning powers. The relative stability of municipal power and its effective control over planning processes often suppress or obscure the contested nature of intra-party–state coordination. The extended process of negotiation and contestation that unfolded in Hailong thus provided an important window into the fundamentally coordinative nature of Chinese planning. Unlike the claims of scientific rationality, in which planning powers are supposed to *regulate* the free exercise of fragmented property rights, the actual implementation of planning powers serves to *coordinate* the various agents of the fragmented party–state that exercise property rights. Planning is therefore not external to the exercise of property rights but rather an integral part of the ongoing process of negotiation by which control over powers, resources, and rights are balanced among various party–state actors. Backroom bargaining and negotiation are at the heart of Chinese planning, and the direction of planning may have as much to do with who ultimately controls the material transformation of the built environment as with who directs the planners. In this alternative narrative of planning, the planning process is more important than the plan itself, and this process does not end with the plan.[14] Rather, the trading of planning powers for planning gain and other resources embeds planning in the wider network of resource trading and power balancing produced through fragmented authoritarianism. The division of Hailong into two separate planning areas helped subdue the conflict between Hailong's cadres and the municipal government, but only temporarily. Indeed, the bifurcation of the village by the urban construction boundary and its artificial division into separate urban and rural territories further underlined the unresolved contradiction in Hailong's development, with two rival party–state actors pushing the village in different directions. As discussed in the following chapter, the gap in Silong Mountain was just the first of many moves enacted by Hailong's cadres as they sought to evade the discipline of municipal regulators and realize their alternative vision of urban–rural coordination.

CHAPTER 5

Village-as-the-City

Land Commodification, Shareholding, and Self-Urbanization

Yu Gong led the way past the crumbling mud-and-timber house where he had been born, now full of honking geese. At the end of his driveway, just beyond a rusty yellow dump truck and a stand of bamboo, a footpath disappeared up the hillside. We climbed single file through the underbrush—Yu, me, and a trio of other village cadres who had been out shrimping in one of Hailong's reservoirs that morning. It was Golden Week of 2011, a weeklong holiday following China's National Day celebration. After a lunch of shrimp, eaten on the airy second floor of Yu's well-appointed home, the air crackled with laughter at Wang Ge's dirty jokes. Yu wanted to take advantage of the crisp October sky to show me Hailong's future, so we climbed unsteadily up the hill. Above the bamboo and brush, we followed a paved nature trail along the top of Hailong's second ridge. Hailong's cadres had built the path a year earlier, when they finished paving the adjacent road that led into the village's interior. The path was ostensibly a contribution to the municipality's Green Chongqing campaign, and it provided a quiet place for young factory workers to take romantic walks. But it was also a showpiece, designed to give clear views of the two innermost valleys where village leaders were planning Hailong's relaunch. As we neared the end of the path, Yu pointed westward at a lone two-story house and a weathered tree, holdouts in a sea of mud and broken brick where Xu Jianguo had once lived. "There," Yu said, pointing at the house. "That is where the new village office building will go. Six stories tall, and *this* big around." He stretched his arms as wide as they would go. "And a plaza three times the size of Hailong Square. Big enough to fit all our villagers." He then pivoted northward, conjuring

Figure 37. Hailong City. A design rendering showed a bird's-eye view of the new residential area surrounded by verdant greenery and misty mountains.

each row of 12-story apartment buildings, which would fill the valley to our west. Yu vividly described a high-rise idyll, set among citrus groves and grape orchards, protected from the odorous wave of industrialization crashing against the western slopes of Silong Mountain. It was difficult for me to imagine amid the rubble and the distant echo of machine work, but Yu spoke with the confidence of a man who saw the future: "When the plan is approved in a few weeks, we'll start building. In just a few years, the whole village will be completely transformed!" As it turned out, final approval of Hailong's statutory plan was still two years away, but Yu had in fact already seen the promised city in the hills—not in a vision but in an architectural rendering, which the village commissioned in overly optimistic anticipation of their imminent planning approval.

Two years later, in June 2013, I saw the idyll for myself at the entrance to Hailong's dusty construction site. Plastered across a billboard, the architectural rendering offered a bird's-eye view of the real estate development, bathed in golden light, nestled in forested hills, and wreathed in mist—common design idioms that emphasized the site's rurality and obscured the complexities of context (Figure 37). It stood amid a series of

Figure 38. Construction Billboard. A billboard at the front of the construction site for the new village center displayed the following message: "In Hailong City, activity is everywhere."

billboards featuring the luxurious lifestyles residents would enjoy amid renderings of high-rise apartment buildings, fountain-filled plazas, and smiling pedestrians. One billboard caught my eye: "In Hailong City, activity is everywhere" (Figure 38). I soon found the phrase "Hailong City" (*hailong cheng* 海龙城) featured in all of the village's promotional materials, including its real estate sales pamphlet: "Hailong City will become a new urban center of Baishiyi." Administratively, Hailong was still a rural village, with rural land, population, and governance, but the Hailong portrayed by these billboards was no longer just a village. Nor was it just a city. Hailong's leaders sought to transcend the limitations of China's urban–rural dichotomy, combining the best of both the urban and the rural to transform the village into something that was simultaneously both and neither.

Was this ideal of urban–rural transcendence possible, or did the realities of urban–rural difference make it a utopian fantasy? China's 1998 Land Management Law (subsequently revised in 2004) forbids the use of rural land for urban development, meaning that for commercial real estate to be built on Hailong's land, it must first be expropriated by the state and then converted to urban status. Through a strict quota system, the law also limits the conversion of agricultural land to nonagricultural uses. By removing construction land from villages and transferring it to urban areas, urban–rural coordination and Chongqing's land reform policy have made village-driven development projects even more difficult. In this context, the only way for villages to develop urban functions is through the black market. Flouting the Land Management Law and bypassing government expropriation, some village collectives have transferred land directly to outside investors or have developed their land independently (Ho and Lin 2003; Lin 2009, 95–96; Yeh 2005). The resulting developments, colloquially known as "small property rights housing" (*xiao chanquan fang* 小产权房), often look just like standard commercial housing and may even undergo formal planning processes, but the housing cannot be registered with the government to obtain formal title, meaning that purchasers' property rights are not protected by law and the development is subject to government expropriation (Deng 2009; Lai, Chan, and Choy 2016; Paik and Lee 2012). As a result, small property rights housing is priced well below the commercial housing market, with discounts sometimes reaching as high as 80 percent (Paik and Lee 2012). Demand for such housing is driven by the very restrictions that prevent rural land use intensification and that grant municipal governments local monopolies over the provision of land for real estate development, thereby constraining supply and driving up housing costs in the formal market (Deng 2009; Paik and Lee 2012). Small property rights housing thus materializes the tension between the messy reality of sociospatial transformation and the Chinese government's artificial separation of urban and rural land. It is an expression of China's urban–rural contradictions, not an escape from them.

This chapter explores how Hailong was nevertheless able to pursue urban–rural transcendence by navigating the gaps opened up by urban–rural coordination. By creatively repurposing the municipality's newly reformulated policies, Hailong's leaders achieved objectives contrary to those of the municipality but without overtly challenging the government's authority. These efforts proceeded on two parallel tracks that urbanized both the village's landscape (as real estate) and its inhabitants (as shareholders). First, Hailong used the principles underlying Chongqing's land reform policy to consolidate control over its collective landholdings and turn them into real estate. Taking advantage of policy changes that regularized the transaction of some rural land use rights, Hailong engineered a partial escape from the conventional constraints on rural urbanization. Rather than risking government expropriation and demolition, the commercial housing in Hailong City would be built on collective land and would enjoy recognition by government regulators. Second, Hailong used the principles underlying Chongqing's household registration reform policy to transform its villagers into shareholders whose moral claims on the village and its land could be replaced by financial claims on collective revenue. By converting collective membership into shares in village shareholding organizations, Hailong's leaders replaced villagers' moral claims to rural welfare—represented by the use value derived from their allocated land use rights—with financial stakes in the future development of Hailong City. By incorporating the village without converting villagers' household registration to urban status, Hailong's leaders consolidated their control over the village's collective assets, ensuring villagers' economic dependence and undercutting potential resistance. Together, these two initiatives provided the basis for the realization of Hailong City, which embodied a utopian aspiration to transcend China's urban–rural contradictions in a single self-contained site. To achieve this transcendence, Hailong's leaders had no choice but to maximize the village's value within the market system, erasing the use values of the existing village and turning it into a spatial abstraction ready for commodification. Thus, in the very act of saving the village from municipal expropriation under urban–rural coordination, Hailong's leaders inadvertently achieved much the same result, emptying the village of its sociospatial functions and ethical principles of organization and transforming it into a simulacrum of itself. While the village collective continued to exist as an administrative entity, Hailong's residents no longer recognized their surroundings as a village.

Rescaling and Reimagining Urban–Rural Coordination

When the State Council designated Chongqing as an experimental area for urban–rural coordination in 2007, Hailong's senior cadres fiercely debated the implications for the village. Many cadres thought urban–rural coordination meant Hailong's inevitable annexation by the expanding city. The village had achieved impressive results over the last half decade, but there was no point in further investment if it would all be torn down anyway. Indeed, the municipal government's deployment of urban–rural coordination directly challenged village-based development initiatives like Hailong's, as discussed in chapter 1. The municipality's two marquee reform programs systematically shifted resources away from villages and toward cities: Household registration reform encouraged villagers to give up their village membership in exchange for urban citizenship, and land reform encouraged villagers to give up their village housing and land in exchange for financial compensation. Hailong's party secretary, Yan Jing, led a rival faction of cadres who were reluctant to abandon the village's achievements and instead advocated harnessing the policy regime in service of village development. With the recent completion of Easy Street and Hailong Square as material testimony, Yan's faction won out, and Hailong embarked on yet another new path of village development, becoming the first village in Chongqing to produce its own development plan for urban–rural coordination.

With urban–rural coordination, Yan Jing took on his greatest challenge yet: reversing the effects of municipal policy without contradicting it. The State Council's designation of Chongqing as an experimental site for urban–rural coordination granted the municipal government extraordinary powers to recalibrate urban–rural relations in the municipality's favor. But this very process of institutional recalibration also opened the door for other actors to reappropriate urban–rural coordination in pursuit of their own ends. To write new institutional rules, municipal policy makers first had to destabilize existing institutions of urban–rural difference, such as household registration and land rights. While the municipality's governmental powers and prerogatives ensured that its proposed replacements took precedence, this was a function of political power, not logical necessity. The experimental nature of urban–rural coordination meant that Chongqing's policies were provisional, and their success or failure was contingent on the approval and support of national leaders. Moreover, to provide sufficient room for experimentation, the national articulation of urban–rural coordination was deliberately vague. Urban–rural coordination could mean any number of things, and the specifics of its implementation depended on the discretion of local cadres. As an intoxicated village official shouted during dinner one night, “None of China’s top leaders know! None of them know how to implement urban–rural coordination!” Just as it threatened Hailong’s village-based development initiatives, urban–rural coordination thus also created an opportunity for village leaders to propose their own alternatives to replace the old system of urban–rural relations.

In laying out his village-scale vision of urban–rural coordination, Yan Jing emphasized that Hailong would not pose a challenge to the municipality’s urban–rural coordination program. For instance, the village’s development would still undergo government regulation and approval, as expressed through the statutory planning process. As he argued in the village newspaper, Hailong’s project of urban–rural coordination should be considered a supplement, rather than an alternative, to government-led urbanization: “In the places that the government cannot cover, Hailong’s self-urbanization will take on social responsibility.” But in the next sentence, he suggested that Hailong’s approach was somehow superior to Chongqing’s: “For those areas that the government has not perfected, we, the village, will perfect them.” And in the preface to Hailong’s exhibition hall, Yan wrote, “We are the forerunner of urban–rural coordinated development.” The phrase suggested not only a temporal but also a logical precedence: Hailong’s development was not a part of urban–rural coordination, urban–rural coordination was a part of Hailong’s development. Despite Yan’s diplomatic rhetoric, Hailong’s interpretation of urban–rural coordination thus presented a direct challenge to the municipal reform program.

Hailong’s approach to household registration reform exemplified cadres’ views of urban–rural coordination. As Assistant Party Secretary Wen Jiancai explained, Hailong saw its own development as an alternative to the municipal program: “Our next objective is to turn our villagers (*cunmin* 村民) into urbanites (*shimin* 市民). What does this mean? It means that even without transferring your household registration, you will be able to enjoy the status of an urban citizen. Just like in urban–rural coordination, you’ll get health insurance, elder care, you name it.” Another cadre, Cai Guangyu, claimed that the importance of household registration would simply disappear. No one would care because all the things that household registration represented would already be provided.

All this was at least consistent with municipal goals, but when I asked Cai if Hailong was able to achieve this because of its participation in Chongqing's household registration reform program, he became frustrated by my lack of understanding and quipped, "We're participating, all right. All those rural migrants coming to Chongqing under urban–rural coordination? Hailong can give them housing and jobs." Cai's comment inverted the logic of the municipal reform program. Rather than becoming a *source* of rural–urban transfers (the anticipated role for villages under the Chongqing program), Hailong would be a *destination* for the migrants targeted by the municipality. In 2012, Hailong began a streamlined application process for rural residents wishing to transfer their household registration to the village. According to municipal policy, these migrants should have been living in the city proper, either in market-rate housing or in one of the municipality's new public housing projects. Chongqing's urban–rural coordination program was meant to eliminate villages like Hailong, not spur their expansion.

Rural Land Reform: Collective Operational Construction Land

Even after the municipal planning bureau approved Hailong's statutory village plan, including the negotiated location of the urban construction boundary, plans for Hailong City were still on hold. Early in Hailong's statutory planning process, the Jiulongpo District land management bureau had appended a document to the draft plan noting that it would "support the appropriate expansion of the scale of village construction land in Hailong." The use of the word "appropriate" (*shidang* 适当) reflected the political balancing act in which the land management bureau was engaged. Jiulongpo's leaders had instructed the local land management bureau to support Hailong Village's development by accommodating its need for additional construction land, but the land management bureau was statutorily charged with protecting agricultural land and limiting the expansion of construction land in rural areas.[1] The word "appropriate" euphemistically indexed the future resolution of this contradiction at a higher level of political authority, as would be expected in the context of fragmented authoritarianism (Lieberthal and Oksenberg 1988). Unfortunately for Yan Jing, the downfall of Hailong's chief political patron, Bo Xilai, in March 2012 weakened political support for the village's development, and the rigors of China's land quota regime forbade the plan's proposal to transform a large portion of agricultural land into construction land. In the summer of 2012, Yan and his deputy, Wen Jiancai, attended a series of meetings with the municipal planning and land management bureaus to resolve the issue, but the talks stalled, and village cadres reported that Yan always came back from the meetings in a foul mood.

Hailong was not the first village to encounter the challenge of rural land use conversion. In the 1970s and 1980s, early efforts to enable village-based industrialization through township and village enterprises (TVEs) focused on regularizing nonagricultural activities on collective-owned land by designating certain parcels as "collective operational construction land" (*jiti jingying xing jianshe yong di* 集体经营性建设用地), which were authorized for industrial use (Gao 2014; Liu 2014; Wang 2011). With the consolidation of the TVE sector in the late 1990s, the unregulated transfer of these parcels became widespread, particularly in the Yangtze River Delta, where the TVE sector had been strongest. Municipalities in the region, most notably Suzhou, began authorizing the transfer of use rights to these parcels—or, in some cases, expropriating the land using market-based compensation rates (Li 2013; Sun and Xu 2011). At the same time, collective operational construction land also became the basis for new forms of rural industrialization driven by diverse combinations of state, collective, and private capital.[2] By taking advantage of preexisting regulatory exemptions granted for the use of collective operational construction land by TVEs, these approaches became popular mechanisms for the marketization and urbanization of village land along China's coast (Huang 2014; Po 2008).

As the central government launched urban–rural coordination in the early 2000s, it began looking for ways to integrate rural land into urban land markets while still protecting agricultural land, and local experiments with collective operational construction land offered useful precedents. The State Council's first mention of collective land transfers came in 2003 as a response to the demands of TVE reform (Lin 2009, 163). After this, the State Council began making annual proclamations gradually liberalizing the regulation of rural land use rights but without lifting the general ban on the transfer of rural land imposed by the Land Management Law (Sun and Xu 2011). In 2008, the State Council made the symbolically important decision to allow the transaction of collective operational construction land on the same basis and with the same rights as urban land, but only in areas not already covered by land use plans, meaning that it had relatively little practical impact (Li 2013; Liu 2014; Wang and Cai 2012). In late 2013, the Third Plenum of the 18th Central Party Committee extended the 2008 measure to all areas, effectively establishing equal rights and status for state-owned and collective-owned land and allowing the full marketization of use rights to collective operational construction land (Gao 2014; Liu 2014). Nevertheless, these reforms were constrained by existing laws and regulations, meaning that small property rights housing was still ineligible for formal title and legal protection, and the government continued to play a leading role in controlling the transfer of rural land through the land use planning and land conversion quota systems. The gradual regularization of rural land transfers therefore functioned as a tool of political and economic discipline. The previous ban on rural land transactions had driven these activities into the black market, hiding them from government regulators. By regularizing these transactions, the government made them transparent and accessible to regulation, thereby constraining the ability of village leaders to sell off agricultural land without government permission. As with other efforts at marketization (Haila 2007; Lin 2009, 10; Wu 2018), liberalizing rural land transactions has been about increasing government control, not relinquishing it to the market.

This new regulatory environment resulted in two distinct approaches to integrating rural land into urban land markets: the transfer of development rights (TDR) and the transfer of use rights. In China, TDR was first applied to rural land in 2004 in Chengdu's Pixian County, which allowed the transfer of construction land from villages to urban areas (Sun and Xu 2011).[3] Chengdu subsequently expanded this program to the entire municipality as part of its urban–rural coordination program, using village consolidation to reduce construction land in villages and increase construction land at the edges of urban areas in the same county or district (Huang et al. 2013; Shi and Tang 2020). In Chongqing's marquee land reform program, a similar process of village consolidation produces a "land note" (*dipiao* 地票), a financial instrument that allows the purchaser to apply to have an equivalent amount of agricultural land elsewhere in the municipality expropriated by the state, converted to urban status, and made available for sale (X. Cai 2010; Yep and Forrest 2016; Zhang 2018). The TDR programs implemented by Chengdu and Chongqing—and subsequently imitated across China—represent an expansion of the government-led expropriation process, reinforcing the government's monopolistic control over rural land development and further subordinating village-led growth initiatives to state-led urbanization. The programs allow municipal governments to expand the legal provision of urban construction land without reducing the total amount of agricultural land within the municipality's territory, making it possible to stockpile valuable land conversion quotas and expand development capacity at the same time (X. Cai 2010; Gao 2014). While TDR allows residents of even the most distant villages to monetize the value of their land use rights (Liu et al. 2016), it comes at the cost of villages' long-term development capacity (Zhang 2018), effectively mortgaging the future to pay for the present.[4] As we saw in chapter 1, Chongqing's planners responded to these constraints by reifying rural villages as pastoral playlands. Elsewhere, participating villages have been transformed into industrial farms as part of the vertical integration of Chinese agriculture, giving agribusinesses substantial control over village land—and in some cases proletarianizing villagers (Abramson 2016; Huang et al. 2013; Zhang and Donaldson 2010).

By contrast, the transfer of use rights enables villages to catalyze their own development. According to advocates of this approach, the Central Party Committee's recognition of equal rights for collective construction land in 2013 legitimized the marketization of collective operational construction land (Gao 2014; Liu 2014). These commentators have argued for the greater efficiency and equity of collective-led development and small property rights housing, which breaks governmental land monopolies, reduces the revenue extracted by real estate developers, and liberates the capital bound up in rural land for use in village development (Gao 2014; Zhang 2013; Zhang 2015). But the collective-led approach still violates existing legal prohibitions on the use of rural land for commercial housing, which some have criticized as a means of protecting profitable governmental monopolies (Liu 2014; Sun and Xu 2011; Zhang 2015). The significant financial returns municipal governments earn from providing land to developers have meant that use rights transfers have been implemented less widely than TDR, with most experiments pursued by enterprising village leaders, like Yan Jing, who have taken advantage of the ambiguity of regulatory reform to push the policy envelope.

Self-Urbanization and Self-Expropriation

On August 26, 2013, with Hailong's statutory plan close to gaining final approval, Yan Jing penned an editorial in the village newspaper introducing the idea of "self-urbanization" (*zizhu chengshihua* 自主城市化). Yan borrowed the term from an academic debate about Zheng'ge, a village in periurban Beijing that became famous for the commercial transfer of use rights and the urban development of its collective operational construction land.[5] In his commentary, Yan explained how excited he was when he first read about self-urbanization, believing it to be the best path forward in Hailong's pursuit of urban–rural coordination. Through self-urbanization, the village would be able to urbanize without government investment, government expropriation, or the conversion of the village's land, population, or governance to urban status.[6] Quoting his own rhetoric from the early 2000s, Yan claimed that Hailong faced yet another critical juncture. "If we fail to seize this opportunity," Yan warned, "it will be a sin against Hailong Village. We will have failed in our responsibility to the whole municipality and even the whole nation in the development of urban–rural coordination!" Yan's excitement in response to self-urbanization reflected his desperate search for a breakthrough in Hailong's stalemate with the land management bureau, which continued to insist on the illegality of Hailong's land use plans. As Yan argued in the introduction to the article on self-urbanization, "China's current law has two valid but irreconcilable perspectives on land transfers." A few months later, Yan found his opening. On November 15 the Central Party Committee announced its passage of the measure that granted equal rights and status for state-owned and collective-owned land and made the eventual establishment of a single market for land use rights national policy. Just two weeks later, on December 3, the land management bureau gave Hailong its blessing, and the municipal government formally approved the village plan. Several days later, on December 12, Yan gave an interview with the village newspaper reiterating Hailong's commitment to self-urbanization and directly referencing the new policies promulgated by the Central Party Committee in November.

Following the example of Zheng'ge, Hailong consolidated control over village land by renting households' allocated land use rights, converting the agricultural portion of that land into construction land, converting that construction land into collective operational construction land, and finally transferring the land use rights to the village development corporation.[7] Like Zheng'ge, Hailong was able to convert its agricultural land into construction land only after an equivalent amount of construction land was converted to agricultural use somewhere else. Yan Jing accomplished this by convincing the town of Baishiyi to allow Hailong to purchase the excess construction land produced by Xindian, a nearby village that was already in the process of consolidation and relocation. Hailong's transformation thus also drew on the precedent established by Chongqing's land reform program, in which excess development capacity produced through village consolidation can be transferred to other locations. Through the use of TDR, Chongqing "implicitly introduced 'land development rights' into Chinese legal practice" (Cui 2011, 658), legitimizing the village-to-village transfer from Xindian to Hailong even though the municipal land reform program required land notes to be transacted on the municipality-wide exchange. In Chongqing's land reform program, the purchase of a land note also necessitated municipal expropriation at the target site, but in its pursuit of self-urbanization, Hailong rejected the government-led expropriation process. Assistant Party Secretary Wen Jiancai even went so far as to turn the logic of government expropriation on its head: "We want to use our collective assets to *expropriate our land ourselves.*" Wen did not mean this literally. There would be no point in the village collective expropriating land from itself. Rather, Wen was making a claim for the equal status of Hailong's ownership rights. Just like state-owned land, Hailong's collective-owned land would be eligible for the market-based transaction of use rights. Hailong combined the backdoor TDR process with a transfer of use rights, contracting the village's newly created collective operational construction land to the village development corporation for real estate development.

Hailong's resolution of the land conversion problem thus opportunistically combined a variety of new practices made possible by both central and local land reforms. By creating instability and flexibility in the existing regulatory system, these reforms made it possible for villages like Hailong to achieve outcomes contrary to those envisioned by the reforms' architects.

Real Estate Development Planning and the Intensification of Village Land Use

The approval of the land management bureau was crucial to Hailong's pursuit of self-urbanization. Without it, Hailong City would be just like any other instance of small property rights housing: vulnerable to regulatory intervention, government expropriation, and demolition. Instead, by subjecting itself to the urban planning and land use planning processes, Hailong secured legitimacy for its development among the regulatory agencies of the municipal government. Even though Hailong's land was not undergoing the government-led expropriation and conversion process, neither would it be at risk of government seizure and demolition. This arrangement enabled Hailong to capture the land rent increment produced by converting its agricultural land into commercial real estate. Instead of the local government capturing the land rent increment and then passing on some of its earnings to the village as compensation for expropriation, the profit produced by commercially developing the village's land would accrue directly to the village development corporation. The corporation would then pass on some of these profits to the village collective, which would transfer a portion of its income to the government in the form of taxes and fees. This reduced Hailong's dependence on the government's fiscal generosity, and it broke the municipal monopoly over land provision for real estate development. As one municipal planner observed, "That village has become like a small city. It even has its own real estate development company. It uses it to build new buildings, which become their property."

Despite the extensive statutory planning process discussed in chapter 4, the village's leaders expressed little concern about the constraints such regulation might place on Hailong's development. When I asked village official Cai Guangyu whether he was satisfied with the statutory plan, he shrugged his shoulders. “Sure,” he said, “because it’s not set in stone. It will be adjusted for each stage of development. It’s not like after the plan is finished, every little thing is going to be done according to what is said in the plan. It’s not like a machine!” For Cai, the statutory plan was just a starting point, a declaration of principles. The real decisions would come afterward, as Hailong iteratively adapted and adjusted to the challenges of turning the village into a city. But Hailong’s leaders did not even wait that long. Early in 2011, months before the first draft of the statutory plan was completed, Hailong started a parallel process of real estate development planning. The village leaders commissioned the Chongqing University College of Construction Management and Real Estate to conduct a feasibility study for developing the 11.53 hectares of collective-owned residential land demarcated in the statutory plan.

The 110-page document produced by Chongqing University was much more than a simple elaboration of the village plan. The feasibility study adopted the basic lot boundaries and land use designations defined by the statutory plan—changing these parameters would have risked condemnation from municipal regulators, necessitating new rounds of negotiation—but the feasibility study completely reimagined what would happen inside this framework, reintroducing elements of the village’s expansive development plan. The original development plan had proposed a total built area of 200,000 square meters, at a cost of approximately 500 million RMB, which the statutory plan had revised down to 108,760 square meters and 10 million RMB. The feasibility study returned these figures close to their original levels—186,700 square meters and 499.5 million RMB. It effectively rescaled the village’s residential area according to the maximalist (and despatialized) vision of the development plan but within the much narrower spatial constraints set by the statutory plan, creating an intensity of land use that was not envisioned by either the development plan or the statutory plan. Hailong’s final construction plan for the residential development increased the total built area still further, to 380,000 square meters, more than double the feasibility study’s recommendation.

The feasibility study arrived at this intensification by reorienting the statutory plan toward the demands of the market. Mo Ying, one of the planners responsible for preparing Hailong’s statutory plan and the coauthor of Chongqing's suburban village planning report, explained how difficult it was to satisfy the market-based incentives that motivated village planning in Chongqing. Town governments only commissioned village plans to attract investment, and the only plans that were implemented relied on commercial development. As Mo admitted, the standard approach to statutory planning had proven ineffective in attracting investment, and at a cost of more than 100,000 RMB, fewer and fewer village plans were being commissioned. He concluded by quoting a frustrated town official: "We've spent all this money, and yet we've gotten nothing for it!" By contrast, the feasibility study embraced the market logic of planning, beginning from an analysis of market demand for real estate products that Hailong might be well positioned to supply. Whereas the statutory planning process treated Hailong's official population of 1,953 registered villagers as its key independent variable, which then determined the size and scale of the village's infrastructure and services, the feasibility study treated the village population as a dependent variable, ultimately adding another 6,300 residents to the existing registered population. This dramatic expansion was made up of three main components—migrant housing, retirement housing, and vacation villas—each of which was identified as a strategic area of unmet demand in Chongqing's housing market. In a development that included 50,000 square meters of luxury villas, a 300-room hotel, an office building, a conference center, and a full-service club, only 25,000 square meters was reserved for villagers' housing, representing just 13 percent of the total built area.

The residential development outlined in the feasibility study was one of four main elements in the village's larger development strategy, which also included an agritourism park, an industrial park, and a commercial street. The first of these projects was launched in October 2010, when Hailong's development corporation began collectivizing more than 350 *mu* (23.3 hectares) of hilly agricultural land in the rear of the village to build an orchard of citrus trees and grapevines. The village also planned to build a high-rise industrial park that would be aimed at high-value-added industries, excluding the village's existing labor-intensive and space-extensive manufacturers in favor of high-tech companies. In this respect, Hailong's high-rise industrial park competed directly with the municipal government's High Tech Zone, which was planning to expand into the western third of the village. Finally, the village's commercial street represented its most aggressive competitive strategy. One end of this shopping arcade occupied the entrance to the new residential area, offering retail, services, and entertainment to residents and visitors. But in negotiations over Hailong's statutory plan, village cadres also convinced the municipality to zone the two sides of Hailong's access road for commercial use, extending the shopping strip all the way to Bai-Peng Road. This part of the village was on the municipality's side of the urban construction boundary and was designated for eventual government expropriation. But as the statutory plan neared approval in 2013, Hailong's leaders expressed their intention to transgress the boundary and preempt the municipality by developing the commercial land themselves. When Yan Jing described Hailong's development strategy, he compared it to a battle plan in their fight to protect the village against municipal expansion: "Each of our four big projects is a weapon."

Selling the Village

All of Hailong's proposed development projects made strategic use of the village's urban–rural liminality. Where the statutory village planning process had sought to separate urban and rural functions, the feasibility study celebrated the integration of urban and rural qualities. The real estate consultants defined Hailong's market niche as "a new kind of urban–rural coordinated village" that combined the clean, stable, modern living of the urban with the clean air, healthfulness, and natural environment of the rural. The design guidelines for Hailong's new residential area further underlined the strategic mixing of urban and rural. The document proposed a living environment that provided urban diversity and convenience while also enabling residents to escape the pressures of the city. One enthusiastic villager echoed the new branding: "People in Baishiyi don't want to live in Baishiyi. They want to live here, near nature. . . . In Hailong you can eat the vegetables without worrying about pesticides and chemicals." Another villager expressed a similar sentiment: "The air is better, and the vegetables are fresher. Years ago we envied city life. Now the city people envy us." Assistant Party Secretary Wen Jiancai put it in more practical terms: "Why would I want to live in the city? My office here is just as good. And the air is cleaner than what you breathe in Chongqing. Plus, it's easy to park your car!"

To sell this urban–rural utopia, Hailong subcontracted with a real estate marketing agency, which initially took over the village exhibition hall as their showroom. When I returned in 2018, much of the first phase of construction had been completed and the sales staff had moved to the first floor of the newly built clubhouse. Promotional materials advertised the development's convenient location and its competitive pricing—between 5,000 and 6,000 RMB per square meter, less than half the average price for apartments in downtown Chongqing. After a brief introduction to the scale model, a sales representative took me on a tour of several model units. Residents of Baishiyi and investors from elsewhere in Chongqing had already purchased most of the desirable apartments, and only smaller units of 70 or 80 square meters remained. My tour guide, an 18-year-old villager on her summer vacation, showed me a duplex apartment that looked out on a leafy garden path. She was only a year old when Yan Jing first took over the village and just 10 years old when Hailong's relaunch began, and she raved about the benefits of Hailong City. It was quiet and green, with beautiful walking trails through the agritourism park just behind the development. It was also exciting and convenient, with access to retail and nighttime activities. Soon there would be a light rail station opening at the end of the village access road. As she argued, Hailong City had everything that a high-end real estate development could offer, and the combination of urban and rural amenities was hard to beat. Indeed, from the look of the sparkling showroom and the professional pamphlets, it would be easy to mistake Hailong for any other commercial real estate project in Chongqing.

After my tour, I spoke with the sales manager and asked about how secure the property rights were. Despite the planning approvals granted by municipal regulators, the Land Management Law and the continued prohibition on the use of rural land for commercial housing meant that Hailong's real estate project was still considered small property rights housing and could not be granted government-backed property certificates. The sales manager acknowledged my concerns and admitted that Hailong's apartments did not come with a property certificate. The village was still in the process of finding a resolution to the property rights issue, but, the manager claimed, "It doesn't matter anyway. What do you need a property certificate for? You want to know your building won't be demolished, and you want to know you can resell your apartment." The regulatory approvals from the municipal planning and land management bureaus were prominently displayed in the showroom to reassure buyers on both counts, and many of the units had already been resold on the secondary market. "Weren't the cheap prices a reflection of insecure tenure?" I asked. "No, no," he insisted. "The cheap prices are just because it's a good deal!"

Turning Villagers into Shareholders: Cooperatives and Corporations

As Hailong's leaders worked to ensure the success of the village's real estate ventures, they also had to figure out what role villagers would play in Hailong City. In part this was a question of resource redistribution: how would the village allocate the profits of development? But it was also about how to handle the village collective's relationship with villagers now that the collective had transformed itself into a for-profit real estate developer. What claims would villagers be able to make on collective assets, and what status would they enjoy once they were living shoulder to shoulder with the new residents of Hailong City? The first indications of the tension between corporation and community had already begun to emerge in the early days of development, and they became even more intense as the village embarked on the construction of Hailong City.

To resolve these questions, Hailong's leaders turned to an established tool of village transformation: shareholding. According to Yan Jing, at the heart of self-urbanization was the transformation of rural people into urban people and the transformation of villagers into shareholders. Shareholding was a necessary response to fundamental issues raised by the marketization and development of collective-owned land, including the disambiguation of the collective and the redistribution of profits (Liu 2014; Sun and Xu 2011). But Hailong's pursuit of shareholding also reflected an effort to increase the concentration of power and capital in the hands of village cadres. Since the very beginning of the village's development, Hailong's leaders had used shareholding as a way to attract investment, reward investors, and control decision making. As work on Hailong City moved ahead, they returned to these strategies, using shareholding to reduce villagers' claims on collective assets and insulate cadre decision making from villagers' influence. Shareholding became another method cadres used to transform the village from a welfare-oriented collective into a profit-oriented real estate company.

The Village Shareholding Cooperative

China's "village shareholding cooperatives" (*nongcun gufen hezuo she* 农村股份合作社) date to the early years of the reform era, when they were used to manage collective assets in the context of de-collectivization. Many of these efforts therefore originated in China's south, where economic opportunities and the growing TVE sector created a need for new mechanisms of economic management (Wong 2016). This included, for instance, the re-collectivization of village land, and some of the earliest experiments in village shareholding took place in Guangdong's Nanhai District, which also led the way in village land consolidation (Chung and Unger 2013; Po 2008; Zhu and Guo 2015). The establishment of village shareholding cooperatives therefore represented a return to the collectivist principles of the commune system, with shareholding cooperatives replacing production teams as the legal holders of collective assets (Kan 2016; Wong 2016). The central government endorsed village shareholding practices in 1985, introduced a regulatory framework for the organizations over the course of the 1990s, and began promoting them as a tool for village governance in the 2000s (Chen 2016; Kan 2016; Wong 2016). As village shareholding became more widespread, municipal governments also started using shareholding cooperatives to manage the distribution of land compensation from government expropriation and to avoid responsibility for public goods and grassroots governance as village collectives were turned into urban neighborhoods (Chung and Unger 2013; Lai, Chan, and Choy 2016; Po 2008, 2012; Tang 2015; Wong 2016). Founded in 2013, Hailong's shareholding cooperative was similarly mandated by the Chongqing government as part of urban–rural coordination. Like other municipal governments, Chongqing used shareholding to standardize rural governance and impose discipline on wayward cadres. Municipal policy makers also saw shareholding as a key element of Chongqing's land reform and household registration reform programs, allowing rural residents to transfer their land use rights to their village's shareholding cooperative in exchange for shares and the promise of future dividends. The municipality thus intended village shareholding cooperatives as a way to facilitate the liquidation of Chongqing's villages.

In implementing Chongqing's shareholding directive, Hailong's cadres resurrected Yan Jing's collectivist rhetoric from the early 2000s and touted the shareholding cooperative as a way to ensure that all villagers enjoyed their fair share of the proceeds from development. Like shareholding cooperatives elsewhere in China (Chan, Madsen, and Unger 2009, 340; Chung and Unger 2013), shares in Hailong's cooperative were allocated on the basis of official household registration in the village and could not be alienated or inherited. In theory, this should protect villagers' interests by excluding outsiders from accessing village resources, preventing the dilution of share value, and guarding against the loss of shares to predatory lenders or unscrupulous profiteers. Such organizations thus often function as redistributive welfare organizations serving clearly bounded communities of interest (Chung and Unger 2013; Kan 2016; Tang 2015; Zhu and Guo 2015). Retained profits are used to finance the provision of public goods and services (Chung and Unger 2013; Kan 2016; Lai, Chan, and Choy 2016; Po 2012; Tang 2015; Wong 2016), while the relatively even distribution of dividends constitutes a community-sponsored welfare subsidy (Chung and Unger 2013; Kan 2016; Po 2008, 2011). Shareholding cooperatives can also promote the transparent governance and democratic accountability that are lacking in other village institutions, such as the village party branch and the villagers' committee (Chen 2016; Po 2008). By granting shareholders the right to elect board members and cooperative managers (Kan 2016; Lai, Chan, and Choy 2016; Po 2011), shareholding reforms can rein in cadre corruption, resolve village governance crises, and even bolster enthusiasm for village democracy (Chen 2016; Po 2011; Tang 2015; Wong 2016). On paper, at least, Hailong's shareholding cooperative offered these benefits and protections: shareholders were entitled to a yearly dividend, and each share gave shareholders a vote on the leadership and management of the cooperative.

In practice, however, the village shareholding cooperative allowed Hailong's cadres to consolidate their control over village assets and exclude villagers from decision-making processes.[8] Cooperative shares entitled villagers to claims on collective-owned assets, but the public announcement of the cooperative's establishment left the exact nature of these assets unclear: "Because assets and their value vary with the market and could even disappear, the specific value and definition of these assets will not be specified, including location, area, specifications, dimensions, etc." The property rights for most of these assets were technically held by one of Hailong's development corporations, while the village collective only had rights to income based on the number of collective-held shares in those companies. These shares were granted to the collective in exchange for the use of the village's collective-owned land, but the number of these shares and their value were never publicized. This meant that the value of villagers' shares in the cooperative depended on agreements between the village collective and its various corporations, all of which were managed by Yan Jing and his team. Hailong villagers therefore had relatively little power to influence the course of village development or the disposal of village assets. And because villagers' cooperative shares were inalienable, they had no way to escape their dependence on village cadres. This shareholding shell game allowed Hailong's cadres to protect their control over the organizations where most of the village's wealth and power were ultimately concentrated: the village shareholding corporations.

The Village Shareholding Corporations

As China's village shareholding experiments evolved, new organizational forms emerged, including shareholding cooperative associations, shareholding cooperative companies, and shareholding corporations (Kan 2016; Po 2012). These organizations often exist side by side in the same village, producing complicated, multitiered organizational structures like that found in Hailong. In most documented cases, however, shareholding cooperatives precede the establishment of such corporate entities and often maintain their autonomy in managing village land and other assets (Chung and Unger 2013; Kan 2016; Po 2012). Shareholding companies thus typically serve to complement and extend the functions of existing shareholding cooperatives, not to displace them. This was not the case in Hailong, where the first village shareholding company was established more than 10 years before the shareholding cooperative. In Hailong, it was the profit-oriented incentives of the village shareholding corporations that drove the logic of village development, not the collectivist principles of its shareholding cooperative.

In 2002, Hailong's cadres were desperate for capital and incorporated the land management corporation as the village's first shareholding company, raising 1.3 million RMB by offering investors a 100 percent return in five years. This then produced a liquidity crisis in 2007, as Hailong was rapidly running out of developable land and cadres feared they would not be able to repay their investors, including local members of organized crime. To resolve this crisis, they started another shareholding corporation, raising more than 2 million RMB on more favorable terms—returning just 18 percent after two years and then 24 percent annually thereafter. Much of this second round of capital was used to pay off the first round of investors, while the remainder was used to build Easy Street and Hailong Square. By turning toward a more intensive form of property development, expressed in the semidetached, midrise townhouses that lined Easy Street, Hailong's cadres pursued a "spatial fix" to the declining returns of industrial development (see chapter 2). The greater density and higher rate of return offered by the apartment buildings and commercial spaces allowed Hailong to earn enough income to continue paying off its investors, even as the village ran out of collective-owned land. Once begun, however, this strategy's only hope of success was the continual intensification of village land use through denser, taller buildings, the logical result of which was the construction of Hailong City. To fund this increasing intensification, Hailong's cadres had to keep raising more capital, and they founded another shareholding corporation in 2010. Because each round of fund-raising involved the establishment of a new shareholding company with new bylaws, the value of the shares varied. In general, the terms favored the village's earliest investors, including the cadres themselves. Each subsequent round of investment offered investors lower dividends and fewer decision-making rights. Many villagers complained about this arrangement, which exacerbated intravillage wealth disparities in favor of the very people who ran the shareholding corporations and determined the annual dividends.

In 2013, as village cadres prepared to break ground on Hailong City, they incorporated yet another shareholding company, the Hailong Corporation. Unlike prior rounds of fund-raising, villagers were given a choice of which development projects they wanted to invest in, meaning villagers would be more directly exposed to the risks of the market. Concerned by the low initial return on the 2010 investment round and confused by the parallel shareholding systems, many villagers balked. One villager compared village shareholding to a pyramid scheme: "There's no way I would be willing to invest. It would be like asking to get mugged. It's a fly-by-night operation. There's a lot of risk involved!" As the village continued to struggle with liquidity problems, a new round of fund-raising for villagers was offered in 2014, but turnout was meager. A month later, Hailong's leaders wrote an open letter to villagers asking them to reconsider their financial priorities and increase their investments. Their insistence reflected the extent to which Hailong's development had become dependent on periodic infusions of cash from new shareholding corporations in 2002, 2007, 2010, 2013, and 2014. Hailong's need for capital was accelerating.

Paying back each group of investors was an important motivation for the village's development. Only by continually intensifying Hailong's land use with a larger number of taller buildings that would produce greater revenue streams could village cadres hope to stay ahead of their ever-increasing debts. At the same time, however, the imperative of serving the corporations' investors also threatened the sustainability of village development, as further intensification became more expensive and villagers grew wary of investing more of their savings. By the summer of 2014, construction on Hailong City was already racing ahead, but rumors swirled about construction delays and budget shortfalls. One Monday I found construction workers hanging out and drinking beer in the middle of the day. "No electricity," they complained. "Again," one of them added after taking a swig of his beer. No one knew for sure, but some whispered that the recent electricity problems were more than mere outages and that the bills were not getting paid. When the conversation turned to the question of pay, the grumbling got angrier. Even when the electricity was running, the construction management company had been withholding wages. Three years later, as the first phase of construction finally neared completion, the consequences of these repeated liquidity crises became clearer. Relocated villagers complained about construction shortcuts, cheap materials, and changes from the original design. The prominent water feature from the promotional materials had disappeared, the apartment buildings were packed closer together, and half of the underground parking lot had been rented to a manufacturer, leading to noise complaints. While money had been lavished on the village's new office building—the first structure to be completed—much of the villagers' residential area felt like an afterthought. This was not the urban–rural arcadia they had been promised.

Corporate Governance

Hailong's use of shareholding corporations insulated decision making from villager influence and reduced responsiveness to villager priorities. The rules governing village shareholding cooperatives require democratic decision-making processes, with equal representation for all villagers. They also limit profit-making activities, requiring cooperatives to focus on providing services and managing collective assets. The rules for shareholding companies are much more flexible, allowing the inclusion of diverse shareholders, the use of complex decision-making procedures, and the unbridled pursuit of profit. As with Hailong's earlier shareholding companies, Yan Jing held ultimate decision-making power at the Hailong Corporation, and the same team that staffed the village party branch and the village committee offices also ran the company's day-to-day operations. The result was a Möbius strip–like ownership structure found in many Chinese villages, where the boundaries between collective and corporate property are often blurred (Selden 1998, 27). The size and importance of the corporation's real estate venture meant that the village's leadership team became increasingly preoccupied with its corporate responsibilities to shareholders and clients, leading to a conflict between community and corporate interests.[9] This tension dated back to 2003, as the village party branch sought to transform itself into a "professionalized service team" that would serve as a one-stop shop for everything a small or medium enterprise might need to succeed. According to village leaders, this initiative moved the village "from its original mode of primitive accumulation toward the corporatized operation of capital." As the village party branch proclaimed in its monthly newspaper: "Serving the party means serving business. . . . If a business needs something, we are there to provide it."

As village leaders launched construction on Hailong City, villagers voiced concerns about the consolidation of economic and political power within the shareholding corporation. With the impending demolition of the existing village, including households' sideline businesses and rental properties, villagers would become increasingly dependent on redistribution from shareholding companies that lacked both transparency and accountability, resulting in substantial anxiety: "Will our leaders actually be able to accomplish what they say they are going to do? We have no choice but to rely on them." Yan Jing alluded to these concerns in an open letter in the village newspaper: "Besides managing the company, we are also an administrative village, and we still need to serve the villagers, provide security, protect the environment, and increase green space. . . . We need to coordinate corporate and village work." Hailong's leaders tried to persuade villagers by arguing for the benefits they would reap from Hailong City. Reiterating the logic of the unfunded mandate, Assistant Party Secretary Wen Jiancai insisted that Hailong's real estate development activities were necessary for village welfare: "For 2,000 villagers, relocation housing will cost one or two hundred million. The only way to fill this gap is to build commercial housing on our collective operational construction land."

For Hailong's cadres, the ultimate resolution of the conflict between community and corporate interests meant changing villagers' perceptions, not the village's actions (Smith 2019a). To accomplish this, Hailong pursued a socialization program, building on initiatives like the marching band to train villagers to behave like urban people with "high quality." By giving villagers internet access and taking them on trips to developed urban areas, such as Beijing and Taiwan, village leaders introduced villagers to different customs and lifestyles: "We took them to see how people in developed areas do things: how they live, what they do during the day, what they do at night. We tried to change their thinking, to change their backward, fossilized ideas." As one village official explained, the party was called on to serve the people and act in accordance with the villagers' wishes, but not all their needs could be satisfied. Many villagers were simply too selfish. Instead, he insisted, it was necessary to educate villagers to take on new values—the values of the market and the party. These market-based values would prepare villagers for their transformation into shareholders, through which their moral claims on the collective as an organization of self-governance and redistributive welfare were reduced to financial claims equivalent to—and often less than—those of the village's investors.[10] In villages that are expropriated and replaced by urban neighborhoods, village shareholding organizations sometimes become the last vestige of collective life, taking on the rights and duties of the liquidated administrative village (Kan 2016). In Hailong, cadres succeeded in forestalling this fate, preserving the formal institutions of the village collective. But in saving the village, Hailong's cadres also emptied it of much of its substance for villagers. The formal category of the village and its rural status had instead become a container for the profit-oriented interests of the cadres' shareholding corporations.

Village-as-the-City

China's planners and policy makers often point to urbanized villages like Hailong as embodiments of the contradictions between the nation's urban and rural categories (Huang 2014). This was certainly the case in Chongqing, where Hailong served as an important foil for planners' implementation of urban–rural coordination. The term "village-in-the-city," which Chongqing's planners used to characterize Hailong, inscribes this pejorative view into planning discourse. Indeed, it is no accident that the term emerged in the mid-1990s just as these settlements were identified as a problem for urban development (Yang 1996; J. Zheng 1997). By combining the characters for the mutually opposed terms "city" (*cheng* 城) and "village" (*cun* 村), the neologism portrays villages like Hailong as contradictory, illogical, and aberrant pieces of the city (Smith 2014a). As previously discussed, the pathologization of urbanized villages often motivates proposals for scientific rational planning and state-led renewal. Village organizations, such as shareholding corporations, frequently participate in the implementation of village redevelopment by organizing demolition and relocation activities, but planners and policy makers generally regard such actors as lacking the skills, expertise, and concern for public welfare needed to lead and plan such projects (Cheng 2003; Tian 2005). In particular, planners fear that village-led renewal risks recreating the spatial disorder it is intended to replace (Shi 2011). The result is the reification of villages as passive spaces that lack the potential to contribute value to processes of urbanization. Even the most dynamic of rural villages are thus dependent on municipal intervention for their redevelopment and revalorization.

Hailong's self-urbanization project turned the pejorative logic of the village-in-the-city discourse on its head, a reversal I have sought to capture with the term "village-as-the-city." This equally oxymoronic turn of phrase highlights villages' potential to originate processes of urbanization that are integral to China's urban future. Other villages, particularly in China's south and along its coasts, have pursued similar projects of village-scale urbanization (Smith 2014a), and Yan Jing explicitly cited those precedents, such as Huaxi and Zheng'ge, in justifying his self-urbanization strategy. Hailong's cadres went one step further: not only would the village be a productive source of urbanization, it would also achieve urban–rural coordination. Rather than embodying China's urban–rural contradictions, Hailong would resolve them. No longer would Hailong be stuck in the trap of China's urban–rural dichotomy, in which villages are either fetishized as agricultural and poverty-stricken or pathologized as messy and illegal. Instead, Hailong would transcend the structure of urban–rural difference, simultaneously combining urban and rural functions in the territory of a single village—a village-scale reimagination of urban–rural coordination.

The pursuit of urban–rural balance in a single settlement reflects a long tradition of utopian urbanism, perhaps best expressed by Ebenezer Howard's 1902 Garden City and the "town–country magnet" that was meant to embody the best of both city and countryside. More recently, the term "agropolitanism" has been used to describe a balanced form of urban development rooted in the livelihoods and lifeways of Asia's rural populations (Friedmann 1988, 229–30). Though Hailong's approach departs significantly from these proposals, its emphasis on rural self-reliance and its rejection of urban dominance resemble both the Garden City and agropolitanism. The central question in each of these approaches is not so much the balance between urban and rural functions but between different interests. Agropolitanism emphasizes the establishment of a grassroots political authority subject to democratic oversight and with the legitimacy to resolve inevitable conflicts of interest (Friedmann 1988, 217). In his proposal for the Garden City, Howard (1902) sought to escape the power of land speculators and real estate developers to ensure that development served the interests of residents. Similar issues troubled Hailong City, where cadres' efforts to overcome China's urban–rural contradictions and save the village ultimately contributed to its disappearance. While the administrative category of the village remained, its sociospatial transformation in the service of investors emptied Hailong of its substantive content as an organization of collective welfare and excluded the interests of the very inhabitants it was intended to serve.

CHAPTER 6

The End of the Village

Experiences of Displacement

In the summer of 2013, bulldozers were already cutting swaths of rubble through the heart of the village, and teams of construction workers swarmed the concrete foundations of Hailong City (Figure 39). But the cacophonous *bing-la-bong* of Hailong's advancing future felt far away from Li Xiaowei's kitchen. Li was one of the guests at the Wangs' lunch table in chapter 3. Now she was playing host, and the sizzle of the wok and the fragrance of Sichuan peppercorns filled her kitchen. Over lunch, Li caught me up on everything that had happened in the past year, narrating a battle of millimeters—fine distinctions of principle calculated to divide and persuade the intractable (whether for or against the village's relaunch). At other times, it was a battle for actual millimeters—those separating kitchens like hers from the bulldozer's blade. For years, Hailong's relaunch had been little more than a distant possibility as cadres shepherded the village plan through protracted statutory and real estate planning processes. But with demolition starting in earnest, the effects of Hailong's self-urbanization program were suddenly very real. Villagers faced the imminent loss of their homes and neighborhoods. In exchange, they were promised new apartments in a housing complex they had never seen, with neighbors they had never met.

"Are you willing to move?" I asked. "No! Of course I'm not willing to move!" Li Xiaowei paused and looked over her shoulder at her comfortably furnished living room. "My heart is sad. It's really a pity to have this house demolished. We have our own garden. It's quiet. If your family had a house like this, would you be willing to see it torn down?" Her house offered more than greenery and peaceful quiet. For Li, as for many

Figure 39. Demolition. A migrant from Hechuan helped to take apart one of the factories standing in the way of Hailong Boulevard.

Hailong residents, her house (and the land on which it was built) was the glue that held her family and her community together.[1] Downstairs, in a specially built room to one side of the main entrance, Li's mother clung to life. For Li, the house was her mother's life support.

Despite her melancholic rejection of relocation, Li Xiaowei grew animated when I mentioned the village's new housing project. Li was retired from a career working for a wealthy state-owned enterprise, and like many middle-class Chinese, she was an avid real estate speculator. Without reliable alternatives for investment, middle-class families with extra cash have eagerly fueled China's ever-inflating real estate bubble (Zhang 2012). Li already owned several properties around Chongqing and was enthusiastic about her recent purchase of a unit in Hailong City. With the preferential rate given to villagers, Li had paid just 250,000 RMB for her 85-square-meter apartment, at least a third less than what she would have paid on the open market. Li even accompanied me to the sales office to try and convince me to buy the unit next to hers, arguing that she could take care of it for me while I was away. Perhaps my parents would like to buy one of the semidetached villas as a retirement property? She was an even better salesperson than the sales staff. Leading me by the hand to inspect the different apartment layouts, Li continued, "And if you end up not liking it, you can always sell it for a good profit! All those people in Baishiyi and Chongqing, they all want to live in developments like this, in the midst of nature but close to the city." As we perused the scale model of the development's first phase, Li bargained fiercely on my behalf with the head salesperson, who wavered, nonplussed. Could I get the special villager discount? It seemed not.

"Aren't people resistant to living so close to the public cemetery on Longju Mountain?" I asked. "I've heard there are ghosts." It was a complaint I had encountered more and more frequently from Hailong's residents, circumspectly whispered or drunkenly shouted, but rarely elaborated upon. The public cemetery, once part of Hailong's territory, overlooked the site of the new residential development. Li Xiaowei cut in before the salesperson had a chance to object: "Why do people choose Longju Mountain to bury their dead? Because the feng shui is excellent. No one has this kind of resistance. Quite the contrary—the foot of a mountain is the best possible place to have a house!" Her defense of the development's geomancy was passionate and dismissive. Talk of ghosts had no place in real estate.

A year later, in the summer of 2014, Li Xiaowei and I were back at her house, this time eating the last of her New Year's sausages and a selection of stir-fried vegetables from her garden. Her mother had passed away in the intervening year, and Li was now spending less time in Hailong and more time with her daughter in central Chongqing. I asked her how her new apartment in Hailong City was coming along, and Li shook her head. She had already sold it, making a tidy profit of 41,500 RMB (though much less than the 100 percent return she had anticipated). Li's change of heart caught me by surprise: "So you don't want to move into one of the new apartment buildings anymore?" She shook her head: "I'm afraid. There are ghosts over there. You couldn't pay me to go." Li quickly pivoted to a new topic, but the chill in her voice lingered. What could explain this reversal from just a year before? In June 2013, Li had touted Hailong City as a wise investment and rejected any mention of ghosts. A year later, she had already unloaded her apartment, citing both resale value and ghostly influence in the same whispered breath. Where she had once mourned the loss of her village house, in 2014 she actively avoided both the village and the house, visiting only for weekly rehearsals of the ladies' marching band and the occasional game of mahjong. Was Li so mercurial? Was her appeal to ghosts just a rationalization for a calculated financial decision? Or was her revised valuation of her investment a cover for stubborn superstition? What had changed in the intervening year?

In the months between our shared meals in 2013 and 2014, Li Xiaowei was forced to confront the reality of Hailong's transformation, including the threat it posed to her existing social networks and the lies that village cadres had told her about it. Across Hailong, other villagers experienced similar misgivings as demolition moved forward and the gap between village cadres' promises and the reality of Hailong's impending future became too obvious to ignore. Like Li, many of these villagers channeled their unease into talk of the ghosts haunting Hailong City. The first time I heard ghosts mentioned in Hailong was in February 2012, just after village cadres began demolishing the front of the village to make way for the new access road for Hailong City. Talk of ghosts only increased as the scope of demolition widened and more and more villagers grappled with the likelihood that they too would eventually lose their homes and be forced to relocate. During this period, when I asked villagers whether they were willing to move to Hailong City, those I knew well would sometimes respond by shaking their heads and simply explaining, "There are ghosts." But when I urged them to continue, they would change the subject. Mention of ghosts was the end of the conversation, not the beginning. In other cases, I would overhear snippets of conversation in which ghosts were mentioned—a young girl who had died at the construction site, a distant relative who had been disinterred to make way for Hailong City's foundations. But the speaker would suddenly grow quiet as soon as I pulled up a chair. In the months and years following February 2012, talk of ghosts in Hailong was both undeniably pervasive and frustratingly elusive.

Through "ghost talk," villagers found a way to voice feelings of unease and opposition that were otherwise difficult to express. In many parts of China, criticism of local development would be couched in the rhetoric and ideology of the CCP, a practice known as "rightful resistance" or "raising the red flag" (O'Brien and Li 2006). But villagers had trouble framing their dissatisfaction in these terms when Hailong's leaders had already shrouded the village's transformation in the aura of the CCP and recruited the endorsement of the party's most powerful figures (Y. Cai 2010). The possibility of reprisals from village cadres also made many villagers reluctant to challenge plans for Hailong City directly. Like other villagers without recourse to outright revolt, Hailong's villagers expressed their resistance to Hailong City through the manipulation of cultural symbols, such as those offered by religion.[2] In Chinese folk religion, the dead are divided into "ancestral spirits" (*shen* 神) and "ghosts" (*gui* 鬼). The distinction between the two categories is a matter of social position. Ancestral spirits are those who have been ritually remembered and properly resituated in networks of family and community as revered ancestors with social rights and duties. Ghosts are those who have been forgotten, who are not properly socialized, or who die as part of some other group. They are strangers without rights or duties, and their ritual locations demarcate the peripheries of the community. In the world of the living, ghosts are compared to beggars or brigands, and like these social outcasts, they are considered dangerous, capable of causing illness and death (Feuchtwang 1974, 2010; Wolf 1974).[3] Villagers' use of ghosts as a basis for their expressions of resistance thus reached beyond the ideological principles of the CCP to appeal to more fundamental principles of social solidarity and community membership rooted in *renqing*, consanguinity, and filiality (Fei [1948] 1992; Yang 1994)—precisely the principles that had previously ensured villagers' stability and survival.

By manipulating these cultural symbols, villagers engaged in the practice of "spatial poetics," through which actors manipulate the apparent givenness of space, simultaneously denaturalizing the dominant power relations inscribed into space and enabling the articulation of new, alternative spatialities (Smith 2020).[4] Ghosts are commonly associated with specific locales and landscapes, connecting remembered pasts or persistent but displaced social worlds to the spaces they would have occupied in the present in order to continue into the future. In this way, talking about ghosts can reveal the incompleteness of new urban forms by giving presence to the absent and forgotten, thereby undermining linear narratives of planning and progress through the representation of alternative accounts of both past and future (Edensor 2008). As absent presences, ghosts re-present what was and what might have been, colocating these alternative urban narratives alongside the social forms that have been newly inscribed in space. Ghost talk can therefore be understood as a form of guerrilla urbanization, a way to inscribe a rebellious sociality in space and project it into the future. In the case of Hailong, villagers' ghost talk highlighted the artificiality and inequality of urbanization patterns the party–state claimed were natural and inevitable outcomes of development. Moreover, these guerrilla practices exposed the unreal rurality of the village plans advanced by municipal officials and village cadres, who had emptied Hailong of its sociospatial substance in favor of abstracted spaces primed for real estate development and shareholding profits. Like Xu Jianguo's poetic reformulation of "urban–rural coordination" as "urban–rural equal pay," villagers' talk of ghosts in Hailong City helped to repoliticize processes of urbanization that had been represented as inevitable and incontestable. Ghost talk destabilized the dominant linear narrative of urbanization by insisting on the persistence of divergent stories and values, thereby creating opportunities for other actors to reshape the process of urban transformation.[5]

What happens when the spatial infrastructure of social life is disrupted, forcing people to resituate themselves in a landscape at once familiar and strange? As a result of urban–rural coordination and the ensuing process of demolition and relocation, villagers' *renqing* networks were dislodged from Hailong's spatial fabric, transforming the village into a space of anonymous strangers and antisocial relations—in other words, a space of ghosts. This chapter treats ghost talk as a sociospatial diagnostic for villagers' deterritorialization, or "the process of losing physical, socioeconomic, and discursive control over homes and villages, [which] is brought about through involuntary relocation" (Hsing 2010, 217). Villagers' ghost talk testified to the sociospatial world lost in the process of urbanization, voicing villagers' nostalgic desires to return to the relationships and practices disallowed by Hailong's new form of urbanization (Feuchtwang 2010; Yang 2004). At the same time, Hailong's ghost talk also manifested the traumatic violence of deterritorialization, whereby sociospatial transformations beyond villagers' control produced feelings of vulnerability, exploitation, and disorientation (Feuchtwang 2010; Ong 1987; Yang 2004). When Li Xiaowei and other villagers said that Hailong City was full of ghosts, they were doing much more than indicating its proximity to the public cemetery on Longju Mountain. To invoke the presence of ghosts was both to mourn the loss of Hailong's past sociality and to identify asocial behavior that was seen as dangerous to the community. Ghost talk thus marked the beginning of the end of the village in Hailong, as villagers' mutual support networks and urban–rural entanglements were displaced by the rural simulacra advanced by village cadres and municipal officials as part of urban–rural coordination. Villagers' responses to this experience of deterritorialization and their efforts to sustain the village's organizing principles ironically served to accelerate the erosion of its sociospatial institutions, as residents increasingly departed Hailong's weakening *renqing* networks in favor of communities with more promising futures.

Profit-Driven Responses to Expropriation

Li Xiaowei's experience was especially revealing because her shifting perspective spanned the spectrum of villagers' positions, from active support for Hailong City to impassioned opposition. Like Li in 2013, some villagers embraced Hailong's relaunch and its transformation into Hailong City. These villagers generally belonged to the two extremes of Hailong's political spectrum: the most excluded and the most included. Villagers who lived on Hailong's outskirts looked forward to the new village center because they had been marginalized in the existing village and had little to lose. By contrast, those who actively participated in the shaping of Hailong's relaunch were emotionally and financially invested in its success. Together, these groups' exclusion from the existing village or inclusion in the development of the new village thus inverted the experiences of the much larger body of villagers who were uneasy about Hailong's new path of urbanization. This latter group was closely integrated into the village's existing sociospatiality, and they felt alienated from a future they had no part in shaping.

Most residents lived in the relatively flat, accessible, and economically dynamic western half of the village, but a few dozen families still lived on the rugged lower slopes of Zhongliang Mountain, the ridge separating Hailong from central Chongqing. Unlike the larger residential communities in the rest of the village, these families were isolated from their neighbors, perched on hillsides wherever they could find a few square meters of flat ground. Accessible only on foot or by motorbike, they also lacked strong connections to the rest of the village, and they often referred to their distant, lonely houses as "cold," the opposite of social heat (Steinmüller 2013, 74–76). These villagers enjoyed neither the economic opportunities brought by Hailong's last decade of industrialization nor the networks of mutual support that formed the village's most important social safety net. Some households even went without reliable electricity and clean water. Many of these remote families therefore welcomed the village's new development initiatives. For instance, the Shi household was one of Hailong's most remote, tucked into a fold of the mountainside near the Longju cemetery. Weaving his motorbike along the treacherous footpath, Shi Nuo's commute was twice as long as his fellow construction workers. When I asked him if he was willing to move to Hailong's new residential development, Shi responded immediately: "Of course! It will be more convenient over there, because there will be more people, right?" As his response illustrated, the support for Hailong's relaunch was in part pragmatic. The new village center offered all the conveniences they currently lacked, including transportation, shopping, electricity, internet, and running water. But most importantly, it was social. Moving to Hailong City offered the Shi family what they missed most: access to the social heat and *renqing* networks that were the lifeblood of village communities.

Even more enthusiastic than Hailong's have-nots were the village's insiders, the members of the village administration and party apparatus who were driving the relaunch forward. Compared to other villagers, party members were more likely to recognize Hailong as a community rather than an artificial administrative jurisdiction. Party members were regularly briefed on Hailong's plans, and they held decision rights over village policy (though ultimate decision-making power remained with Hailong's party secretary, Yan Jing). They were also the earliest and largest investors in Hailong's shareholding corporations, giving them a financial stake in the success of the village's relaunch. Party members and their relatives were therefore some of the most vociferous advocates of Hailong City. Up until 2014, this had also described Li Xiaowei. As a retiree, she was not the most active participant in village affairs, but she was a longtime party member with robust relationship networks in both the village and town party organizations. She had even sponsored her brothers for party membership. And she was a fierce advocate of Yan's vision for Hailong's transformation. Li divided the village between "us"—Yan and his supporters—and "them"—all who opposed him. Like many other party members, Li saw Yan as a terrific leader, a champion of the community, and the best hope for Hailong's future.

According to a survey conducted by Hailong's planners in 2011, 95 percent of villagers agreed with Shi Nuo and Li Xiaowei and were willing to move into the new residential area. As Hailong's leaders claimed in the village newspaper, "Villagers are willing to move because they can live together more easily and look after each other." This narrative, which built on village *renqing* principles and the attraction to social heat, suggested that the village-wide consensus about the benefits of the relaunch was already proof of the project's success in community building. But as I interviewed villagers in 2011 and 2012, it became clear that Hailong's leaders and planners had overestimated support for relocation. As more details of the relaunch emerged, resistance grew, finally coming to a head during a village meeting in May 2012. Li Xiaowei described the confrontation with horror: "Yan Jing prostrated himself in front of the people. If you don't believe it, go ask anyone. But they all refused to change their minds. They swore at him. They cursed him!"

Hailong's leaders were quick to paint the opposition as narrowly self-interested. As Yan Jing argued, greedy villagers were placing their individual profit ahead of village-wide prosperity: "They want to keep their own profits, and they don't understand what benefit they will get from the new development. They think public goods don't have anything to do with them because they won't use them. They don't believe in their leaders, and they don't trust the collective."[6] These arguments played on existing socioeconomic divisions within the village, encouraging villagers to blame their wealthier neighbors for being overly greedy. For instance, Li Xiaowei bewailed the selfishness of neighbors who had gotten rich by building migrant dormitories: "They all have buildings that they rent out. They make money, as much as several thousand *kuai* each month. . . . If you demolish those buildings, then they won't have any income." Zheng Zhihui, who lived in the rear of the village and was one of the first villagers to lose his house to demolition, articulated the distinction spatially: "People in the front of the village have benefited from development. They built houses and rented them out to make money. But people here in the back of the village haven't seen any benefit." After a pause, Zheng continued, "And now the village wants to tear our houses down!" This last exclamation exposed the limitations of cadres' efforts to divide the village into those choosing individual profit and those committed to collective welfare. Zheng may have been upset about the inequitable distribution of resources within the village over the previous decade, but he was even more upset by the prospect of losing his house, as well as the paltry compensation he would receive as a result. Likewise, Li may have blamed her wealthier neighbors for being selfish, but she was just as eager to maximize her returns from Hailong's redevelopment and just as reluctant to part with her house. Far from making a binary choice between individual profit and community welfare, villagers' complex reactions made them real, multidimensional people doing their best to navigate the challenges of rapid sociospatial change. No linear narrative of urbanization could succeed in capturing this complexity. Instead, the cadres' arguments served to simplify villagers' complex reactions in ways that fit the village's impending transformation into a profit-making real estate development.

Like displaced residents anywhere in China (Yep 2013; Zhao and Webster 2011), villagers did their best to earn as much money as they could from the disruption of urbanization. For some—like the residents of Hailong's back hills or the village's party insiders—this presented a relatively simple choice: accept the compensation and embrace Hailong's transformation. But for those who harbored alternative visions for Hailong's urban future and alternative definitions of what constituted community welfare, the choice was more complicated. For them, the desire for financial security could not fully explain their reluctance to relocate. But Hailong's linear narrative of village-scale self-urbanization left no room to express ambivalence. For these villagers, ghosts accounted for the social and moral significance of the village that was not addressed by calculations of profit and loss (cf. Evans-Pritchard 1937; Sargeson 2013). At the same time, talk of ghosts did not exclude villagers from participating in more pecuniary considerations. Hailong villagers like Li Xiaowei could simultaneously speak the language of market value and the language of ghosts without contradiction.

Nostalgia for Lost Homes and Communities

I first encountered Zheng Zhihui lingering at the site of his demolished home, barely aware of the foreigner who had just sat down next to him. Zheng had been neighbors with the outspoken Xu Jianguo. Both had been among the first villagers to lose their houses to demolition, part of a small cluster of buildings that occupied the proposed site of Hailong City. That was in February 2011, days after the Chinese New Year. A year later, in March 2012, there was still just dirt and rubble. All that remained of the old neighborhood was a single house opposite a lone tree. Zheng sat on a stool outside the house, rocking back and forth while staring at the empty space where his home once stood.

"Is this your house?" I asked.

"No, I just come here to visit."

"You used to live here?"

"Yes. My house used to be there. Just next to the tree." Zheng pointed toward the rubble.

"Were you willing to leave?"

"No! I wasn't willing to leave. Who's willing to leave? It's forced demolition! They make you agree!"

"But at least they gave you compensation?"

"Compensation? What fucking compensation? Each month, they give me 200 fucking *kuai* as a bridge subsidy. I lived in that house, and what have they done? The fucking village. . . . They've made everything filthy. Everywhere, it's just dust."

The ferocity of Zheng Zhihui's anguish echoed Xu Jianguo's assault on "urban–rural coordination" and reflected the desperation many villagers felt as they faced the inevitable demolition of their lifelong homes. Insufficient compensation was a common issue. Zheng's bridge subsidy was 200 RMB per month, but rental housing in the village cost him twice that. Although the village promised he would eventually get 30 square meters of new housing, his old house had been more than 200 square meters. But it was more than just a financial loss. I asked Zheng why he came here when there was nothing left. He answered in a low voice: "What else do I have to do? I'm retired. There's nothing. All I have is this empty space where my home used to be." After a few minutes, with the sun slowly setting, I left him, staring at the remembered walls of a house that had been reduced to rubble.

Was Zheng Zhihui mourning the loss of his house, or was it something more? Li Xiaowei's reluctant abandonment of her family's house, still standing in 2018, offered a clue. In 2013, Li was unwilling to give up the house, which she shared with her two siblings' families and their ailing mother. A year later, she had packed up and moved to her daughter's place in Yuzhong. In the intervening year, Li's mother had died. This meant the loss of the single most important relationship tying Li to the house and to Hailong. The Li family's cohabitation, with each branch of the family occupying its own floor of the three-story house, was explicitly intended to enable their collaboration in providing care for their mother. Once she died, decades-old resentments resurfaced, and the three households began to drift apart. Even without being torn down, the social substance of the house—the mutual solidarity and support of the extended family—had faded. Around the same time, Li came to another crucial realization: her community network would not survive the move to Hailong

City. Throughout the latter half of 2013, Li spent much of her time trying to convince her neighbors and friends to buy apartments near hers. Some villagers followed her example, but it soon became clear that many would be leaving. At the end of 2013, only 130 of Hailong's 888 registered households had purchased units in the new development, meaning they would have to depart the village once demolition was complete.

Seen in this light, Zheng Zhihui's return to his old neighborhood can also be read as mourning a lost social world. I had found Zheng on a stool outside the one house left standing. It was also slated for demolition, but in the meantime, it served as a social club for the bygone community. Displaced neighbors came every day to play cards or mahjong, talk about the old days, and complain about Hailong's transformation, reconnecting to the old neighborhood networks of *renqing*. Similar buildings are often referred to as "nail houses" (*dingzi hu* 钉子户) because they look like nails sticking up from the desolate landscape of demolition. But this building would be better termed an "anchor house" (*maojian hu* 锚件户), tethering displaced residents to their lost social world and keeping them from drifting away into the feared anonymity of the city. As the stories of Zheng and Li demonstrate, demolition and relocation were about much more than the loss of a house or use rights to a piece of land. These losses were important, but their ultimate effect was more devastating by far: forced disconnection from the sociospatiality of village life, including the networks of mutual support and risk sharing that ensured the stability and security of villagers' lives.

Fears of the Unknown Stranger

The sting of this loss was clearest in villagers' accounts of what they feared might replace the existing village, anticipating a world in which mutuality and sociality would be replaced by anomie and greed. For some villagers concerned about the possibility of retaliation by village officials, these fears were best expressed in allegory. For instance, when I mentioned village development to Zhu Jianguo, a villager who also lived in the rear of Hailong but whose house had so far been spared, he launched into an impassioned critique of Chongqing's bus system: "What do you think of these buses without ticket attendants?"[7] Zhu continued, "What does it mean for 'serving the people' (*wei renmin fuwu* 为人民服务)? You have the bus driver. He's driving and he's collecting fares. How could he possibly focus on anything else! What about people's safety? It's reckless. It's a question of right and wrong. You have the old, weak, sick, and disabled (*lao ruo bing can* 老弱病残). . . . A ticket attendant should take them by the hand, but there's no one there!" I had seen attendants in action on my daily bus ride to Baishiyi. They helped the elderly onto the bus, asked younger passengers to give up their seats, and ensured that cargo was properly stowed. Zhu shook his head and continued, "These ticketless buses. They're a new thing. Something they brought from America." But Zhu was angry about more than Chongqing's bus system. According to him, Hailong's leaders had prioritized rapid growth over the safety and security of the village's residents. The moral responsibility to "serve the people," a stock phrase dating back to Mao Zedong and frequently invoked by contemporary leaders (Cho 2013), had been abandoned in favor of capitalist profit, metonymically represented by the United States. Without their customary systems of social support, the weak and elderly were left to fend for themselves. Like passengers on a ticketless bus, villagers felt abandoned by Hailong's leaders, who were charged with ensuring their welfare.

Meanwhile, the substance of the village—the social solidarity and mutuality that once ensured residents' survival—was being supplanted by impersonal and exploitative market transactions. Ren Jie, a factory owner from Jiangxi (and thus a capitalist himself), complained, "Already, there's barely any difference between our society and global capitalism. You ask me for a job. I give you a little salary. . . . At most, you make two or three thousand *kuai*. If you want to buy a house for, say, a million, you couldn't possibly buy it in your lifetime." Then he turned to the street and pointed at a passing car: "These capitalists—their BMWs are practically worth a million!" Others described how they had been cheated and fleeced by business people they did not recognize. According to village elder Wang Anshi, these "city people" lacked any *renqing* and were just out to make an extra buck at the expense of their fellow human beings. In the new apartment buildings of Hailong City, villagers feared, the sense of exploitation and alienation would only get worse. Isolated from friends and family—even if they were living in the same building—it would be difficult to rebuild social networks and regain stability (Hsing 2010; Yep and

Forrest 2016). There would be no social safety net to protect them from the anonymous perils of the city and the unknown city people who would be their neighbors. These strangers would not be bound by the social norms of reciprocity and solidarity that once governed Hailong, and new arrivals would mark the end of the villagers' social world.

The threat of losing one's house and one's connection to the land inspired the most impassioned horror. After relating his bus allegory, Zhu Jianguo emphasized the life-and-death stakes of village development: "Today I want to build a house over there. I have the rights [to expropriate the land], but it means tearing down your house. Later, you don't have the money to buy a new house. . . . What do you have left? There's no logic to it! It's a dead end. Your life is over! Human life, it's the most fragile thing on this earth." In this imagined exchange, Zhu played the role of Yan Jing, who Zhu claimed treated villagers like livestock, only caring for them so that he could kill and eat them (and their property) later. Another elderly villager had resigned herself to the loss of her house but still could not bear to part with her garden, suspicious of any food not grown by her friends and family. She indicted the widespread practice of putting pesticides on vegetables just before taking them to market, an easy way for the farmer to save on costs but a potentially life-threatening problem for food safety. As she pondered what to cook for lunch that day, she whispered in a shaky voice, "In today's society, people eat people" (*ren chi ren* 人吃人).

Each of these accounts—from missing ticket attendants to profit-driven farmer zombies—hinged on the dereliction of a social responsibility to one's fellow human beings. Either by putting one's own advancement and profit over the welfare of others or by simply ignoring human suffering, those who denied these responsibilities risked losing their own humanity. Similar to the bloodthirsty cannibals in Lu Xun's "Diary of a Madman" (1990), who were committed to an exploitative set of social principles, the antisocial profit motives of urban strangers and predatory cadres made them less than human. They became living ghosts: they were not part of the village's social networks, and they did not help reproduce Hailong's sociospatiality. And like ghosts, they were vectors of change, danger, and disease. Their actions undermined the solidarity and mutual support that ensured the survival and stability of the village and its members. Their presence marked the edges of the community, and once they entered inside the village, their presence marked the community's end.

Villagers' Exclusion from Planning Processes

As much as villagers were nostalgic for the past and fearful of the future, their opposition to Hailong City was also driven by their sense of powerlessness over the village's present transformation (see also Ren 2014). China's Urban–Rural Planning Law requires villager approval of all village plans but leaves substantial interpretive flexibility. The word used for villager "approval," *tongyi* (同意), indicates passive consent or willingness, in contrast to the word for "approval" by supervising governments, *pizhun* (批准), which indicates authoritative ratification and sanction. Moreover, villager representative committees are often tightly controlled by village party secretaries (Oi and Rozelle 2000), as was the case in Hailong, and legal requirements for participation only apply to the statutory planning process. Modifications to the village plan, or subsequent nonstatutory planning activities, such as Hailong's real estate planning process, did not legally necessitate villager participation.

Hailong officials claimed to have gone through a rigorous participatory process, with extensive villager input and multiple rounds of adjustment. Photographs in the village newspaper and the exhibition hall proudly portrayed village officials explaining Hailong's new land use maps and planning regulations to elderly villagers. But as one village official explained it, this process amounted to little more than a publicity campaign: "We get all the villagers together and explain it to them in a detailed way: why do this, why do that, what are the benefits? Especially the benefits, such as our residential environment. . . . Once they think it's okay, then they vote. Once the majority of people agree (*tongyi* 同意), then we send it up for approval (*pizhun* 批准)." What he laid out was not an iterative process of input and influence but a tokenistic process of manipulation and persuasion in which approval was a foregone conclusion (cf. Arnstein 1969): a vote was taken only once a majority of villagers had already agreed.

The lack of participation made living with uncertainty a part of village life. As one migrant put it, "This place has all been planned. In two years, it probably won't exist." When I asked villagers what was in the village plan, most shrugged their shoulders, "Who knows?" Knowledge of the plan became a unit of social currency, endowing the bearer with prestige and influence. Villagers avidly followed any mention of Hailong in Chongqing's newspapers and television news. Others proudly claimed to have inside knowledge but gave inconsistent accounts. One villager insisted the whole of Hailong was set to become a tourist resort. Another thought it was going to be a public park. When they heard that I was researching village planning, many residents turned the tables and asked if there was anything *I* could tell them about Hailong's plan. Without the opportunity to participate in choosing the direction of development, villagers encountered the unpredictability of Hailong's unfolding sociospatial transformation as a collective trauma, "an experience of being shot into a future that is not entirely one's own" (Caruth 1996, 71). Villagers' constant search for the details of Hailong's plan can therefore be understood as an effort to close the gap left by their exclusion and resituate themselves in the village's trajectory.

The dearth of substantive participation resulted in a series of crises, as each announcement about the village relaunch precipitated new objections and necessitated a fresh round of village meetings. Villagers' lack of input into the relocation and demolition process was especially contentious. When Hailong's demolition regulations were announced, the village offices were swamped with angry villagers. In response, village leaders convened a series of eight meetings with villagers, during which they gathered opinions about relocation. After these meetings, the village's party members, community leaders, and villager representatives voted on a revised set of regulations. In their announcement of the new procedures, Hailong's leaders claimed to have "gained the approval of a majority of villagers in order to balance all interests." For those who were still unhappy, the announcement warned, "their issues will be addressed on a case-by-case basis." As demolition began in earnest, some villagers again expressed frustration and anger: "There's no one to give the people justice. Reporters come, but they're all on the hook. . . . The central government said that forced demolition wasn't allowed, but they went and did it anyway. So who will give us justice?" Others complained about their inability to choose their own leaders, labeling Hailong's village elections as "fake democracy." According to one frustrated villager, the elections always offered a choice between the village idiot and a party lackey. Echoing the crisis of cadre legitimacy that had plagued Hailong in the early 2000s, these protests all pointed to policies or laws that should have protected villager interests in theory but that were conspicuously absent in practice (O'Brien and Li 2006).

As related by Li Xiaowei, the confrontation over relocation came to a head in May 2012, when villagers cursed Yan Jing for betraying their interests. The meeting marked a shift in tactics. Rather than seeking to appease the opponents of relocation, village leaders began portraying them as greedy and antisocial. The tactical change divided villagers against each other, recasting the conflict as a fight between villagers rather than a fight with the village leadership—a tactic common in conflicts over demolition and relocation (Hsing 2010). Isolated from their networks of mutual support, Hailong's most vocal activists backed down, and no further changes to the relocation and demolition procedures were made. It was at this point that many villagers began shrugging their shoulders and voicing the ubiquitous Chinese phrase of resignation and powerlessness: "There's nothing to be done" (*mei banfa* 没办法). It was also around this time that talk of ghosts became more prevalent, providing an alternative outlet for villagers' silenced frustrations.

As construction on Hailong City began in 2013, it soon became clear that what was being built did not resemble cadres' promises. In April 2014, Hailong's leaders finally convened a public meeting for the "airing of grievances," but village cadres expressed little interest in accommodating villagers' requests. It was then that Li Xiaowei's anxieties finally outweighed her faith in Yan Jing's benevolence. In February there had been a new investment round for villagers, but turnout was lower than expected. In March, Hailong's leaders wrote an open letter to villagers, urging them to reconsider their priorities and purchase more shares in the real estate company. To some, these entreaties smacked of desperation, and by June, rumors swirled of construction delays, budget shortfalls, and corruption. With the looming possibility of bankruptcy, Li became antsy about the future value of her newly purchased apartment: "Who knows what property rights the village actually has? There's so much demolition going on here, I'm worried it will all just get torn down!" Without knowledge of the village plan or the compromise that had been struck with the municipal government, Li worried that Hailong would go the way of other villages that relied on "small property rights"—state expropriation and demolition.

Just a year earlier, Li Xiaowei had energetically defended Yan Jing against his critics, but now she condemned him, in much the same whisper as she had hinted at Hailong's ghosts: "He is a bad man, a corrupt official. Yan Jing has deceived us all." The reversal was remarkable. Li was a well-connected party member, which gave her access to details other villagers never knew. This access had made her supremely confident in Hailong's future direction, but when she tried to dispel the rumors and suspicions by asking for more information, she was met with evasion and silence. Li thought she had known where Hailong was headed, but the new future unfolding before her was not one she recognized. At some unknown point, the village's direction had changed, and Yan's ever-present leadership had become a traumatic reminder of her exclusion from that process. After having been silenced during Hailong's planning process, Li and other villagers found a culturally relevant way to give voice to their shared "social suffering" through ghost talk (Morris 1997).

"We Will All Be Hungry Ghosts": Experiences of Displacement

As Hailong's development proceeded, villagers talked about being unable to position themselves in relation to their surroundings and about being out of sync with the rhythm of the village's transformation. Ultimately the experience of being forgotten was expressed in the ritual response to death and villagers' fears of themselves becoming ghosts. In Chinese practice, ghosts often represent those social beings who are neither wanted nor remembered by the current society (Feuchtwang 2010, 169–70), meaning that the distinction between the human and the spectral is just a matter of one's position in relation to prevailing social norms. In this respect, the nostalgia for home and the fear of unsocialized strangers can be reinterpreted as nostalgia for feeling at home and fear of becoming a stranger (Forrest and Kearns 2001, 2135). The encounter with a lost home is painful not only because something has disappeared but also because something remains; the encounter with strangers is disquieting not only because they are unknown but also because they do not know you. The experience of deterritorialization therefore does not require demolition and relocation. If the relationships that make a home homey and a community communal are removed, then leaving the village intact might prove even more alienating than razing it.

Sun Jieshi, a retired construction worker, liked to spend his days reading by the window. Sitting in his study lined with history books, I asked Sun to draw a map of Hailong. Sun protested that he had no artistic talent, but with pen in hand, a delicate landscape emerged (Figure 40). As he drew, Sun's anxieties about the village's uncertain transformation took form on the page. First Sun filled in the cardinal directions, pointing toward the regularity of the sun's rise and fall. Then he sketched the two mountain ranges that bound Chongqing's West City. Unmovable and timeless, they were Sun's only dependable reference points. Between them, Sun left an empty plain, marked only with characters to denote a topographical depression. In this broad blank space, he explained, were fields, houses, and factories, a jumble of transformation too fast-paced and uncertain to draw. The constant state of change meant that no point could be differentiated from any other. In the midst of this unnavigable sea of change, Sun drew a single tiny character representing us. Even that dot could easily be erased. Sun's study was perched just a few meters from the land being cleared and graded for Hailong's relaunch. The house was relatively new, and Sun had yet to settle in, fearful that his home would be demolished to make way for further transformation. When I complimented him on the quality of construction, he dismissed the idea: "It's only temporary, until they tear it down." Sun's world, expressed through the map, was one of continuous, overwhelming uncertainty and transformation: "Today's society changes fast. . . . This year it's one way, you get to the end of it, and next year it's totally different."

Like Sun Jieshi, many villagers compared the opaque and threatening uncertainty of Hailong's transformation to the stability and reliability of nature. Gesturing to the factories opposite his house, villager Chen Siming told me they had all been lotus ponds in his youth: "It used to be so picturesque here. Everything was so clean. You could drink water right out of the pond. You could grab fish right out of the stream." Chen narrated a direct and organic relationship to nature in which nothing

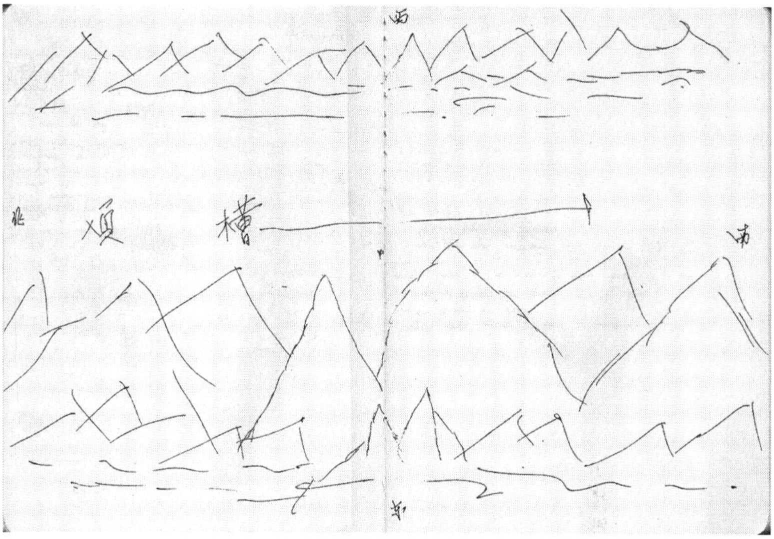

Figure 40. Sun Jieshi's Map. Sun Jieshi's map showed the cardinal directions, the mountains, and a large uncertain plain between them. To the left of the notebook's crease, Sun positioned us by drawing the character for "middle."

was other than what it seemed, and the term he used for "picturesque" (*shan qing shui xiu* 山清水秀) implied clarity and cleanliness. Looking at the factories again, Chen continued, "You can't do development like this. These factories, they affect our health. At the very least they've shortened our lifespans." Hailong's uncertain landscape was full of hidden threats. Chen could only guess which factory's pollution had caused the chronic illnesses afflicting several of his family members.

Villagers also experienced their alienation from their surroundings as a temporal disjuncture, in which they had been left behind by Hailong's transformation. As he criticized Yan Jing's approach to village development, Ma Chuifeng grew heated: "It should be built slowly from the bottom up, step by step. He's done it from high above, so that the results are divorced from reality. What should not be done, he's gone and done. Things that should be done this year, he did last year. . . . It doesn't match the condition of the people." Some of the old men seated around him crowed in approval, and Ma continued with a sweep of his hand that embraced the growing circle of villagers, "Nobody supports this, because it's too soon. We sped up too soon. Too soon!" The sense of being left behind was particularly common among the elderly and the middle-aged. Many had extensive work experience as migrants but could not find jobs in Hailong's factories. Job postings frequently specified age ranges that excluded older workers, whom employers considered obsolete. Factory bosses assumed anyone over 40 would be untrained in the newest technology and incapable of adapting quickly enough. Nor could these older villagers return to farming because most of Hailong's agricultural land had already been used up. Many were stuck working in construction gangs, or what they referred to as "coolie labor" (*kuli laodong* 苦力劳动), a transliteration of the colonial term for physical, low-value work. Not only had they been left behind by Hailong's urban transformation, but their labor and even their value to society had been relegated to a bygone era.

For some, these anxieties became all too real. In the front of the village, a few days after Hailong had begun its "low-key" process of demolition, I stumbled on a funeral. The deceased had lived in one of the newly demolished buildings, and people whispered that the shock of the loss had killed him. The Taoist ceremony was performed on the ground floor of the last building left standing (Figure 41).[8] On the dirt, tables and chairs were arrayed for a banquet. People smoked and chatted in low voices. With gallows humor, someone joked that the old man had saved himself the cost of furnishing an apartment in Hailong City: he would still have the same view from the Longju Mountain cemetery. His neighbor gave him a biting look and snapped, "Shut it. We'll all be hungry ghosts soon enough." Once the funerary rites were over, they drank and ate where their homes had once stood, celebrating the memory of a man who lost his life to Hailong's future. The ritual of the funeral confronted the participants with their all-too-provisional escape. In Chinese religious practice, "mourning is not only the internalizing of loss, it is also a reminder of one's own continued life, one's own fear of a bad death, of insignificance and one's own efforts to assure the three r's of continuation and extension: reproduction, remembrance, and recognition" (Feuchtwang 2010, 141). But villagers' institutional means of continuation had been deracinated, and like ghosts—the beggars of the afterlife—they had been cast aside.

Figure 41. A Funeral amid Demolition. Funerary offerings lay against the marketing billboards that guarded the demolition site.

Ghosts as Plans: Villagers' Preparations for Exit

This chapter has investigated Hailong's ghost talk as a sociospatial diagnostic, exploring how villagers' experiences of deterritorialization were expressed both as nostalgic loss and as traumatic exclusion. As poetic manipulations of cultural essentialisms (Herzfeld 2005), talk of ghosts might be considered little more than catharsis, the village's last gasp before its disappearance. In the context of the party–state's political dominance, it would be easy to see such talk as mere rhetorical reappropriations that lack the ability to offer a true sociospatial alternative (Castells 1983, 327). But these symbolic expressions are more than cathartic escapes to the realm of fantasy (Amin and Thrift 2002, 122–24). Cultural dissent "represents an alternative moral universe in embryo . . . which helps unite its members as a human community and as a community of values. In this sense, it is as much a beginning as an end" (Scott 1976, 240). Ghost talk is thus more than a diagnostic tool that reveals the sociospatial inequities and political excesses of urbanization. By troubling teleological narratives of urbanization, ghost talk creates opportunities for other actors to reshape the city. It exposes something damaged or undone and is thus oriented toward the need for repair and completion (Edensor 2008, 331; Gordon 1997, 201–6). It not only attests to the past but also asks something of the future. Ghosts prescribe action. Ghosts are plans.

In Chinese practice, ghosts demand ritual worship and the repair of ancestral homes, altars, and tombs—activities that can help to transform ghosts into ancestral spirits. These practices also serve to reproduce the relationships that ensure the family's continuity into the future (Feuchtwang 2010). By gathering family members at grave sites or ancestral altars, ancestor worship and the expiation of ghosts provide opportunities not only for the assertion of existing groups but also for the creation of new groups, enabling the articulation of alternative social relationships and power arrangements (Watson 1988). Indeed, the siting and construction of graves can offer opportunities to defy governmental authority when more direct political action is impossible or dangerous (Watson 1988). Talk of ghosts thus provided a framework through which villagers could turn their silenced opposition to Hailong City into action, including through ritual worship, network building, and departure. Far from being in conflict with concerns about compensation and profit maximization, ghost talk complemented such pecuniary considerations by "selecting the cause that is socially relevant . . . since it is the only one that allows intervention and determines social behaviour" (Evans-Pritchard 1937, 25). Villagers could not change the development of Hailong City, but through their responses to Hailong's ghosts, they could change their families' own survival strategies.

In part because of the political potential represented by graves and ghosts, Hailong cadres insisted that there were no grave sites left in the village. According to their account, all the village's dead had already been reburied in the Longju Mountain cemetery. But in 2012, the village was still full of graves. They were hidden in overgrown hillsides, wedged between factory walls, and perched precariously in road embankments (Figure 42). During the Qingming Festival, when Chinese families clean their ancestors' graves and make offerings to the dead, a heavy pall of incense hung amid the acrid smoke of crackling fireworks. Walking through Hailong on the day of the festival in 2012, I came upon the Cheng family—four

Figure 42. Village Tombs. Tombs were scattered throughout the village, and the intensity of Hailong's development often pushed up against them. This photograph depicts a tomb adjacent to a migrant dormitory.

brothers and their father—whom I had never met. Hailong was their ancestral home, but they had given up their land and household registration to move into the city. All that remained were their grandparents' graves, and they returned to Hailong every year to honor them. I watched as they burned the brush that had grown in the past year, lit candles, and set off firecrackers. Then each man knelt and prayed, incense between his hands. When the last of them paid his respects, they piled back into their minivan to leave, the father grumbling that this was the only time they all managed to gather in one place. Would they manage it again next year? Across the valley from their ancestors' graves, one of Hailong's demolition cranes stood parked, waiting. As Hailong's leaders proceeded with the relaunch, cleansing the village of past values and attachments, fewer and fewer graves were left undisturbed. For those with descendants around to claim them, remains were exhumed and reinterred in the public cemetery on Longju Mountain. A few ancestors were prominently reburied on the slopes of the same valley where Hailong City was being built, becoming visible expressions of villagers' moral critique of the village's relaunch. But for the vast majority of graves, they were bulldozed into the ground, where they became the spectral foundations of the future village. Through talk of ghosts, villagers articulated the threat that Hailong City posed to ritual practices of ancestor worship and thus to the principles of filiality and *renqing* that formed the basis of village society.

As their homes, neighborhoods, and even their graves were demolished, many villagers followed the example of the Cheng family: They left. In an environment where the past had been erased, the present was unrecognizable, and the future was unpredictable, it became impossible for families to ensure their stability. Shi Chunliang complained that village and municipal "plans" (*guihua* 规划) were making it more difficult for her and her family to make their own "plans" (*jihua* 计划), and as a result, they were planning to leave. When I asked her what the difference between the two types of planning was, Shi explained that *guihua* plans were divorced from reality, while her *jihua* planning meant anticipating the needs of the future based on her family's experience of the past.[9] The exclusion of villagers' voices from village planning processes had led her family to exit the village (Hirschman 1970). By choosing exit, villagers abandoned their disappearing community networks and sought to consolidate their social worlds through their extended families. Li Xiaowei sold her new Hailong apartment and moved to Yuzhong to live with her daughter. Zhu Jianguo planned to move to Guangzhou to live with his children. And the Lin family talked about moving to Chengdu, where the eldest son, Lin Yi, ran a factory. Meanwhile, Shi Chunliang's family opted into a municipal relocation program for families in dilapidated housing. As he espoused the benefits of the program, which required the family to leave Hailong, Wang Dai rejected the village's new development as a city of ghosts: "The dead and the living shouldn't be so close together. I don't want to wake up in the morning and see ghosts walking by along the hillside!"

The End of the Village

In the summer of 2018, the first phase of Hailong City was already complete. Where a village alleyway full of snack stalls and pool halls had once stood, and where in 2012 Hailong's cadres had started the process of demo-

Figure 43. The Front Plaza after Demolition. In 2012, on the first day of demolition for the construction of Hailong Boulevard, the edge of Hailong abutting Bai-Peng Road was cleared of structures. A migrant-run eatery quickly adapted and reopened out of a pushcart.

lition for the village's relaunch (Figure 43), there now extended six lanes of asphalt: Hailong Boulevard (Figure 44). At the other end of the road, through the gap Hailong's cadres had blown in Silong Mountain, an imposing six-floor building housed the new offices for the village committee and the Hailong Corporation, which looked over a vast public square twice the size of the once-celebrated Hailong Plaza (since repurposed as a parking lot). From the entrance of a sumptuously appointed kindergarten, squealing children bounced into the waiting arms of parents and grandparents. Some of these were the children of Hailong villagers, but many were new residents of Hailong City—the sons and daughters of middle-class families who had purchased apartments in the newly completed high-rises arrayed in uneven rows down the valley. Some village families had also bought apartments in the commercial part of Hailong City, but poorer villagers who had lost their homes to demolition lived at the back of the development, crowded in the last two buildings, which had been designated for Hailong's relocation housing. There I found groups of elderly villagers gathered on the steps of each entryway, in search of the social heat of courtyard life but unsure where to find it in this strange

Figure 44. The Front Plaza after Development. After the construction of Hailong Boulevard in 2018, the grand entrance to the village stretches away from Bai-Peng Road, with the roofs of Hailong City in the far distance. Photograph by Sara M. Watson.

new landscape. While the grounds surrounding the commercial apartment buildings were green and well manicured, the landscape in this part of Hailong City was still incomplete and unkempt. The villagers I spoke with were nonplussed: "Is this it? Is this what we have waited so long for? It's as dirty and dusty as it was 20 years ago!"

For these villagers, their worst fears about Hailong City had come true. Their homes had been torn down and replaced with high-rise apartments that made it more difficult to connect with their neighbors. Strangers with whom they had no ties had moved in next door, taking over public spaces and facilities for their own uses. Meanwhile, many of their friends and relations had departed Hailong in favor of new lives in central Chongqing or elsewhere in China. And they themselves had been forgotten at the back of the development, living in conditions that—despite the high-rise apartment buildings with running water, electricity, and internet—reminded them of the impoverished conditions Hailong had been struggling to escape for two decades (Figure 45). Hailong Village still existed in name. As a jurisdiction of rural governance, the adminis-

Figure 45. Hailong: Past, Present, and Future. In the rear of Hailong City, residential blocks designated for villagers' relocation housing overlook a still-inhabited village home and an abandoned mud-and-timber structure. Photograph by Sara M. Watson.

trative village continued, and they still counted as rural villagers. Parts of the village even looked quintessentially rural, including the agritourism park where tourists now paid to catch fish or pick grapes. Elsewhere in the village, the Pastoral Inn offered a rural escape for modern-day literati disaffected with urban life. But amid this ersatz rurality, the village's sociospatial reality had disappeared, replaced by a transformation that villagers had no role in shaping. Villagers' ghost talk exposed this disjuncture between the continued existence of the rural village as an administrative category and its sociospatial transformation into something new and unrecognizable, a ghost of its former self.

Conclusion

Disjunctural Urbanization

By focusing on actors' conflicting efforts to navigate China's urban–rural contradictions, this book explores the ways in which the dynamic tension between urban categories and urban processes generates urbanization. This disjuncture motivated urban–rural coordination, and it has troubled Chinese urban studies for more than two decades. Likewise, it has confronted actors throughout China in their professional and everyday lives, and their varied responses to these challenges have intersected to produce new and unanticipated forms of urban transformation. In Chongqing and Hailong, this transformational process emerged as different actors competed and collaborated to recalibrate the category–process nexus. In doing so, actors were not necessarily seeking to eliminate the tension between categories and processes but rather to ensure that whatever disjuncture remained served their interests. This involved efforts to extend processes of sociospatial transformation in order to maximize the extraction of resources and simultaneously efforts to concentrate those resources within areas defined by categorical divisions that ensured actors' control by constraining alternative forms of collective action. For instance, Chongqing's planners and policy makers sought to redirect rural economies toward the production of goods and services for urban consumption, while concentrating rural populations within cities and towns where they would contribute to urban growth and be subjected to the redistributive discipline of the party–state. Hailong's cadres, meanwhile, demolished and rebuilt the rural landscape to attract industrial, real estate, and financial capital into the administrative village, which they reorganized to reinforce cadres' discretionary control over and reduce villagers' claims on collective resources. Finally, through practices such as migration and entrepreneurship, Hailong's inhabitants sought to gather diverse resources for redistribution within rural households, kinship groups, and community networks governed by relationships of reciprocity rather than party–state paternalism. Through their efforts to navigate the tensions produced by the disjuncture between the categorical and processual dimensions of urban change in contemporary China, the actors in Chongqing and Hailong pursued dialectical strategies of extension and concentration that are hallmarks of urbanization (cf. Brenner and Schmid 2015; Lefebvre [1970] 2003).

The resulting process of disjunctural urbanization rearranged and redistributed resources and opportunities not according to the abstract, disembodied, and inexorable logic of development but according to the specific agendas of those with the power to effect sociospatial change—though not always in the ways they intended. Urbanization inscribed these power relations into Hailong's sociospatial fabric, conditioning the lives and opportunities of inhabitants. The village's urbanization was therefore a political process for the accumulation, consolidation, redistribution, and contestation of resources and power. The artifice of disjunctural urbanization is especially apparent in contemporary China, where the combination of hegemonic urban and rural categories with the party–state's commitment to rapid urbanization has resulted in stark inequities and contradictions. These tensions also come into clear relief at sites of urban–rural intersection, like Chongqing's peripheral zone of urban expansion known as West City. But to what extent can the political manufacture of urbanization found in Hailong be helpful in understanding processes of transformation in other parts of a polity as large and diverse as China? Moreover, how might Hailong's experience affect how urbanization is studied and conceptualized more broadly, beyond China's territorial boundaries?

This concluding chapter considers the larger implications the preceding investigation of Chongqing and Hailong might hold for the field of urban studies, both within China and beyond. Hailong's context, including its periurban proximity to urban infrastructure and markets, its highly placed political patrons, and its designation as a site of experimentation for village development, necessarily make it unique, and the specific trajectory of its transformation cannot easily be generalized to the experiences of the thousands of villages across China that are geographically more remote, politically less connected, and developmentally less advanced.[1] But the very characteristics that make Hailong so singular also make it a privileged reference point for conceptualizing larger processes by intensifying, distilling, and clarifying underlying principles and dynamics that are likely present, but otherwise obscured, in more typical cases (Eckstein 1992; Ferguson 1990; Mitchell 2011). For instance, Hailong's position at Chongqing's urban–rural edge intensifies the dialectical tension between the categorical and processual dimensions of urban change, making the periphery a particularly productive site for theorization (Roy 2011). Similarly, the drawn-out process of political contestation that unfolded in Hailong provides a temporary window through the opaque facade of "social harmony" that often obscures social and political discord within the Chinese polity, allowing a glimpse of the messy politics and unharmonious reality of urban transformation everywhere (Turner 1972, 93). As a site of experimentation, where actors debated and tried out different combinations of administrative categories and transformational processes, Hailong also offers a privileged opportunity to investigate sociospatial phenomena that easily disappear from view once stabilized (Latour 2005, 79–81). Hailong's urban–rural liminality, political intensity, and experimental innovation thus make it a productive site for interrogating the conceptual and theoretical assumptions used to understand processes of urbanization more broadly. In other words, Hailong is a privileged case not because it provides a functional model for the transformation of other Chinese villages but because it is "good to think" with (Lévi-Strauss 1963, 89).

Rural China's Urban Futures

Seen through the eyes of the actors on the ground, the implementation of urban–rural coordination in Chongqing and Hailong revealed something quite different from the rhetorical claims of the party–state, which represented urbanization and urban–rural inequality as naturally occurring outcomes of the process of development. In Chongqing and Hailong, urbanization was instead an emergent outcome of politically contested choices arising from actors' efforts to instrumentalize the spatial continuities and discontinuities of social life to concentrate and control access to resources. By destabilizing the economic determinism of party–state rhetoric, actors' experiences in Chongqing and Hailong raised questions about the larger goals of urban–rural coordination, which the party–state claimed would use the principles of scientific rational planning to resolve the inevitable contradictions of urbanization. Instead, the party–state's planning processes under urban–rural coordination contributed to further urbanization, intensifying urban–rural difference and compounding its inequalities. This was most evident in Hailong's statutory planning process, which unfolded not according to the objective scientific principles touted by the party–state but according to the fuzzy science of political horse trading, as municipal planners and village cadres negotiated who would ultimately control which aspects of Hailong's urbanization. The outcome of these negotiations produced two separate plans for the village, one urban and one rural, thus highlighting both the artificiality of urban–rural difference and its disjunctive catalyzation of urban transformation. This episode of planning politics made clear the extent to which the urban construction boundary, rather than serving to ensure the rational relationship between urban and rural development, actually functioned as a tool for the promotion of state-led urbanization. While the redrawing of the urban construction boundary indeed redistributed the benefits of urbanization, it did so according to the internal logics of the party–state, as actors with different political and economic resources bargained for their own share of urban expansion. Like the rules of the game governing market institutions (Knight 1992; North 1990), planning processes tend to serve the interests of the powerful (cf. Harvey 1978).

In contemporary China, the most powerful interests are those of the party–state, which has deployed urban–rural coordination to consolidate its control over rural areas by eliminating de facto processes of urban–rural integration and extending its de jure regime of state-led urbanization. This underlying agenda was evident in municipal plans for village development, which proposed the depopulation of Chongqing's most remote hinterlands, the concentration of development within a one-hour circle around the main city, and the transformation of any remaining villages into touristic playscapes or industrialized farms to provide goods and services for urban consumers. Similarly, policies such as land reform and household registration reform helped to concentrate resources and population in Chongqing's cities and towns while limiting the possibility of village-led development in the countryside. China's leaders proposed urban–rural coordination as a way to ameliorate the inequities arising from supercharged urbanization in the 1990s, but after being refracted through the power structures and incentives of the local party–state, urban–rural coordination ended up promoting the further expansion of urbanization and the widening of urban–rural difference. Just as the tension between China's de jure urban categories and its de facto urban processes allowed the party–state to accelerate urbanization in the 1990s, so did the rearrangement of these relationships under urban–rural coordination serve to expand state-led urbanization still further.

The party–state's implementation of urban–rural coordination and the expansion of state-led urbanization have had profound implications for the distribution of resources and the possibility of collective action in rural China. The incipient displacement and disappearance of China's villages has amounted to a fundamental rewriting of the nation's social contract, which for decades has been rooted in the de jure separation of urban and rural areas. That urban–rural coordination posed an existential challenge to rural lives and livelihoods can be seen in the stiff resistance Chongqing's reform policies encountered in Hailong. The only way Hailong's cadres had escaped China's rural development crisis was through the re-collectivization of village land, a strategy that was directly challenged by Chongqing's land reform program. Similarly, residents' survival strategies in the face of rural exploitation were rooted in their rural use rights to housing construction land and their opportunistic engagement with urban–rural networks of migration and entrepreneurship—strategies that Chongqing's household registration reform program threatened to disrupt. Through these and other policies, from the abolition of agricultural taxes to the consolidation of village settlements, urban–rural coordination often ended up compounding the challenges villages and villagers faced as a result of China's rural development crisis. By deracinating existing village mechanisms of resource redistribution and collective action and by displacing villagers toward lives that are less hybrid and more tightly integrated into urban processes dominated by the party–state, urban–rural coordination potentially threatens the stability and survival of rural families and communities.

The stark consequences urban–rural coordination has for rural lives and livelihoods means that the program's implementation has been hotly contested. While there is broad agreement within China that the exploitative rules governing urban–rural relations should change, there is significantly less agreement on what the new rules should be and even greater apprehension among China's villagers that the ultimate outcome may be worse. In most parts of China, the hierarchical ordering of the party–state and the dearth of political and economic resources in rural villages means that the versions of urban–rural coordination advanced by local government actors, such as Chongqing's municipal government, enjoy greater efficacy. In Hailong, however, cadres' early success in catalyzing rural development and navigating the CCP's political patronage networks made it possible to challenge the municipal regime of urban–rural coordination. Hailong's cadres appropriated and rescaled municipal policies, pursuing village-scale versions of land reform and household registration reform that concentrated resources within the administrative village and reinforced cadres' redistributive powers. The result of these village-scale initiatives was an alternative form of urban intensification, this time led by the village party branch instead of the municipal government.

In the context of urban–rural coordination and the expansion of state-led urbanization, the only viable way to avoid the village's transformation into a peripheral extension of Chongqing's High Tech Zone was to preempt state expropriation with the development of Hailong City. Ironically, the very act of saving the village also contributed to its disappearance, as neighborhood networks of mutual support were replaced by forced relocation into high-rise housing and as moral claims on collective welfare gave way to shareholding contracts and marketized mechanisms of redistribution—much the same fate that villagers confronted under Chongqing's urban–rural coordination program. Rather than face this future, many of Hailong's residents chose a different path, exiting the village in favor of reconstituted networks of kinship and mutual support in China's cities—much the same outcome the municipal government sought to promote through household registration reform. Indeed, by leaving for the city, villagers themselves inadvertently contributed to the disappearance of the village, as each departure incrementally eroded the network effects of Hailong's informal social insurance systems. Thus, even where the implementation of urban–rural coordination diverges from the pattern of state-led urban expansion, the result may still mean the urbanization of the Chinese countryside.[2]

While the implementation of urban–rural coordination in Chongqing and Hailong tended toward the expanding urbanization of the countryside, not all of these urban futures are alike. "Urbanization" may mean very different things when conceived and enacted by different people: rural depopulation and city-centered expansion for municipal planners and policy makers, village-centered land use intensification and self-urbanization for village cadres, and local, regional, and national networks of resources and opportunities for village inhabitants. Apparent quantitative increases in urbanization therefore obscure substantial qualitative heterogeneity, as different types of urbanization, enacted by different actors in the service of different ends coexist in the landscape. Even as the implementation of urban–rural coordination and its successor, new-type urbanization, asymptotically expands urbanization to the entirety of China's territory and population, the simultaneous diversification of urban trajectories means the party–state's control over those processes will necessarily be incomplete. The effort to replace de facto urban–rural integration with de jure state-led urbanization is inevitably conditioned by the fact that urbanization never fits neatly into fixed categories. No matter how the party–state redefines China's urban and rural categories, urbanization will always exceed them.

The inherent heterogeneity of urbanization also has implications for future research within the field of Chinese urban studies. If both the categories and processes of urbanization are contested and variable, then any effort to arrive at a single resolution to the tension between the two may prove frustratingly elusive. Each actor offers a different understanding of the problem and a different approach to resolving it, and any coherence between these varied perspectives is provisional. In other words, it matters very much which actors are the subjects of research. For instance, the parallel deployment of categorical redefinition, complication, and recombination by both urban scholars and grassroots actors suggests the extent to which scholars of Chinese urbanization depend on the interpretive perspectives of their interlocutors. Analytical interventions that redefine the rural as a source of bottom-up urbanization have often been driven by a desire to understand the processes of village-scale development that have escaped the government's land use controls (Gu and Li 1998; Lin 2009; Ma and Fan 1994). Similarly, many efforts to complicate the rural through the introduction of village typologies have started from the concerns of municipal planners, who must deal with a wide range of rural actors in the course of urban expansion (Chung 2009; Hsing 2010; Wang, Wang, and Wu 2009). Finally, the recombination of urban and rural categories has reflected an effort to accurately represent the transitional, adaptive, and hybrid experiences of China's rural–urban migrants (Fan 2008; Kipnis 2016). Grassroots actors' attempts to grapple with China's urban–rural contradictions are thus already implicit in the various analytical efforts to address the conceptual insufficiency of the nation's urban and rural categories. By working across the varying accounts and practices of different actors, this book is equally indebted to the concepts and theories of those working on the front lines of Chinese urbanization. In peeling back the homogenizing rhetoric of social harmony, I have sought to enable planners, cadres, and villagers to take their rightful places as the protagonists of China's urban futures. As Xu Jianguo's substitution of "urban–rural equal pay" for "urban–rural coordination" so effectively exposed, what urban–rural coordination ultimately means all depends on whom you ask.

Toward an Asian Agenda for Urban Studies

To what extent can the preceding analysis of Chongqing and Hailong inform the investigation of urbanization beyond contemporary China? Within the field of urban studies, scholars have long treated China as either exceptional or convergent. For some, the legacy of socialism makes China too unique for any meaningful comparison to other contexts; for others, the process of market reform means China is inevitably becoming more like the rest of the world (i.e., Europe and North America) and therefore has little new to contribute to urban studies (Chan and Wei 2019; Hamnett 2020; Lin 2007; Pow 2012). Both of these positions are based on normative comparisons between China and the assumed universality of Euro-American urbanism, an assumption that has increasingly been challenged by critical urban scholars (Leitner and Sheppard 2015; Peake 2015; Robinson and Roy 2015). At the heart of such universalizing theory is the reification of urban and rural as pregiven, apolitical, and empirically self-evident categories defined in opposition to each other (Brenner 2013; Brenner and Schmid 2014, 2015). Just as in China, these categories are ontologically unstable, lacking a defensible theoretical or empirical foundation and often relying on artificial boundaries produced by administrative fiat (Brenner and Schmid 2014). Nevertheless, this approach has formed the basis for an uncritical urban triumphalism that has become "an all-purpose, largely depoliticized ideological rubric around which, in diverse contexts, aggressively market-oriented and/or authoritarian contemporary projects and prescriptions of urban transformation are being narrated, justified, and naturalized" (Brenner and Schmid 2015, 158). There is therefore a clear resonance between the Chinese party–state's naturalistic rhetoric of urban–rural coordination and larger patterns of both scholarly analysis and political practice. The deep and pervasive entrenchment of urban–rural difference in China's social and spatial fabric, along with the party–state's mobilization of urban–rural coordination as a way to depoliticize the dramatic expansion of state-led urbanization, thus makes China a revealingly extreme example of a much more widespread phenomenon. By rejecting claims of a single explanatory model as a universal standard of comparison, it becomes possible to reengage the field of urban studies through a critical Chinese lens. Just as the very qualities that make Hailong so singular also make it good to think with, so do many of the things that are apparent Chinese "exceptions"—including the evident artificiality and political contingency of urban–rural difference—make it a privileged site for reconsidering the role of urban categories in processes of urbanization. As I will argue in these concluding pages, this alternative narrative of urbanization is by no means unique to China, and it may be particularly helpful for understanding rapidly urbanizing areas in Asia.

The contemporary explosion of urbanization beyond the bounds of the city and the nation-state to encompass transnational and even planetary patterns of transformation has inspired a range of scholarly efforts to escape inherited analytical categories. If urbanization is unbounded, then it is no longer meaningful to privilege the role of cities or to define the urban in opposition to an ontological other, such as the rural (Brenner and Schmid 2015, 174). Instead, some scholars have advocated an analytical focus on the processes of sociospatial transformation that supersede the apparent fixity of urban categories and settlement typologies (Brenner and Schmid 2014, 20). This same explosion of urban diversity has led other scholars to emphasize the inescapable consequences of urban categories, including the dominant Eurocentric categories of analysis that discipline divergent cities into urban development processes that do not fit their needs (Robinson 2006). These scholars have thus sought to provincialize and destabilize the universal claims of urban theory (Leitner and Sheppard 2015), thereby enabling new categorical groupings that reflect both local actors' understandings of urbanization and the local practices that produce urban difference (Robinson 2006; Roy 2009, 2016). This has precipitated both a reflexive interrogation of urban categories and a reexamination of the rural—not as the nonurban, but as an alternative mode of sociospatial organization that is inevitably entangled with the urban (Roy 2016, 816–17). The account of Chinese urbanization presented in this book reveals the extent to which these two perspectives—both the processual transcendence of urban categories and their reflexive rearticulation—are mutually dependent, with each accounting for half of a dialectical process that can only be understood as a whole.[3] In China, it is precisely the dynamic tension between artificial urban and rural categories and expansive processes of sociospatial transformation that is generative of contemporary urbanization.

Is the generative tension between urban categories and urban processes found in China exceptional? A conventional comparison to dominant accounts of urbanization in, for instance, Europe or North America might conclude so. In these contexts, where the rate of urbanization has slowed and urban–rural relations have largely stabilized, urban and rural categories no longer seem so meaningful or so actively contested. But if instead a comparison is made with China's Asian neighbors, different patterns emerge. This more regional approach follows postcolonial calls for new geographies of theory and a reinvigoration of the "comparative imagination" within urban studies (McFarlane and Robinson 2012; Robinson 2011; Roy 2009; Ward 2008). It also adopts the perspective of "Asia as method," through which "societies in Asia can become each other's points of reference" rather than forever responding to Euro-American practices as the hegemonic basis of comparison (Chen 2010, 212). Seen through this lens, characteristics that are often thought to make China exceptional or convergent, including its socialist past and its transition toward free-market capitalism, become less determinative (Chen 2010, 252). Instead, China's struggle to respond to its urban–rural contradictions might become a definitional reference point for understanding the experiences of other rapidly urbanizing contexts, much as Shanghai and Shenzhen have become reference points for other Asian cities in the process of urban "worlding" (Ong 2011).

For instance, Indonesia and the concept of the *desakota* often serve as reference points for discussions of nonnormative forms of rural urbanization in Asia, including China. Formulated in an effort to escape the prescriptions of Euro-American urban models that assume a linear transition between clearly differentiated urban and rural areas, the term *desakota* combines the Indonesian terms for "village" *(desa)* and "town" *(kota)* in order to describe the intense mixture of economic activities and land uses found in the nation's urban peripheries (McGee 1991). In *desakota* zones, it is argued, "the rural–urban dichotomy ceases to exist" (McGee 1991, 20). But in Indonesia, the categories of *desa* and *kota* are still commonly used in everyday parlance, and relatively few people beyond the intellectual elite have heard the word *desakota.* Moreover, categorical legacies of the Dutch colonial period continue to condition processes of urban transformation by producing persistent disjunctures in the treatment of land. While these categories are not straightforwardly urban and rural like those found in China, they are intimately intertwined with historical patterns of urban–rural difference. Dutch laws were applied to land administered by the colonial regime, including cities' formally planned European quarters and more remote sites of industrialized agriculture and resource extraction; all other land, including indigenous village settlements in both cities and the countryside, was governed by customary law (Zhu and Simarmata 2015). In the contemporary period, these categorical divisions in land administration have helped produce urban peripheries characterized by intense fragmentation and exclusion, as real estate developers seek to acquire and convert customary land for the development of gated high-rise developments that are juxtaposed with urban villages (Zhu and Simarmata 2015). Far from a paradigmatic example of urban–rural transcendence, therefore, Indonesian urbanization is characterized by the persistent tension between artificial categories of land governance and the transformational processes of land use intensification.

Similar patterns of division and connection can be found elsewhere in Asia. In Malaysia, migration patterns have produced complex hybrid identities that transcend urban and rural categories and ensure the mutual interpenetration of their ideologies and lifeways (Thompson 2007). Meanwhile, legal frameworks inherited from the British colonial regime restrict the sale of land in Malay villages, resulting in disjunctive patterns of urbanization, with villages alternately surrounded by urban development or overtaken by new forms of rapid land use intensification (Brookfield, Hadi, and Mahmud 1991). In Vietnam, the legacy of socialism has produced institutional arrangements and categories analogous to those in China, resulting in the rapid urbanization of some villages even as economic reforms are allowed to transgress certain urban–rural divisions but not others (Leaf 2002). Idealized categories of urban and rural have also produced an uneven and shifting periurban geography, which residents and real estate developers strategically transgress, navigate, and reorganize depending on their differential access to economic and political resources (Harms 2011, 2016). These actors engage in practices of "spatiotemporal oscillation," producing an experience of "edginess" that both offers a potential escape from the dominant binary and also reproduces the hegemony of urban and rural categories (Harms 2011, 25–26). In India, urban and rural discontinuities serve as disciplinary tools that reinforce gendered and class-based power dynamics, but the interstices and interconnections between these categories also enable an emancipatory politics that challenges entrenched power differentials through embodied practices of mobility (Roy 2003). Meanwhile, the sociospatial transformations wrought by infrastructure expansion produce varied forms of urbanization as they leave cities and intersect with different types of political organization in rural areas, a highly uneven landscape that emerges from the path-dependent transformation of distinct urban and agrarian politics (Balakrishnan 2019). Finally, the disjunctures between urban categories and transformational processes are perhaps best illustrated by Singapore, where national borders categorically divide the island city-state from a region to which it is intimately connected through the flow of people, goods, and capital (Bunnell, Muzaini, and Sidaway 2006; Sparke et al. 2004). Singapore's urban intensity is at least in part a product of these divisions and connections, as the city concentrates within its borders resources extracted through extended processes of transformation across the region, including from industrial estates, palm oil plantations, sand mines, and migrants' home villages.

These rapidly urbanizing contexts, from Indonesian *desakotas* to the Singapore–Johor–Riau (SiJoRi) region, are often analyzed as a result of transformational processes that transcend or erode categorical divisions and boundaries. This is reflected, for instance, in the widespread application of the *desakota* model as a means of escaping conventional urban and rural categories, including in China (Guldin 1996; Heikkila, Shen, and Yang 2003). It can also be seen in calls to move beyond the city centrism of much urban (and rural) scholarship and to engage less familiar forms of transformation in sites that are more peripheral or difficult to access (Bunnell and Maringanti 2010; Rigg 2019; Roy 2011). This book joins in these critical efforts to examine Asia's novel sociospatial transformations from new perspectives and with new conceptual tools. Seen through the lens of contemporary China and the politics of urban–rural coordination, however, it also becomes clear that categorical divisions continue to be central in shaping processes of urban change across Asia. These divisions and their effects might look quite different from those found in China. For instance, China's socialist history has resulted in urban and rural institutions that are distinct from nations more indelibly marked by colonial histories. The political hegemony of the CCP and the relative efficacy of the state bureaucracy also mean that China's urban and rural categories often have a more direct impact on people's lives and livelihoods than they do in nations that are less politically integrated. Perhaps most importantly, China's developmental trajectory over the last century has produced categorical divisions that are more unambiguously defined along urban and rural lines than those found in other contexts. For instance, the division between Dutch and customary land laws is correlated but not coextensive with urban–rural difference in Indonesia, and Singapore's urban boundaries are simultaneously the boundaries of an island city-state. Nevertheless, the clarity of China's urban–rural divisions helps to cast the unevenness of Asia's urban transformations in a new light. The intensity with which the rapidly urbanizing contexts of Asia are challenging conventional urban and rural categories should not necessitate the abandonment of those categories but rather catalyze an interrogation of the ways in which the dialectical tension between categorical divisions and integrative processes generates new forms of urban transformation and urban politics. From developmental states to motorcycle taxi drivers (Pempel 1999; Sopranzetti 2014), actors across Asia are actively manipulating the contradictions between urban categories and processes and thereby manufacturing new forms of urbanization. This book has sought to sketch the contours of an Asian agenda for urban studies that helps to bring these contested politics of disjunctive urbanization into focus.

This Asian agenda for urban studies also entails a renewed engagement with the rest of the world, in which the Eurocentrism of urban theory is abandoned in favor of emergent comparisons that span the globe and privilege the novel urban transformations of contexts in Asia, Africa, and Latin America as a basis for relativizing and reexamining the experiences of Europe and North America.[4] As in Asia, recent changes in patterns of urban development in Europe and North America have often been framed in terms of fluid processes of networking and rescaling that make conventional categorical distinctions such as territorial boundaries and place attachments less relevant (Brenner 2004; Castells 1996; Robinson 2002). While these new processes of interconnection may challenge existing categorical regimes, they do not necessarily supplant them. The potential for destabilization posed by globalized networks can also reinvigorate, for instance, place-based localisms and territory-based nationalisms (Appadurai 1996). Using China as a lens to reengage with the rest of Asia, it becomes clear that the categorical divisions that shape urban transformation need not be unambiguously urban and rural. An Asian agenda for urban studies thus calls more generally for the reflexive examination of the dialectical tension between the categorical and the processual dimensions of urban change. In other words, the processes of networking and rescaling can only be understood in relation to, rather than as substitutes for, the categorical divisions of territories and places.[5] Applied to the United States, this can be seen in the politics of incorporation and annexation, through which territorial categories are used to inscribe divisions in urban processes that unfold across metropolitan regions (Low 2008; Young 1999). Through these politics, residents may exert greater control over resources drawn from larger urban processes or, alternatively, avoid paying taxes used to support urban infrastructure networks and service systems. Interjurisdictional fragmentation is also in dynamic tension with efforts to provide mass transit and regional infrastructure in Los Angeles and the articulation of growth boundaries in Portland, Oregon (Aoki 2005; Soja 2014). At the micro scale, gated communities create categorical divisions in public goods provision (Blakely and Snyder 1998), while at the macro scale, international conflicts over migration and trade can be understood as efforts to make national territories selectively permeable to transnational processes of transformation (Houtum and Pijpers 2007).

Finally, an Asian agenda for urban studies also offers an opportunity to reflect on China and the implications of its current path of urbanization (Chen 2010, 253). For instance, elements of urban–rural coordination are reminiscent of the most intense period of British land enclosure (1760–1820), when existing categorizations of rural life that privileged small holding and commoning were undone to make way for urban-oriented relations of property and citizenship (North, Wallis, and Weingast 2009, 100–101; Thompson 1963). The transformational processes these changes unleashed were central to both the industrial revolution and the rapid urbanization of Britain and continental Europe, as displaced rural residents increasingly migrated to cities for manufacturing jobs. China's ongoing transformation might also be compared to the suburbanization of the United States in the mid-twentieth century, when urbanization was radically rescaled and extended beyond existing cities to resolve political and economic crises through the expansion of consumption and the absorption of economic surplus (Harvey 2008, 27–28). Here too the tension between categories and processes played a defining role, as suburban incorporation, restrictive covenants, and discriminatory lending and sales practices enabled white middle-class populations to escape and ignore the perceived dangers of racially and economically diverse cities while still benefiting from proximity to urban commercial and business networks (Fishman 1987; Fogelson 2007). Both of these cases represented epochal social realignments, when the rules of the social contract were rewritten through the recalibration of urban and rural categories and the pursuit of new processes of sociospatial transformation. At the same time, these periods of rapid urbanization also sowed the seeds of later crises, contributing to social instability and civil unrest in subsequent decades (Harvey 2008, 27–28).

Will urban–rural coordination have similarly profound consequences for Chinese society? If Hailong's transformation is any indication, China's near future may be unrecognizable to its current inhabitants. For a nation long defined by its rural institutions and culture (Fei [1948] 1992), the loss of its villages would represent a fundamental change. The implications for the globe may be just as far-reaching. The rapid urbanization of both Europe and the United States was driven in part by the international extension of transformational processes through colonial and neocolonial networks (Harvey 1975; King 1990). These processes exploited colonial territories and populations, extracting resources that were then concentrated within the territorial boundaries of the colonial metropoles. This rescaling of the dialectical tension between categories and processes also seems to be unfolding in China, where the party–state has combined urban–rural coordination and new-type urbanization with the Belt and Road Initiative. This program, formally announced in 2014 but consistent with initiatives of transnational integration that were originally conceived and experimentally implemented in the 2000s alongside urban–rural coordination, is designed to extend Chinese-led infrastructure, agriculture, industry, and real estate into neighboring parts of Asia and beyond, enabling the extraction and concentration of resources at a regional and even global scale. Alongside its military and diplomatic dimensions, this massive sociospatial transformation is therefore poised to supercharge Chinese urbanization once again, much as the exploitation of China's rural areas contributed to accelerated urban growth in the 1990s. Unlike that earlier period of transformation, however, the resulting developmental contradictions could potentially produce much more than "three rural problems." The next crisis of Chinese urbanization may be global.

Acknowledgments

Like all books, this book was born of a specific place and time. When I arrived in Chongqing in June 2011, the city was just entering its hottest summer on record. Experiencing the full force of that heat as I walked the winding pathways of Hailong was an important part of inhabiting the spatiality of the village's residents. The heat became an ever-present companion, and through it, I began to understand what it meant to be from Chongqing: the taste for spicy food, the flair for fiery argument, the search for social heat. The process of writing was just as much a product of climatological extremes, from the snowiest winter in Boston to the haziest fall in Singapore. As I wrap up the last of my revisions in late 2020, we all now are caught in the existential grip of a global pandemic. These inclement seasons have kept me at my desk, retracing my steps through Chongqing's outer hills—a provisional escape from the endings anticipated by experiences of global crisis and local extremity. How will our ways of life change in the face of shared challenges like climate change and global health? How will *we* change? Much the same questions faced my interlocutors in Chongqing, who were caught up in the onslaught of Chinese urbanization. These planetary processes of transformation often seem beyond our individual and collective capacities of comprehension. In the end, they become real only through the indelible and idiosyncratic ways they land in each place and time, at the intersection of globalization and community.

I am indebted to my fellow travelers on this journey, without whom this book would not have been possible. At Harvard University, the mentorship of Eve Blau, Susan Fainstein, Michael Herzfeld, and Peter Rowe proved invaluable. The Graduate School of Arts and Sciences, the Graduate School of Design, and the Fairbank Center for Chinese Studies at Harvard all provided organizational and financial support. I relied on comments and feedback from the Political Ecology Working Group, the Fairbank

Graduate Student Associates, and a variety of informal writing groups. In particular, I would like to thank the generous input of Sai Balakrishnan, Ted Bestor, Neil Brenner, Marco Cenzatti, Nicolas Sternsdorff Cisterna, Jean Comaroff, John Comaroff, Margaret Crawford, Namita Dharia, Barbara Elfman, Chenghe Guan, Har Ye Kan, Kyle Jaros, Jerold Kayden, Ahn-Thu Ngo, Sun-Young Park, Federico Perez, Elizabeth Perry, Meg Rithmire, Ajantha Subramanian, Anand Vaidya, and Delia Wendel. In the offices on Sumner Road, Matt Gin's and Sun-Young Park's engagements with French architectural history offered a productive counterpoint to the rhythms of Chinese urbanization. At an even earlier stage in my time at Harvard, the encouragement and guidance of Peter Bol, Eric Mortensen, Parimal Patil, Michael Puett, and Eugene Wang helped set the course of the scholarly inquiry that has culminated in this book.

In 2011 and 2012, I visited the College of Architecture and Urban Planning at Chongqing University, where I found a welcoming and supportive community of planners and scholars, including Huang Ling, Xu Jianfeng, and Yang Yuhuan. I am particularly grateful to Yang Yuzhen, who served as my mentor at Chongqing University and who arranged my initial introduction to Hailong. Without his support, little of this book would have been possible. In China, I also relied on a network of colleagues who supported me in my research endeavors. This included Hou Li and Zhang Fei at Tongji University, Qin Bo and Ye Yumin at Renmin University, and Liu Jian at Tsinghua University. Portions of the book were also shared at the annual conferences of the International Association for China Planning, at numerous symposia and colloquia at Chongqing University and Tongji University, at the Urban Planning and Land Resources Commission in Shenzhen, and at the Municipal Planning Design Institute and the Municipal Design Institute in Chongqing.

After completing my fieldwork, the Oxford China Centre offered financial support and a quiet nook for starting the writing process. While there, I encountered a friendly and supportive interlocutor in Vivienne Shue. Over the following years, I have presented pieces of the book at annual meetings of the Association of Collegiate Schools of Planning, the Association for Asian Studies, the Urban Affairs Association, the American Association of Geographers, the American Anthropological Association, the Association of European Schools of Planning, and the Asian

Planning Schools Association, all of which offered critical and encouraging intellectual communities. I have shared drafts of individual chapters at the International Conference on China Urban Development hosted by University College London, the Journal of Planning Education and Research Writing Workshop hosted by Rutgers University, the International Conference on Urbanization and Land Development in China's Interior and Frontier Regions hosted by Hong Kong Baptist University, the Regional Studies Association China Conference hosted by Zhejiang University, and the Public Symposium on Chinese Urbanism hosted by the University of Buffalo. I am also grateful to have had the opportunity to present portions of the book to the Urban China Seminar at the Massachusetts Institute of Technology, the Urban China Forum organized by the Graduate School of Architecture, Planning and Preservation at Columbia University, the Architecture Department and the Urban Studies Program at Barnard College, the Department of Town and Regional Planning at Sheffield University, the Department of Urban Planning and Design at the University of Hong Kong, the School of Community and Regional Planning at the University of British Columbia, and the Department of Urban and Public Affairs at the University of Louisville. I have also benefited enormously from my membership in the Urban China Research Network, and particularly the insights of Eric Fong, John Logan, Fulong Wu, and Weiping Wu. Across these various contexts, I am especially indebted to a number of colleagues who have provided invaluable feedback on my writing, including Daniel Abramson, Pietro Calogero, Heather Campbell, Nicole Constable, Jennifer Day, Michael Greenberg, Lisa Hoffman, You-tien Hsing, Michael Leaf, Richard LeGates, Al Lim, Mi Shih, and Jonathan Unger. A special thank you goes to Neil Brenner and Erik Harms, who offered unwavering support at critical moments in the book's development.

For much of the past decade I found a welcoming home at Yale–NUS College, and specifically in the urban studies program, whose faculty and students became my intellectual family in Singapore. Ricardo Cardoso, Cheng Yi'En, Chua Beng Huat, Joshua Comaroff, Justin Stern, Yaffa Truelove, Chen Zhang, and Valentina Zuin have been incomparable colleagues and comrades during this time. I am particularly grateful to Jane M. Jacobs for her indefatigable mentorship and thoughtful feedback as I navigated the delicate process of transforming the manuscript into a book. My students at Yale–NUS also deserve enthusiastic thanks, especially those who participated in my class Urbanisation in China and who served as a captive (and critical) audience for many of the ideas in this book. At the National University of Singapore, I found welcoming intellectual communities in the Faculty of Arts and Social Sciences Global Urban Studies Cluster and the Asia Research Institute Asian Urbanisms Cluster, where I am particularly grateful for the support of Tim Bunnell and K. C. Ho. I also presented draft work to the NUS East Asia Institute and the Future Cities Laboratory at the Singapore-ETH Centre.

Most recently, I have enjoyed getting to know a new community of colleagues and students in the Barnard College architecture department and the Barnard–Columbia urban studies program. In particular, I am grateful for the encouragement of Gergely Baics and Karen Fairbanks, who recognized the promise in this work and provided timely support in the final stages of its publication.

I received technical assistance from a variety of people, without whose help my project would have been much longer and more laborious. Yuan Yi, Xiong Tianshou, and Li Juan all helped to transcribe interviews. Wu Longfeng and Wei Lin contributed to the renderings of buildings and site plans, and Dave Lim and Ernest Tan produced the final versions of the maps. Sara M. Watson took many of the photographs and contributed to the processing of the images in the book.

A number of institutions provided critical financial support during the process of research and writing. Research was conducted with grants from the U.S. National Science Foundation Graduate Research Fellowship Program (DGE1144152), the Wenner-Gren Foundation Dissertation Fieldwork Grant (8331), the Whitney and Desmond Shum Fellowship, the Fairbank Center for Chinese Studies, the Foreign Language Acquisition Scholarship, the P.R.C. Ministry of Education, and the P.R.C. Ministry of Science and Technology (2012BAJ22B03). The book's publication was made possible through a publication subsidy grant from the Chiang Ching-kuo Foundation. Portions of the book were previously published as journal articles in the *Journal of Urban Affairs, Cities, Journal of Planning Education and Research,* and *International Development Planning Review,* where I am thankful for the comments from the editors and the anonymous reviewers.

The book has ultimately found a welcoming home at the University of Minnesota Press and its Globalization and Community series. I am enormously grateful to Pieter Martin and Susan Clarke for seeing the importance of this story and for guiding the project to completion. I am also indebted to the anonymous readers who took time to engage with and respond to the book. Special thanks to Anne Carter, Karen Hellekson, and the rest of the editorial and production team at the University of Minnesota Press for ensuring that no t is uncrossed.

Most important, I want to thank the residents, officials, and planners with whom I worked during my research. Their patience, trust, and generosity made this project possible. I hope that this book will enable deeper understanding of the challenges they face and provide an input into the development of new approaches to the planning, development, and survival of China's villages.

Finally, my heartfelt gratitude goes to Sara M. Watson and Linda C. Smith, without whose moral support and editorial expertise this book would not exist.

Notes

Introduction

1 "Coordination" and "equal pay" are pronounced identically except for their tones. In "coordination," *tongchou* (统筹) is pronounced third–second, while in "equal pay," *tongchou* (同酬) is pronounced second–second.

2 In the following discussion, I rely extensively on the description of urban–rural coordination offered in the training manuals developed by the Party Organization Committee for CCP cadres (Chen 2009; Ma 2006). These manuals provide a fuller account of the reasoning behind urban–rural coordination in language that is meant to be accessible to low-level party cadres, thus dispensing with much of the obtuse rhetoric and decontextualized phrasing that characterizes the national government's official policy documents (CCP Central Committee 2003; State Council 2003).

3 As urbanization concentrates people and resources in new centers, connecting some people and places and excluding others, inequality is unavoidable (cf. Harvey 1973; Soja and Tobin 2007).

4 While aspects of urban development may follow seemingly inevitable pathways like those naturalized by the party–state's interpretation of Marxism (Smith 2008), the redistributive effects of urbanization—and thus the processes by which urbanization is produced—are inherently political (cf. Castells 1977).

5 The term "party–state" describes two interlocking organizations that together govern contemporary China: the Chinese Communist Party and the People's Government. The boundaries between these two organizations are sometimes blurred, and they are often seen to act as a unified governing apparatus. While they overlap, the party and the state also represent distinct

hierarchies of power and operate according to their own organizing principles. The term "party–state" provides a convenient shorthand for this relational ambiguity, representing both the totality and its internal heterogeneity.

6 Announced in the early 2000s alongside urban–rural coordination, the ideal of "social harmony" soon became a tool for the suppression of political contention, as those who criticized party–state policies were "harmonized" (*bei hexie le* 被和谐了) by local cadres and internet censors.

7 This contrasts with the popular belief that imperial China was characterized by an urban–rural continuum (Mote 1977). Evidence from the Shang and Zhou dynasties rebuts this position (Lewis 2006), and it is possible that the perception of urban–rural immanence derives from an Orientalist belief in China's spiritual holism (Puett 2002). Nevertheless, the idea of an imperial-era urban–rural continuum is still widely repeated (Ren 2013, 17).

8 In the 1950s and 1960s, China's policies on urban–rural relations were much influenced by Mao Zedong's idiosyncratic reading of Marxism and the Soviet disurbanist debates of the 1920s, which sought a resolution to the contradiction between town and country (French 1995). The urbanist school focused on self-contained urban centers based on communal living, an approach that ultimately translated into the Chinese work unit (Bater 1980; Bray 2005; French 1995). By contrast, the disurbanist school advocated the dissolution of the town and the functional dispersion of population across the landscape (Bater 1980; French 1995), as seen, for instance, in the construction of Daqing (Hou 2018). While the limitations on urban growth are often taken as evidence of Mao's antiurbanism (Naughton 1995), developmental policy during the socialist era was characterized by a pragmatic concern with urban–rural balance, as seen, for instance, in the rural commune movement and its efforts at distributed urbanism.

9 All Chinese land is divided into two separate urban and rural land regimes, granting ownership rights over urban land to the state, while rural land is owned by collectives.

10 Under the household responsibility system, villages' agricultural land was de-collectivized and land use rights were allocated to individual households for agricultural use. TVEs were encouraged as a way to absorb the excess labor force resulting from de-collectivization, part of an effort to keep urban populations manageable by steering rural migrants away from large cities.

11 For instance, investments in infrastructure focused within cities and along the arteries of the urban network, and the urban planning system extended only to formally designated urban areas. Investments in education, health care, and other services primarily benefited cities, where citizens with urban

household registration were entitled to state-sponsored welfare. Efforts to address the nation's dramatic housing shortage, including the gradual commodification of housing and the development of the nascent real estate industry, were limited to urban areas. Finally, the commodification and marketization of land use rights was also limited to state-owned urban land, while the alienation of collective-owned rural land remained strictly prohibited.

12 The Number One Document, the first policy document of each year, highlights China's rural development challenges and announces policy responses. By relaunching the document series, which had originally run from 1982 to 1986, the central leadership cloaked their policies in nostalgia for the mid-1980s, the golden years of rural development and prosperity.

13 Despite its prominence as a centerpiece of national policy—or, rather, exactly because it is so central—urban–rural coordination eludes precise definition. As the official training manual for CCP cadres explained, "The contents of urban–rural coordination are relatively wide-ranging," involving "many levels and dimensions of policy and organization" (Ma 2006, 78, 94). Such vague expansiveness is not uncommon in China's major national policy initiatives, which often identify broad policy directions and priorities but leave the details to be worked out through specific regulations and the process of local implementation and experimentation.

14 This terminological choice also marked an important departure from earlier proposals, which often used a more generic word for "coordination" (*xietiao* 协调) that connoted harmony and balance rather than comprehensive planning.

15 A large body of scholarship has documented these various consequences of the socialist new countryside (Chuang 2014; Cheung 2012; Looney 2015; Rosenberg 2013; Steinmüller 2013).

16 These institutions include, for instance, the recontracting of rural land use rights to reflect changes in population and land, the construction of self-built housing with migrant remittances, and the expansion of mutual support networks to include ever-wider circles of neighbors and kin. My use of the term "institution" therefore encompasses both formal rules based in Chinese law and informal norms and strategies rooted in historical practice (cf. North 1990; Ostrom 2005).

17 Other scholars have similarly remarked on the potentially existential implications of urban–rural coordination for China's villages. For instance, referring to villages as an "endangered species," David Bray describes the expansion of urban planning practices to rural areas as "the beginning of the end for a distinctive rural way of life" (2013a, 92).

18 Administrative villages are territorial jurisdictions that can vary from several hundred to several thousand officially registered villagers living in one or several natural villages, which are socially and morphologically defined clusters of households. For a further discussion of these designations, see chapter 2.

19 In charting the end of the village, it is important not to romanticize China's villages as a collectivist or counterhegemonic ideal that should be preserved for its own sake; indeed, this kind of nostalgic romanticism is precisely one of the forces that is contributing to the urbanization of rural China. On the contrary, the social institutions embedded in villages are highly exploitative and lead to structural inequities defined by gender, class, and political affiliation. To the extent that village institutions perform systems maintenance functions for China's bifurcated mode of development, they also perpetuate larger patterns of exploitation and inequality. Nevertheless, villages and their institutions provide the basis for rural lives and livelihoods, and the weakening of village institutions may ultimately threaten those survival strategies, representing a profound transformation in the organization of rural life.

20 For a further discussion of the ways in which urbanization and the reframing of the urban–rural binary serves to expand party–state power, see Oakes (2019).

21 The Chinese term *chengxiang yitihua* (城乡一体化) is most commonly rendered in English as "urban–rural integration," but this phrase has historically been used to describe informal processes of village-driven urbanization that escape government control and transcend China's formal urban–rural divisions (Chen 1984). I have chosen an alternative translation here to distinguish this historical phenomenon, which proponents of urban–rural coordination generally disparaged (as further discussed in chapter 1), from the aspirational movement toward a future when there is no longer a formal urban–rural divide and urban and rural areas are both functionally and administratively unified. This also helps to address a terminological confusion within the English-language literature, where "urban–rural integration" is sometimes used as a translation for *chengxiang tongchou* (城乡统筹) (Abramson and Qi 2011; Ye and LeGates 2013, 65).

22 The continuity between urban–rural coordination and new-type urbanization is characteristic of China's leadership transitions. New leaders face pressure to put their distinctive mark on policy, but they cannot simply repudiate the work of their predecessors. The effort to preserve some degree of policy continuity results in the frequent rebranding of fundamentally similar policy initiatives.

23 The implicit tendencies of urban–rural coordination also have been intensified under new-type urbanization. For instance, the programs that have succeeded the socialist new countryside—first the "beautiful countryside" (*meili xiangcun* 美丽乡村) in 2013 and then "rural revitalization" (*xiangcun zhenxing* 乡村振兴) in 2018—have actively encouraged the aestheticization of rural areas as ecological and historical preserves devoid of industry, the consolidation of agriculture under the leadership of corporate capital, and the proletarianization of rural populations through land transfers and retraining programs (State Council 2012, 2018; Wu 2018).

24 Many of Chongqing's experimental policies have attracted the attention of national and provincial Chinese officials, providing inspiration for subsequent rounds of policy rearticulation (Looney and Rithmire 2016, 7). Chongqing's experiments thus represent "partial intimations of the coming whole" (Cui 2011, 647).

25 For an analysis of the inefficacy of large highway projects for driving local rural development, see Donaldson (2011).

26 Registered villagers include those whose household registration designated them as Hailong residents. The category of long-term migrants includes all other people who had been living in Hailong for at least the previous six months.

27 There are compelling reasons to accept the party–state's rhetoric around urban–rural coordination. In the context of Chinese authoritarianism, China-based scholars face significant professional and personal risks in openly challenging state policies, and even relatively critical analyses are often framed as supporting party–state goals (cf. O'Brien and Li 2006; Zha 2012). Some studies of urban–rural coordination have also been funded by local governments, which typically retain approval rights over published findings (Ye and LeGates 2013). Moreover, by accepting the party–state's representation of urban–rural coordination, authors make it possible to pursue alternative analytical goals, such as documenting the ambitious scope of urban–rural coordination (as in some of the more celebratory accounts) or the inner workings of individual policies that might be emulated as best practices (as in many of the more narrowly technical studies).

28 Prevailing scholarly accounts emphasize the rapid growth in the number and size of China's cities during the reform era, often inferring a causal relationship between the introduction of market reforms in the nation's cities and the subsequent acceleration of urbanization (Naughton 1995; Zhu 1999). This has resulted in a tendency to conflate China's urban categories and its urban processes and to assume that urbanization originates in the nation's

cities. For instance, the rural development boom of the 1980s has been ascribed to "the spillover of urban economies from the bounds imposed on them by the command economy" (Naughton 1995, 82).

29 This tension has similarly troubled the wider field of urban studies, where scholars continue to debate the categories with which urbanization is conceptualized (Brenner and Schmid 2014; Robinson 2016; Roy 2016).

30 The fact that such predictions regarding the impending irrelevance of China's urban and rural categories span nearly two decades (Guldin 1997a; Kipnis 2016) suggests both the tenuousness of this claim and the stubborn persistence of these categorical divisions in spite of (or, rather, because of) their incongruity (cf. Chan and Buckingham 2008).

31 For a further discussion of the problematic slippage between categories of analysis and categories of practice in urban studies, see Brenner (2013).

32 This more dialectical approach is reflected in some of the most promising recent explorations of urban–rural coordination and its subsidiary programs. See Chuang (2014) on the extractive politics resulting from the intersection of household registration reform and village resettlement; Chen, Zinda, and Yeh (2017) on the "recasting" of the rural to create new ecological and productive landscapes; and Oakes (2019) on the ways in which the spaces and processes of urbanization push back against the ideological image of urbanization advanced by the party–state.

33 Interviews and field research were conducted in January 2010, June 2011 to August 2012, June to July 2013, June 2014, and June 2015. While the scope of these interviews allows me to identify general patterns and consistencies across a wide range of actors, I rely heavily on the insights of a handful of key informants—people with whom I developed particularly close relationships and who were thus willing to share more intimate and revealing details. The names of all participants have been changed to protect their privacy. The only exceptions to this rule are public figures whose conversations with me were limited to public declarations. So as to grant equal authority to both official and unofficial speech, I have not specified documentary sources for statements by party–state officials, except when necessary for the purposes of clarity.

34 In addition to conversations, I observed, noted, and photographed participants' behaviors, comportment, gestures, clothing, and movements, paying particular attention to the use of spaces, objects, and buildings that play important roles in the process of sociospatial transformation.

35 From planners and officials I collected plans and design renderings of proposed transformations, as well as maps of existing spaces. I had village in-

habitants produce cognitive maps, respond to existing maps and plans, and give tours of village spaces. I also produced sketches and formal design studies of village spaces, representative buildings, and spatial practices, and as a foundational reference, I produced a detailed ground survey of the village, including every structure and pathway.

1. Urbanization by Other Means

1 The inner ring demarcates a territory of approximately 500 square kilometers, and the second ring encircles a territory of approximately 2,000 square kilometers, meaning that the second ring era constitutes a 400 percent expansion in the city's area. These boundaries are morphological rather than administrative. The administrative area of the "main city" (*zhucheng* 主城) is approximately 5,500 square kilometers, which means that the second ring divides the city's territory roughly in half.

2 Even in the liberal democracies of Europe and North America, democratic and participatory practices are not necessarily enough to counteract the powerful combination of scientific expertise and political power (Flyvbjerg 1998, 236; Purcell 2009).

3 Founded in 1928, the Congrès internationaux d'architecture moderne (CIAM), or International Congress of Modern Architecture, was influential in spreading modernist principles of architecture and urbanism during the mid-twentieth century.

4 Andrew Kipnis reports a similar comparison made by a Chinese urban planner, who claims, "City planning is a bit like predicting the future" (2016, 59–60).

5 This analogy provides an affirmative interpretive framework for understanding planning practice in terms of its adherence to ritual, rather than relying on a differential analysis that compares planning practice to a normative ideal of science. The latter approach risks reproducing the ideology of scientific rationality by ascribing any shortcomings in planning practice to its inability to attain scientific ideals. In making this comparison between contemporary Chinese planning and the Chinese tradition of oracular divination, it is also important to avoid the dangers of cultural essentialism. The political and magical dimensions of both planning and divination are not unique to China (Evans-Pritchard 1937; Flyvbjerg 1998).

6 For further discussion of the effects of household registration reform on villager survival strategies, see chapter 3; and for a further discussion of the implications of land reform for village development, see chapter 5.

7 In what became known as the Chongqing model, state-owned enterprises

also took a leading role in driving the municipality's economy, with the government redistributing proceeds through the provision of public goods and services (Huang 2011). In particular, the so-called eight big companies that dominated Chongqing's real estate development sector were all state owned. These firms borrowed cheap money from state-backed banks, while smaller, private firms were faced with interest rates that were two to four times higher.

8 This language echoes similar characterizations of China's rural–urban migrants, who are often described as constituting a "blind flow" (*mangmu liudong* 盲目流动) of people lacking reason or agency.

9 First practiced in Shanghai in the late 1990s (Bray 2013b; Wu 2018), the concentration of villages into more compact settlements has been a primary motivation for much village planning. Originally intended to rationalize land use and enable agricultural industrialization, village consolidation also became a means to bypass government-imposed quotas on the conversion of agricultural land and to transfer development capacity from villages to urban areas (Abramson 2016, 5; Abramson and Qi 2011, 511–12; Bray 2013b; Wu 2018, 10; Huang et al. 2013), a pattern also seen in Chongqing's land reform policy.

2. Village Growth Machine

1 During the period that is the focus of this book, the value of the renminbi fluctuated between 6 and 8 RMB to the U.S. dollar. In the early 2000s, the Chinese government artificially pegged its currency at 8.28 RMB to the U.S. dollar. This policy ended in 2005, and the currency's value eventually declined to a low of 6.05 RMB to the U.S. dollar in 2014. Currencies are indicated in RMB throughout the book.

2 Wang Yang was responsible for Chongqing's designation as a pilot area for urban–rural coordination but was reassigned to Guangdong before his plans for the program could be implemented.

3 Xi Jinping himself can be counted among this number. In 2001, he submitted his doctoral dissertation to Tsinghua University under the title "Research on China's Rural Marketization."

4 Though they are often understood as a single governance apparatus, the party and the government constitute distinct but interwoven organizations, with the party duplicating each level of government and extending beyond the government to penetrate the state-owned, private, and collective sectors. At any given level of the party–state, it is the party that takes precedence, directing the government and at times replacing it (S. Zheng 1997).

5 The integration of successful entrepreneurs into the CCP has been widespread since the 1990s, a phenomenon that is described colloquially as "capitalists wearing red hats." This has extended to village leadership posts, where the boundaries between economic and political leadership have grown increasingly fuzzy (cf. Chen 2014, 282–83; Guldin 2001, 90–97; He 2003, 256–58).

6 Under the household responsibility system, the collective still exercised formal ownership over village land, but use rights to the land were allocated to village households, giving villagers substantial control over land use and the incentive to increase productivity on their parcels (Ye 2015).

7 In fact, Xiaogang was not the first village to take this bold step, but it was the most brazen in its actions, and the attention of China's leaders soon made it famous as the originator of the household responsibility system.

8 The *mu* is an areal unit of land equivalent to 0.06667 hectares, or 666.7 square meters.

9 According to the land use transfer agreement signed by village households, this rent increment was appropriated by the village collective to pay for its operations and for the provision of infrastructure and services, thus constituting a form of community-based land tax or land value capture (George 1884; Hagman and Misczynski 1978).

10 For a further discussion of Hailong's approach to shareholding, see chapter 5.

11 Conversely, strong solidary organizations can also enable village leaders to manipulate villagers and enforce compliance with land consolidation (Mattingly 2016).

12 Superficial improvements implemented for the benefit of higher-level officials are known as "face projects" and are common in rural China, particularly in villages targeted as models or experiments for government development programs (Steinmüller 2013).

13 Red songs, many of which are drawn from the Cultural Revolution, invoke nostalgia for the socialist era and celebrate the ideology of the CCP. During his tenure as Chongqing's party secretary, Bo Xilai promoted the singing of red songs as part of a municipality-wide ideological campaign, and red song teams could be found practicing in public parks, government offices, and village meeting rooms.

14 In Marxist urban theory, the term "spatial fix" refers to a form of capitalist urban development in which declining returns to productive capital produce a crisis of overaccumulation, which owners of capital resolve by reinvesting excess capital in real estate and other forms of spatial development, resulting

in urbanization (Harvey 1981). As the returns to such investments decline over time, further spatial fixes result in the demolition, reconstruction, and intensification of the urban fabric. Hailong's spatial fix reflected both senses of the term, as village leaders sought to shift their investments from industry to real estate and to intensify village land use.

3. Living on the Edge

1 An early survey conducted by Chongqing's Public Security Bureau found that only 10 percent of rural residents were willing to participate in household registration reform (Han 2012).

2 These mechanisms include gift exchange, lending, savings associations, burial societies, and knowledge sharing (Cook 2002; Duckett and Carillo 2011; Lora-Wainwright 2011; Liu 2011; Xu 2001). Rather than contemporary innovations, these practices represent institutional continuities, as families and village communities repeatedly filled gaps in state welfare throughout China's history (Chang 1993; Chang 2013).

3 Similar community-based systems of mutual support can be found beyond China, providing poor villagers with informal social insurance that helps them "smooth consumption" in response to unanticipated challenges that threaten subsistence (Genoni 2012; Morduch 1995; Morduch and Sharma 2002; Townsend 1995). In the context of Southeast Asia, such practices have been described as a "moral economy," in which village-wide norms of reciprocity guarantee basic levels of subsistence for all community members (Scott 1976, 167–77).

4 When I encountered these practices in Hailong, I also initially described them in terms of *guanxi*, but residents uniformly rejected this characterization.

5 I experienced the obligatory quality of *renqing* reciprocity on my last day of fieldwork in Hailong, when a villager I knew well came chasing after me with a red envelope filled with two 100 RMB notes—a gift for my upcoming wedding. I had attended her nephew's wedding earlier in the year and given the same amount to the family as a *renqing* gift. Technically, giving me the exact same amount in return made for bad *renqing*, but in this instance, it served as an appropriate recognition of my departure from the village and the apparent likelihood that I would not return. Giving me the exact same amount closed the books on our mutual obligation and symbolically marked the end of my participation in the family's *renqing* networks.

6 The informal boundaries of these unwalled courtyard spaces were typically policed by household dogs, who would ignore neighbors, family members, friends, and even renters but bark at the approach of any stranger. In this

way, fine distinctions could be made between those who did and did not have access to a social space that might otherwise be unbounded.

7 The Chinese term *renao* (热闹) can be rendered in English in a variety of ways, including "activity," "excitement," "fun," "liveliness," and "merriment." I adopt the more literal "social heat" (Steinmüller 2011, 2013, 74–76), which reflects both the absence of a direct English translation and, more importantly, the colloquial use of the term in everyday discourse—for instance, those sites that lack "social heat" are typically referred to as "cold" (chapter 6).

8 The culturally embedded dyad of "inside" (*nei* 内) and "outside" (*wai* 外) corresponds only imperfectly to the conventional opposition between "private" and "public," etic terms that suggest social relations of fixity, universality, and exclusivity that are not reflected in Chinese cultural practice (Fei [1948] 1992). Instead, inside/outside flexibly denotes relative social position, where those who are inside are more familiar and those who are outside are more other. Thus, a fellow villager might be outside in relation to one's kin group but inside in relation to foreign visitors (cf. Rofel 1999, 64–65).

9 Most houses were just two stories in height, and the only buildings that exceeded three stories were income-generating properties, such as dormitories and factories. Hailong also had a strict six-story height limit imposed by the nearby airfield.

10 Under the program the Wangs qualified for, relocation housing was calculated on a per capita basis rather than as a proportion of the family's existing housing, making it possible to increase the size of their total housing.

11 The gendered division of inside from outside is a long-standing characteristic of Chinese patriarchy, in which women stay inside the domestic sphere while men represent the household outside in the realms of business and public affairs (Evans 2008, 101; Rofel 1999, 64–74). As an effort to turn the outside inside and extend kinship principles beyond the family, *renqing* practices build on this gendered division of labor, and the exchange of gifts and favors with neighbors, kin, and family friends is often considered part of a female domestic domain (Yang 1994, 81–82). This tendency is reinforced by the affinal connections embodied by women through marriage, along with the cultural association of affective expression with femininity (Yang 1994, 316).

12 Peasant resistance to larger systems of exploitation does not necessarily take the form of revolutionary liberation and has often expressed the conservative principles of an entrenched and reliable paternalism (Scott 1976, 188–89).

13 The evidence from Hailong thus destabilizes the presumed opposition between subsistence and profit in the literature on the moral economies of

rural Asia (Popkin 1979; Scott 1976; Walker 2012). Hailong residents were both stability maximizers and entrepreneurial profit maximizers, pursuing a single integrated strategy guided by the ethical principles of *renqing.* (For a further discussion of how villagers integrated moral and market principles, see chapter 6.) In this respect, they also challenged the assumption that high incomes, outside employment opportunities, and migration are likely to undermine the moral economy of village subsistence (Walker 2012; Scott 1976, 25, 213).

14 The cultural and social identification between Hailong villagers and migrants originating from elsewhere in Chongqing or Sichuan therefore goes further than the relative social inclusion of intraprovincial Cantonese migrants in Guangdong, who are still referred to as outsiders but are spared the greater levels of ostracization experienced by those migrating from other provinces (Guldin 2001, 226, 244–45).

15 This language can penetrate otherwise well-intentioned efforts at reform. For instance, in 2011, while discussing strategies to end discrimination against migrants, planning scholars at an elite Chinese university consistently referred to migrants as "amphibians" (cf. Zhou 1997, 23).

16 The importance of this slight difference in language is echoed by the frequent ironization of the word "harmony" in popular discourse, where people mock the slogan with references to "river crabs," which is a homophone for "harmony" (Ren 2013, 37).

17 Earlier experiments in household registration reform have also encountered low participation rates (Zhu 2007).

18 In Southeast Asia, the collapse of a village's moral system of subsistence guarantees can inspire "ferocious resistance" among villagers (Scott 1976, 39–40). Chapter 6 provides a further discussion of villagers' responses to the disappearance of village institutions.

4. Coordinative Planning

1 Yan Jing's use of the cake metaphor echoed the national debate between the Guangdong model, which sought to address poverty by creating economic opportunities and "making the cake bigger," and the Chongqing model, which proposed to solve economic inequality by "splitting up the cake more evenly." Yan was thus implicitly endorsing the Guangdong model and setting up a distinction between Hailong's approach to urban–rural coordination and Chongqing policy.

2 For instance, under China's top-down planning system, a municipal plan should theoretically precede a district, town, or village plan within the municipal planning area. Even if this is not true temporally, it should be true

logically, with municipal plan revisions requiring reevaluations of existing plans at lower levels. Similarly, a social and economic development plan, which establishes general development objectives, should precede a master plan, which should precede a detailed regulatory control plan.

3 Four distinct roles can be identified in the statutory definition of Chinese plan preparation, as expressed in the 1989 Urban Planning Law and the 2007 Urban–Rural Planning Law. Plan "formulation" (*bianzhi* 编织) involves the technical production of urban plans, a role that can only be filled by accredited planning firms and design institutes. Equally important is plan "organization" (*zuzhi* 组织), which is conducted by a legally designated local government, such as a municipality or county. The plan organizer is effectively the client, commissioning and overseeing the plan's formulation. There is also plan "participation" (*canyu* 参与) as well as "inspection and approval" (*shenpi* 审批), which is conducted by a supervising government, such as a province or the State Council.

4 Colloquially referred to as the 12–5 plan, the twelfth five-year plan articulated national development priorities for 2011 to 2015. Local governments then developed their own 12–5 plans to demonstrate how they would enact these priorities within their territories. Because village collectives are not technically part of the state apparatus, villages rarely develop five-year development plans.

5 This "Greater Hailong" strategy echoed the approach of Huaxi Village, in Jiangsu Province, where village leaders had expanded their developmental reach to include surrounding villages.

6 Similar phenomena have been observed in the postsocialist societies of Eastern Europe (Weimer 1997; Pryor 1973).

7 To a limited extent, such proprietary rights have even been enshrined in the nation's 2007 Property Law (Article 53), which recognizes the right of government organs to occupy, use, and dispose of movable and immovable property over which they have direct control, but the law does not specify that these rights constitute ownership (*suoyouquan* 所有权). This more complete set of rights is still reserved by the central state.

8 In China, the homology between rights and powers is further underlined by the fact that both are referred to by a single character, *quan* (权). This character is paired with the character for force, *li* (力), to specify power or authority and with the character for profit, *li* (利), to specify right or privilege. This equivalence is particularly evident in the word for "ownership" *(suoyouquan)*, which can be translated as either the "right of possession" or the "power of possession."

9 In states like China, where the political elite holds a relative monopoly on

power, the distribution of political power has an even stronger influence on the distribution of property rights (North, Wallis, and Weingast 2009, 34–36).

10 This is a simplification of a complex fiscal system that continues to evolve. For instance, the Chinese government has experimented with a more conventional property tax system, but these reforms have stalled (Man 2012; Wildau 2017).

11 The classic form of such contestation arises between municipal governments and centrally or provincially administered state-owned enterprises (SOEs). Many SOEs entered the reform era with land obtained through the administrative allocation process (Hsing 2006, 2010), putting them in direct competition with municipal governments, which pushed to consolidate their control over land by expropriating SOE land within their jurisdictions (Hsing 2006, 2010; Leaf 1998; Shi 2005). Similar conflicts can arise at the urban construction boundary, where state ownership of urban land intersects with collective ownership of rural land (Ho and Lin 2003; Lin 2009).

12 Webster (2009) proposes a related understanding of planning as part of the state's, or the landowner's, sovereign authority.

13 These qualities suggest that Chinese planning powers constitute "stewardship rights," which are assigned, conditional, and inalienable (Pryor 1973, 380).

14 This point is similar to arguments that deliberative and communicative planning processes in the United States engender community-building resources that are just as important as the ultimate planning outcome (Forester 1999; Sandercock and Attili 2010).

5. Village-as-the-City

1 In China's *tiao-kuai* matrix of intergovernmental relations, land management bureaus respond to two sets of incentives: the ministerial bureaucracy prioritizes land use control and the conservation of agricultural land, while local governments prioritize land use intensification and the conversion of agricultural land for urban construction (cf. Hsing 2010; Wu, Xu, and Yeh 2007).

2 For instance, in a model that became popular across the Pearl River Delta, Nanhai District allowed village collectives to transfer operational land to collective-owned corporations, which could then contract the land to third parties through the establishment of joint ventures (Sun and Xu 2011). Other municipalities, such as Kunshan and Wuhu, encouraged the consolidation of villager housing to free up construction land that could then be reclas-

sified as operational land and used for industrialization (Li 2013; Sun and Xu 2011).

3 The transfer of development rights draws on a set of practices originating in the United States in the mid-twentieth century (Cui 2011), in which a landowner is able to sell the development rights from a land parcel to another landowner, who is then able to increase the intensity of development on a receiving parcel (Johnston and Madison 1997).

4 Much of the surplus is appropriated by intermediaries, such as land reclamation firms, and only 15 percent of the net revenue goes to the village collective. By dramatically increasing the overall supply of land available for conversion, these programs also reduce the real market value of collective-owned land, redistributing this surplus from villagers to municipal governments and developers in the form of cost savings (X. Cai 2010).

5 After visiting Zheng'ge in 2008, Liu Shouying, then a researcher at the State Council Development Research Center, coined the term "self-urbanization" to describe the village's distinctive development path (Chen 2014). Similar experimental practices have been documented in other parts of China, including, for instance, the development of "farmers' towns" (*nongmin cheng* 农民城) (Hoffman and Liu 1997).

6 Unlike China's formal urbanization process and Chongqing's urban–rural coordination program, self-urbanization denotes village urbanization without government involvement (Wang and Cai 2012; Zhang 2013). Working within the constraints of planning and land use regulations, the village collective uses its own land for urban functions, transferring land use rights to new land users through market mechanisms (Cheng and Liu 2012; Gao 2014; Li 2013; Wang and Cai 2012). By appropriating the land rent increment produced by urbanization, the village collective is able to provide villagers with public goods and services equivalent to those found in urban areas (Gao 2014; Li 2013; Wang and Cai 2012).

7 In Zheng'ge, the village collective consolidated villagers' housing construction land in 1998 based on a village plan completed in 1996, and it paid an administrative fee to convert nearly all its agricultural land to construction land. The 1998 Land Management Law put this strategy in limbo, and the municipal planning bureau did not approve the 1996 plan until 2005, after the State Council began reliberalizing collective-owned construction land. With this approval, the village collective then transferred its construction land to a village corporation, which used the land to construct commercial housing, tourism facilities, and a high-end industrial estate (Chen 2011).

8 Similar abuses have been documented in China's south, where some cadres

have manipulated the distribution of shares and perquisites to ensure the dependence and obedience of villager clients and to appropriate profits, obscure village assets, and obstruct democratic accountability (cf. Chung and Unger 2013; Kan 2016; Wong 2016).

9 These tensions are faced by many village shareholding organizations, which must balance villager demands for the provision of services and welfare with market incentives for profit maximization and reinvestment (Chung and Unger 2013; Kan 2016; Tang 2015; Zhu and Guo 2015).

10 A similar displacement of the village community and its moral claims on collective welfare also resulted from the land reform and household registration reform programs implemented by the municipal government (cf. Yep and Forrest 2016; Zhang 2018).

6. The End of the Village

1 As described in chapter 3, colocation and cohabitation allowed residents to pursue strategies of economic diversification and mutual support, including the reciprocal provision of care for the sick and elderly.

2 In the context of Southeast Asia, James Scott has described such cultural appropriations as the "weapons of the weak" (Scott 1976, 231–33; 1985). Similar practices have been observed in China, where protesters have appropriated funerary rituals to criticize and even threaten local officials (O'Brien and Deng 2015).

3 Given the cultural association between ghosts and strangers, it is therefore unsurprising that many Hailong villagers would be reluctant to discuss ghosts with me, a stranger. This is especially true for a foreign visitor, because foreigners are sometimes disparagingly referred to as "ghosts." Conversely, my most extensive discussions of ghosts were always with those villagers, like Li Xiaowei, who had integrated me most closely into their social networks. This marker of social distinction, with access to ghost talk representing community membership, can be seen as an intensification of "cultural intimacy" (Herzfeld 2005). The belief in ghosts represented a "social essentialism" that was simultaneously a source of external embarrassment when exposed to outsiders and a basis for common identity when shared internally (Herzfeld 2005, 3).

4 In this respect, my use of spatial poetics is more akin to Michael Herzfeld's understanding of *social* poetics, which draws attention to the ambiguous multiplication of meanings wrought through the manipulation of social conventions and forms (2005, 37, 190). Following Herzfeld, a *spatial* poetics thus involves the creative appropriation of the naturalized meanings of space in

order to highlight their artificiality and reveal potential alternatives—though in the very act of doing so, the hegemony of the original meanings may also be reproduced.

5 Villagers' appeals to ghosts therefore can be understood as "voices from the borderlands," giving expression to the experiences of marginal, displaced, and oppressed people who are excluded from or silenced in more conventional forums of discussion and debate (Sandercock 1998, 110).

6 The demonization of villagers' profit motives reflects a larger pattern in the portrayal of rural resistance to demolition and relocation in China, as discussed in chapter 3.

7 For me, ticketless buses were a matter of convenience: instead of exchanging cash with a ticket attendant, I could simply swipe my refillable transit pass in front of the card reader. So I rejoiced when, in the spring of 2012, the 280 bus that I regularly took to Baishiyi on my way to Hailong went ticketless. All fares were reduced to the citywide one-*kuai* fare, integrating West City more tightly into the urban networks emanating from downtown Chongqing.

8 This was as close as you could get to his home, where, according to Chinese religious practice, the man's spirit would return to be ritually resocialized by his descendants. Unable to return home, the spirit might remain lost and turn into a ghost, haunting the place where the home once stood (Feuchtwang 2010, 136).

9 *Guihua* is a term used for technical planning activities, including urban planning, that are rooted in the technocratic practices of scientific rationality. *Jihua* is a more general term used to refer both to the social and economic planning of the Chinese state (including the command and control planning of the socialist period) and the everyday planning of individuals and households (cf. Heilmann and Melton 2013; Sigley 2006).

Conclusion

1 Whether Hailong's experiences are applicable to other specific cases of transformation is ultimately a question for further research and the process of naturalistic generalization, whereby readers determine Hailong's relevance on the basis of their personal experiences and conditioned by the empirical complexity of the social world (Flyvbjerg 2006, 238; Stake 1978).

2 This may even be true for villages that do not follow Hailong's path of industrialization and real estate development. For instance, agricultural villages that succeed in escaping the state-led industrialization and corporatization of agriculture often end up pursuing village-scaled forms of urbanization (Smith 2019b).

3 Indeed, the main protagonists behind these intellectual movements often remark on their shared critical agenda despite their methodological differences (Brenner 2018; Brenner and Schmid 2015; Robinson and Roy 2015; Roy 2016).

4 This approach draws directly from the arguments of both "Asia as method" and "China as method" (Chen 2010, 252–53; Mizoguchi 2016), as well as engagements with "theory from the South" (Comaroff and Comaroff 2012). It is also inspired by current calls for the "provincialization of Europe" and "new geographies of theory" within urban studies (Leitner and Sheppard 2015; Robinson 2014; Roy 2009).

5 This echoes calls within critical geography for research that deals with the intersections between different dimensions of sociospatiality, such as territory, place, scale, and network, rather than investigations that focus on a single dimension or that argue for the substitution of one dimension by another (Jessop, Brenner, and Jones 2008; cf. O'Callaghan 2012).

Bibliography

Abramson, Daniel B. 2016. "Periurbanization and the Politics of Development-as-City-Building in China." *Cities* 53 (April): 156–62. https://doi.org/10.1016/j.cities.2015.11.002.

Abramson, Daniel B., and Yu Qi. 2011. "'Urban–Rural Integration' in the Earthquake Zone: Sichuan's Post-disaster Reconstruction and the Expansion of the Chengdu Metropole." *Pacific Affairs* 84 (3): 495–523. https://doi.org/info:doi/10.5509/2011843495.

Ahlers, Anna L., and Gunter Schubert. 2010. "'Building a New Socialist Countryside'—Only a Political Slogan?" *Journal of Current Chinese Affairs* 38 (4): 35–62.

Alchian, Armen A., and Harold Demsetz. 1973. "The Property Right Paradigm." *Journal of Economic History* 33 (1): 16–27. https://doi.org/10.2307/2117138.

Alexander, Ernest R. 1992. "A Transaction Cost Theory of Planning." *Journal of the American Planning Association* 58 (2): 190–200.

Alpermann, Björn. 2001. "The Post-election Administration of Chinese Villages." *China Journal* 46:45–67. https://doi.org/10.2307/3182307.

Amin, Ash, and Nigel Thrift. 2002. *Cities: Reimagining the Urban.* Cambridge: Polity Press.

An, Mark Yuying, Wei Li, and Dennis Tao Yang. 2001. *China's Great Leap Forward or Backward? Anatomy of a Central Planning Disaster.* London: Centre for Economic Policy Research.

Anagnost, Ann. 2004. "The Corporeal Politics of Quality (Suzhi)." *Public Culture* 16 (2): 189–208.

Andreas, Joel. 2009. *Rise of the Red Engineers: The Cultural Revolution and the Origins of China's New Class.* Stanford, Calif.: Stanford University Press.

Aoki, Keith. 2005. "All the King's Horses and All the King's Men: Hurdles to Putting the Fragmented Metropolis Back Together Again—Statewide Land Use Planning, Portland Metro and Oregon's Measure 37." *Journal of Law and Politics* 21:397–450.

Appadurai, Arjun. 1996. *Modernity at Large: Cultural Dimensions of Globalization.* Minneapolis: University of Minnesota Press.

Arnstein, Sherry R. 1969. "A Ladder of Citizen Participation." *American Institute of Planning Journal,* July, 216–24.

Baker, Hugh D. R. 1979. *Chinese Family and Kinship.* New York: Columbia University Press.

Balakrishnan, Sai. 2019. *Shareholder Cities: Land Transformations along Urban Corridors in India.* Philadelphia: University of Pennsylvania Press.

Bater, James H. 1980. *The Soviet City: Ideal and Reality.* Beverly Hills: Sage.

Blakely, Edward J., and Mary Gail Snyder. 1998. "Forting Up: Gated Communities in the United States." *Journal of Architectural and Planning Research* 15 (1): 61–72.

Bradnstädter, Susanne. 2003. "The Moral Economy of Kinship and Property in Southern China." In *The Postsocialist Agrarian Question: Property Relations and the Rural Condition,* edited by C. M. Hann, 419–40. Münster: LIT Verlag Münster.

Brandt, Loren, Jikun Huang, Guo Li, and Scott Rozelle. 2002. "Land Rights in Rural China: Facts, Fictions and Issues." *China Journal,* no. 47: 67–97. https://doi.org/10.2307/3182074.

Brandt, Loren, and Matthew A. Turner. 2007. "The Usefulness of Imperfect Elections: The Case of Village Elections in Rural China." *Economics and Politics* 19 (3): 453–80. https://doi.org/10.1111/j.1468-0343.2007.00316.x.

Bray, David. 2005. *Social Space and Governance in Urban China: The Danwei System from Origins to Reform.* Stanford, Calif.: Stanford University Press.

Bray, David. 2013a. "Master Planning the Nation: Elites and the Transformation of China's Built Environment." In *Elites and Governance in China,* edited by Xiaowei Zang and Chien-wen Kou, 73–93. Abingdon, U.K.: Routledge.

Bray, David. 2013b. "Urban Planning Goes Rural: Conceptualising the 'New Village.'" *China Perspectives,* no. 3: 53–62.

Brenner, Neil. 2004. *New State Spaces: Urban Governance and the Rescaling of Statehood.* Oxford: Oxford University Press.

Brenner, Neil. 2013. "Theses on Urbanization." *Public Culture* 25 (1): 85–114. https://doi.org/10.1215/08992363-1890477.

Brenner, Neil. 2018. "Debating Planetary Urbanization: For an Engaged Pluralism." *Environment and Planning D: Society and Space* 36 (3): 570–90. https://doi.org/10.1177/0263775818757510.

Brenner, Neil, and Christian Schmid. 2014. "The 'Urban Age' in Question." *International Journal of Urban and Regional Research* 38 (3): 731–55. https://doi.org/10.1111/1468-2427.12115.

Brenner, Neil, and Christian Schmid. 2015. "Towards a New Epistemology of the Urban?" *City* 19 (2–3): 151–82. https://doi.org/10.1080/13604813.2015.1014712.

Brookfield, Harold C., Abdul Samad Hadi, and Zaharah Mahmud. 1991. *The City in the Village: The In-Situ Urbanization of Villages and Their Land around Kuala Lumpur, Malaysia.* Oxford: Oxford University Press.

Bunce, Michael. 2003. "Reproducing Rural Idylls." In *Country Visions,* edited by Paul J. Cloke, 14–30. Upper Saddle River, N.J.: Prentice Hall.

Bunnell, Tim, and Anant Maringanti. 2010. "Practising Urban and Regional Research beyond Metrocentricity." *International Journal of Urban and Regional Research* 34 (2): 415–20. https://doi.org/10.1111/j.1468-2427.2010.00988.x.

Bunnell, Tim, Hamzah Muzaini, and James D. Sidaway. 2006. "Global City Frontiers: Singapore's Hinterland and the Contested Socio-political Geographies of Bintan, Indonesia." *International Journal of Urban and Regional Research* 30 (1): 3–22.

Cai, Fang. 2011. "Hukou System Reform and Unification of Rural–Urban Social Welfare." *China and World Economy* 19 (3): 33–48. https://doi.org/10.1111/j.1749-124X.2011.01241.x.

Cai Xuming. 2010. "Nongcun jiti jianshe yongdi liuzhuan de zhuti he liyi fenpei—Chongqingshi he Chengdushi nongcun jiti jianshe yongdi liuzhuan de zhengzhi jingji xue fenxi" [Profit distribution and the subject of rural collective construction land transfer—A political and economic analysis of rural collective construction land transfer in Chongqing and Chengdu]. *Xuexi luntan* [Tribune of study] 26 (7): 59–62.

Cai, Yongshun. 2003. "Collective Ownership or Cadres' Ownership? The Non-agricultural Use of Farmland in China." *China Quarterly* 175:662–80.

Cai, Yongshun. 2010. *Collective Resistance in China: Why Popular Protests Succeed or Fail.* Redwood City: Stanford University Press.

Cartier, Carolyn. 2005. "Scale Relations and China's Spatial Administrative Hierarchy." In *Restructuring the Chinese City: Changing Society, Economy and Space,* edited by Laurence J. C. Ma and Fulong Wu, 21–38. London: Routledge.

Caruth, Cathy. 1996. *Unclaimed Experience: Trauma, Narrative and History.* Baltimore, Md.: Johns Hopkins University Press.

Castells, Manuel. 1977. *The Urban Question: A Marxist Approach.* Cambridge, Mass.: MIT Press.

Castells, Manuel. 1983. *The City and the Grassroots: A Cross-Cultural Theory of Urban Social Movements.* Berkeley: University of California Press.

Castells, Manuel. 1996. *The Rise of the Network Society.* Cambridge: Blackwell.

CCP Central Committee. 2003. "Guanyu wanshan shehui zhuyi shichang jingji tizhi ruogan wenti de jueding" [Decision on several questions regarding the perfection of the socialist market economy]. http://www.people.com.cn/GB/shizheng/1024/2145119.html.

Chan, Anita, Richard Madsen, and Jonathan Unger. 2009. *Chen Village: Revolution to Globalization.* Berkeley: University of California Press.

Chan, Kam Wing. 1994. *Cities with Invisible Walls: Reinterpreting Urbanization in Post-1949 China.* Oxford: Oxford University Press.

Chan, Kam Wing. 2010. "The Household Registration System and Migrant Labor in China: Notes on a Debate." *Population and Development Review* 36 (2): 357–64. https://doi.org/10.1111/j.1728-4457.2010.00333.x.

Chan, Kam Wing. 2012. "Crossing the 50 Percent Population Rubicon: Can China Urbanize to Prosperity?" *Eurasian Geography and Economics* 53 (1): 63–86. https://doi.org/10.2747/1539-7216.53.1.63.

Chan, Kam Wing, and Will Buckingham. 2008. "Is China Abolishing the Hukou System?" *China Quarterly* 195 (September): 582–606.

Chan, Kam Wing, and Yanning Wei. 2019. "Two Systems in One Country: The Origin, Functions, and Mechanisms of the Rural–Urban Dual System in China." *Eurasian Geography and Economics* 60 (4): 422–54. https://doi.org/10.1080/15387216.2019.1669203.

Chang, Kyung-Sup. 1993. "The Confucian Family Instead of the Welfare State? Reform and Peasant Welfare in Post-Mao China." *Asian Perspective* 17 (3): 169–200.

Chang, Shu. 2013. "Discourse, Morality, Body: Radical Socialism in a Chinese Model Village (1946–1978)." Ph.D. diss., Harvard University.

Chen, An. 2014. *The Transformation of Governance in Rural China.* Cambridge: Cambridge University Press.

Chen, An. 2016. "The Politics of the Shareholding Collective Economy in China's Rural Villages." *Journal of Peasant Studies* 43 (4): 828–49. https://doi.org/10.1080/03066150.2015.1078318.

Chen Cheng. 1984. "Shi shehui zhuyi chengshihua, haishi chengxiang yitihua" [Is it socialist urbanization, or is it urban–rural integration?]. *Qiusuo* [Seeker], no. 6: 7–12.

Chen, Jia-Ching, John Aloysius Zinda, and Emily Ting Yeh. 2017. "Recasting the Rural: State, Society and Environment in Contemporary China." *Geoforum* 78 (January): 83–88. https://doi.org/10.1016/j.geoforum.2016.03.014.

Chen Jingsi. 2011. "Tudi jiti jingying zhi zu bu shou—Beijing Zheng'ge zhuang zizhu chengshihua zhi lu de diaocha" [Land the collective operates and only rents but does not sell—Research on the self-urbanization of Zheng'ge Village in Beijing]. *Nongcun gongzuo tongxun* [Rural work news], no. 2: 26–27.

Chen, Kuan-Hsing. 2010. *Asia as Method: Toward Deimperialization.* Durham, N.C.: Duke University Press.

Chen Pengming, ed. 2009. *Kexue fazhan guan xuexi duben* [Scientific development platform reader]. Beijing: Renmin chubanshe [People's press].

Chen Weibang. 2003. "Zhongguo chengshi kexue 20 nian" [20 years of urban science in China]. *Chengshi fazhan yanjiu* [Urban studies] 10 (5): 8–14.

Cheng Jianping. 2003. "Nongcun chengshihua yu nongmin shiminhua" [Village urbanization and the urbanization of rural people]. *Jishu jingji yu guanli yanjiu* [Techno-economics and management research], no. 2: 18.

Cheng Shiyong and Yang Liu. 2012. "Nongmin zizhu chengshihua de zhidu kongjian yu mianlin kunjing" [Challenges and opportunities for villager self-urbanization]. *Shangye shidai* [Journal of commercial economics], no. 12: 14–15.

Cheung, Chi-Pui. 2012. "The Paradox of China's Urban–Rural Integration: The Hukou System, Rural Policy, and Rural Land Development." *Urban Anthropology and Studies of Cultural Systems and World Economic Development* 41 (2–4): 293–328.

Cho, Mun Young. 2013. *The Specter of "the People": Urban Poverty in Northeast China.* Ithaca, N.Y.: Cornell University Press.

Chuang, Julia. 2014. "China's Rural Land Politics: Bureaucratic Absorption and the Muting of Rightful Resistance." *China Quarterly* 219:649–69. https://doi.org/10.1017/S030574101400068X.

Chung, Him. 2009. "The Planning of 'Villages-in-the-City' in Shenzhen, China: The Significance of the New State-Led Approach." *International Planning Studies* 14 (3): 253. https://doi.org/10.1080/13563470903450606.

Chung, Him, and Jonathan Unger. 2013. "The Guangdong Model of Urbanisation: Collective Village Land and the Making of a New Middle Class." *China Perspectives,* no. 3: 33–41.

Coase, Ronald H. 1937. "The Nature of the Firm." *Economica* 4 (16): 386–405.

Coase, Ronald H. 1960. "The Problem of Social Cost." In *Classic Papers in Natural Resource Economics,* edited by Chennat Gopalakrishnan, 87–137. London: Palgrave Macmillan.

Cody, Jeffrey W. 1996. "American Planning in Republican China, 1911–1937." *Planning Perspectives* 11 (4): 339–77.

Cole, Daniel H., and Peter Z. Grossman. 2002. "The Meaning of Property Rights: Law versus Economics?" *Land Economics* 78 (3): 317–30.

Comaroff, Jean, and John L. Comaroff. 2012. *Theory from the South: Or, How Euro-America Is Evolving toward Africa.* Boulder, Colo.: Paradigm.

Cook, Sarah. 2002. "From Rice Bowl to Safety Net: Insecurity and Social Protection during China's Transition." *Development Policy Review* 20 (5): 615–35.

Cui, Zhiyuan. 2011. "Partial Intimations of the Coming Whole: The Chongqing Experiment in Light of the Theories of Henry George, James Meade, and Antonio Gramsci." *Modern China* 37 (6): 646–60. https://doi.org/10.1177/0097700411420852.

Dahlman, Carl J. 1979. "The Problem of Externality." *Journal of Law and Economics* 22 (1): 141–62. https://doi.org/10.1086/466936.

Dai Feng. 2004. "Tantan chengshi guihua guanli zhong de zhiye daode wenti" [A discussion of professional planning ethics in the course of urban planning implementation]. *Chengshi guihua* [City planning review] 28 (1): 25–27.

Dai Yue. 2000. "Guanyu gongzhong canyu de huati: shijian yu sikao" [Regarding public participation topics: Practice and reflection]. *Chengshi guihua* [City planning review] 24 (7): 59–61.

Davidoff, Paul. 1965. "Advocacy and Pluralism in Planning." *Journal of the American Institute of Planners* 31 (4): 331–38.

Day, Alexander. 2008. "The End of the Peasant? New Rural Reconstruction in China." *Boundary 2* 35 (2): 49–73.

Demsetz, Harold. 1967. "Toward a Theory of Property Rights." *American Economic Review* 57 (2): 347–59.

Deng, Feng. 2009. "Housing of Limited Property Rights: A Paradox Inside and Outside Chinese Cities." *Housing Studies* 24 (6): 825–41. https://doi.org/10.1080/02673030903223625.

Deng, F. Frederic, Peter Gordon, and Harry W. Richardson. 2007. "Private Communities, Market Institutions and Planning." In *Institutions and Planning,* edited by Niraj Verma, 187–205. Amsterdam: Elsevier.

Donaldson, John A. 2011. *Small Works: Poverty and Economic Development in Southwestern China.* Ithaca, N.Y.: Cornell University Press.

Du Yu. 2014. "Cunzhuang jianshe jinfang 'qian cun yimian'" [Village construction needs to beware of "all villages looking the same"]. *Nongcun, nongye, nongmin* [Villages, agriculture, peasants], no. 6: 6.

Duany, Andres, Jeff Speck, and Mike Lydon. 2010. *The Smart Growth Manual.* New York: McGraw Hill.

Duckett, Jane, and Beatriz Carillo. 2011. "China's Changing Welfare Mix: Introducing the Local Perspective." In *China's Changing Welfare Mix: Local Perspectives,* edited by Beatriz Carrillo and Jane Duckett, 1–19. New York: Routledge.

Eckstein, Harry. 1992. *Regarding Politics: Essays on Political Theory, Stability, and Change.* Berkeley: University of California Press.

Edensor, Tim. 2008. "Mundane Hauntings: Commuting through the Phantasmagoric Working-Class Spaces of Manchester, England." *Cultural Geographies* 15 (3): 313–33. http://dx.doi.org.libproxy1.nus.edu.sg/10.1177/1474474008091330.

Edin, Maria. 2003. "State Capacity and Local Agent Control in China: CCP Cadre Management from a Township Perspective." *China Quarterly* 173:5–52. https://doi.org/10.2307/20058957.

Esherick, Joseph. 2000. "Modernity and Nation in the Chinese City." In *Remaking the Chinese City: Modernity and National Identity, 1900–1950,* edited by Joseph Esherick, 1–18. Honolulu: University of Hawai'i Press.

Evans, Harriet. 2008. *The Subject of Gender: Daughters and Mothers in Urban China.* Lanham, Md.: Rowman & Littlefield.

Evans-Pritchard, Edward E. 1937. *Witchcraft, Oracles and Magic among the Azande.* Oxford: Clarendon Press.

Fan, C. Cindy. 2008. *China on the Move: Migration, the State, and the Household.* New York: Routledge.

Fan, C. Cindy, and Wenfei Winnie Wang. 2008. "The Household as Security: Strategies of Rural–Urban Migrants in China." In *Migration and Social Protection in China,* edited by Ingrid Nielsen and Russell Smyth, 155–83. Singapore: World Scientific.

Farías, Ignacio. 2012. "Introduction: Decentring the Object of Urban Studies." In *Urban Assemblages: How Actor-Network Theory Changes Urban Studies,* edited by Ignacio Farías and Thomas Bender, 1–24. New York: Routledge.

Farrer, James. 2002. "'Idle Talk': Neighborhood Gossip as a Medium of Social Communication in Reform Era Shanghai." In *Social Connections in China: Institutions, Culture, and the Changing Nature of Guanxi,* edited by Thomas B. Gold, Doug Guthrie, and David L. Wank, 197–218. Cambridge: Cambridge University Press.

Faure, David, and Helen F. Siu, eds. 1995. *Down to Earth: The Territorial Bond in South China.* Stanford, Calif.: Stanford University Press.

Fei, Xiaotong. (1948) 1992. *From the Soil, the Foundations of Chinese Society: A Translation of Fei Xiaotong's Xiangtu Zhongguo.* Translated by Gary G. Hamilton and Zheng Wang. Berkeley: University of California Press.

Fei Xiaotong. 1991. "Tan chengxiang xietiao fazhan" [A discussion of urban–rural coordinated development]. *Liaowang zhoukan* [Outlook weekly], no. 47: 8–10.

Feng Hua. 1983. "Qianyi chengxiang xietiao fazhan" [A superficial discussion of urban–rural coordinated development]. *Jianzhu xuebao* [Architectural journal], no. 4: 1–7.

Ferguson, James. 1990. *The Anti-politics Machine: "Development," Depoliticization, and Bureaucratic Power in Lesotho.* Cambridge: Cambridge University Press.

Festa, Paul. 2007. "Mahjong Agonistics and the Political Public in Taiwan: Fate, Mimesis, and the Martial Imaginary." *Anthropological Quarterly* 80 (1): 93–125.

Feuchtwang, Stephan. 1974. "Domestic and Communal Worship in Taiwan." In *Religion and Ritual in Chinese Society,* edited by Arthur P. Wolf, 105–30. Stanford, Calif.: Stanford University Press.

Feuchtwang, Stephan. 2010. *The Anthropology of Religion, Charisma, and Ghosts: Chinese Lessons for Adequate Theory.* New York: Walter de Gruyter.

Fischel, William A. 1987. *The Economics of Zoning Laws: A Property Rights Approach to American Land Use Controls.* Baltimore, Md.: Johns Hopkins University Press.

Fishman, Robert. 1987. *Bourgeois Utopias: The Rise and Fall of Suburbia.* New York: Basic Books.

Flad, Rowan K. 2008. "Divination and Power: A Multiregional View of the Development of Oracle Bone Divination in Early China." *Current Anthropology* 49 (3): 403–37. https://doi.org/10.1086/588495.

Flyvbjerg, Bent. 1998. *Rationality and Power: Democracy in Practice.* Chicago: University of Chicago Press.

Flyvbjerg, Bent. 2006. "Five Misunderstandings about Case-Study Research." *Qualitative Inquiry* 12 (2): 219–45. https://doi.org/10.1177/1077800405284363.

Fogelson, Robert. 2007. *Bourgeois Nightmares: Suburbia, 1870–1930.* New Haven, Conn.: Yale University Press.

Forester, John. 1999. *The Deliberative Practitioner: Encouraging Participatory Planning Processes.* Cambridge, Mass.: MIT Press.

Forrest, Ray, and Ade Kearns. 2001. "Social Cohesion, Social Capital and the Neighbourhood." *Urban Studies* 38 (12): 2125–43. https://doi.org/10.1080/00420980120087081.

Freedman, Maurice. 1971. *Chinese Lineage and Society: Fukien and Kwangtung.* New York: Humanities Press.

French, Richard Anthony. 1995. *Plans, Pragmatism and People: The Legacy of Soviet Planning for Today's Cities.* London: UCL Press.

Friedmann, John. 1973. *Retracking America: A Theory of Transactive Planning.* Norwell, Mass.: Anchor Press.

Friedmann, John. 1988. *Life Space and Economic Space: Essays in Third World Planning.* Brunswick, N.J.: Transaction Books.

Gao Fuping. 2014. "Chongqi jiti jianshe yongdi shichanghua gaige de yiyi he zhidu xuqiu" [The importance and systemic need for the rebooting of marketization reform for collective construction land]. *Dongfang faxue* [Oriental law], no. 6: 74–85.

Ge Zhengpeng. 2006. "'Shimin' gainian de chonggou yu woguo nongmin shiminhua daolu yanjiu" [Research on the reconstruction of the 'urban person' concept and China's path of urbanization of rural people]. *Nongye jingji wenti* [Issues in agricultural economy], no. 9: 63–67.

Genoni, Maria Eugenia. 2012. "Health Shocks and Consumption Smoothing: Evidence from Indonesia." *Economic Development and Cultural Change* 60 (3): 475–506. https://doi.org/10.1086/664019.

George, Henry. 1884. *Progress and Poverty: An Inquiry into the Cause of Industrial Depressions, and of Increase of Want with Increase of Wealth, the Remedy.* London: Reeves.

Gordon, Avery. 1997. *Ghostly Matters: Haunting and the Sociological Imagination.* Minneapolis: University of Minnesota Press.

Gore, Lance L. P. 2012. "The Fall of Bo Xilai and the Seduction of the Chongqing Model." *East Asian Policy* 4 (2): 53–61. https://doi.org/10.1142/S1793930512000153.

Griffiths, Michael B., Malcolm Chapman, and Flemming Christiansen. 2010. "Chinese Consumers: The Romantic Reappraisal." *Ethnography* 11 (3): 331–57. https://doi.org/10.1177/1466138110370412.

Gu Jijian. 2011. "Huji zhidu gaige de chongqing shijian" [Chongqing's practice of household registration system reform]. *Chongqing shehui kexue* [Chongqing social sciences], no. 9: 95–100.

Gu Shengzu and Zhengyou Li. 1998. "Zhongguo zixia er shang chengzhenhua de zhidu fenxi" [An analysis of the system of bottom-up urbanization in China]. *Zhongguo shehui kexue* [Social sciences in China], no. 2: 60–70.

Guldin, Gregory Eliyu. 1996. "Desakotas and Beyond: Urbanization in Southern China." *Ethnology* 35 (4): 265–83.

Guldin, Gregory Eliyu, ed. 1997a. *Farewell to Peasant China: Rural Urbanization and Social Change in the Late Twentieth Century.* Armonk, N.Y.: M. E. Sharpe.

Guldin, Gregory Eliyu. 1997b. "Urbanization with Chinese Characteristics." In *Farewell to Peasant China: Rural Urbanization and Social Change in the Late Twentieth Century,* edited by Gregory Eliyu Guldin, 265–74. Armonk, N.Y.: M. E. Sharpe.

Guldin, Gregory Eliyu. 2001. *What's a Peasant to Do? Village Becoming Town in Southern China.* Boulder, Colo.: Westview Press.

Guo Wuxia. 2004. "Tan guihuashi de zhiye daode" [A discussion of planners' professional ethics]. *Chengshi guihua* [City planning review], no. 2: 88.

Guo, Xiaolin. 2001. "Land Expropriation and Rural Conflicts in China." *China Quarterly* 166: 422–39.

Guo, Zhenglin, and Thomas P. Bernstein. 2004. "The Impact of Elections on the Village Structure of Power: The Relations between the Village Committees and the Party Branches." *Journal of Contemporary China* 13 (39): 257–75.

Habermas, Jürgen. 1970. *Toward a Rational Society: Student Protest, Science, and Politics.* Boston: Beacon Press.

Habermas, Jürgen. 1973. *Theory and Practice.* Boston: Beacon Press.

Hagman, Donald G., and Dean J. Misczynski. 1978. *Windfalls for Wipeouts: Land Value Capture and Compensation.* Chicago: American Society of Planning Officials.

Haila, Anne. 2007. "The Market as the New Emperor." *International Journal of Urban and Regional Research* 31 (1): 3–20.

Hamnett, Chris. 2020. "Is Chinese Urbanisation Unique?" *Urban Studies* 57 (3): 690–700. https://doi.org/10.1177/0042098019890810.

Han Binhui. 2012. "Chongqing huji zhidu gaige de sikao" [Thoughts on Chongqing's household registration reform]. *Nongcun jingji yu keji* [Rural economy and science-technology] 23 (8): 32–33.

Han Kunyu. 2013. "Yin di zhi yi jinxing nongcun shequ jianshe" [Constructing new rural communities by suiting measures to local conditions]. *Henan gongcheng xueyuan xuebao* [Journal of Henan Institute of Engineering], no. 1: 19–21.

Han Zenglin and Tianbao Liu. 2009. "Chengshi guihua zhuanxing de zhengtixing he xitongxing" [Systematicity and wholeness of urban planning in transition]. *Chengshi wenti* [Urban problems], no. 4: 12–17.

Harms, Erik. 2011. *Saigon's Edge: On the Margins of Ho Chi Minh City.* Minneapolis: University of Minnesota Press.

Harms, Erik. 2016. *Luxury and Rubble: Civility and Dispossession in the New Saigon.* Berkeley: University of California Press.

Harvey, David. 1973. *Social Justice and the City.* Atlanta: University of Georgia Press.

Harvey, David. 1975. "The Geography of Capitalist Accumulation: A Reconstruction of the Marxian Theory." *Antipode* 7 (2): 9–21. https://doi.org/10.1111/j.1467-8330.1975.tb00616.x.

Harvey, David. 1978. "On Planning the Ideology of Planning." In *Planning Theory in the 1980s: A Search for Future Directions,* edited by Robert W. Burchell and George Sternlieb, 213–33. New Brunswick, N.J.: Center for Urban Policy Research.

Harvey, David. 1981. "The Urban Process under Capitalism: A Framework for Analysis." In *Urbanization and Urban Planning in Capitalist Society,* edited by Michael J. Dear and Allen John Scott, 91–122. New York: Methuen.

Harvey, David. 2008. "The Right to the City." *New Left Review,* no. 53 (October): 23–40.

He, Shenjing, Yuting Liu, Christopher J. Webster, and Fulong Wu. 2009. "Property Rights Redistribution, Entitlement Failure and the Impoverishment of

Landless Farmers in China." *Urban Studies* 46 (9): 1925–49. https://doi.org/10.1177/0042098009106015.

He, Shenjing, and Fulong Wu. 2005. "Property-Led Redevelopment in Post-reform China: A Case Study of Xintiandi Redevelopment Project in Shanghai." *Journal of Urban Affairs* 27 (1): 1–23. https://doi.org/10.1111/j.0735-2166.2005.00222.x.

He, Xuefeng. 2003. *Xiangcun zhili de shehui jichu—zhuanxing qi xiangcun shehui xingzhi yanjiu* [The social foundation of rural governance—A study on the nature of rural society during transition]. Beijing: Zhongguo shehui kexue chubanshe [China social sciences press].

He, Xuefeng. 2007. *Xiang cun de qian tu: Xin nong cun jian she yu Zhongguo dao lu* [The future of the countryside: New village development and China's path]. Jinan: Shandong ren min chu ban she [Shandong people's press].

Healey, Patsy. 1996. "The Communicative Turn in Planning Theory and Its Implications for Spatial Strategy Formations." *Environment and Planning B: Planning and Design* 23 (2): 217–34. https://doi.org/10.1068/b230217.

Heikkila, Eric J., Ti-yan Shen, and Kai-zhong Yang. 2003. "Fuzzy Urban Sets: Theory and Application to Desakota Regions in China." *Environment and Planning B: Planning and Design* 30 (2): 239–54. https://doi.org/10.1068/b12820.

Heilmann, Sebastian. 2011. "Policy-making through Experimentation: The Formation of a Distinctive Policy Process." In *Mao's Invisible Hand: The Political Foundations of Adaptive Governance in China,* edited by Sebastian Heilmann and Elizabeth J. Perry, 62–101. Cambridge, Mass.: Harvard University Asia Center.

Heilmann, Sebastian, and Oliver Melton. 2013. "The Reinvention of Development Planning in China, 1993–2012." *Modern China* 39 (6): 580–628. https://doi.org/10.1177/0097700413497551.

Hershkovitz, Linda. 1993. "Tiananmen Square and the Politics of Place." *Political Geography* 12 (5): 395–420. https://doi.org/10.1016/0962-6298(93)90010-5.

Herzfeld, Michael. 2005. *Cultural Intimacy: Social Poetics in the Nation-State.* 2nd ed. New York: Routledge.

Hillman, Ben. 2014. *Patronage and Power: Local State Networks and Party–State Resilience in Rural China.* Stanford, Calif.: Stanford University Press.

Hirschman, Albert O. 1970. *Exit, Voice, and Loyalty: Responses to Decline in Firms, Organizations, and States.* Cambridge, Mass.: Harvard University Press.

Ho, Peter. 2001. "Who Owns China's Land? Policies, Property Rights and Deliberate Institutional Ambiguity." *China Quarterly* 166: 394–421.

Ho, Samuel P., and George C. S. Lin. 2003. "Emerging Land Markets in Rural and Urban China: Policies and Practices." *China Quarterly* 175: 681–707.

Hoffman, Lisa, and Zhongquan Liu. 1997. "Rural Urbanization on the Liaodong Peninsula." In *Farewell to Peasant China: Rural Urbanization and Social Change in the Late Twentieth Century*, edited by Gregory Eliyu Guldin, 151–82. Armonk, N.Y.: M. E. Sharpe.

Hou, Li. 2018. *Building for Oil: Daqing and the Formation of the Chinese Socialist State.* Cambridge, Mass.: Harvard University Asia Center.

Hou, Xiaoshuo. 2013. *Community Capitalism in China: The State, the Market, and Collectivism.* Cambridge: Cambridge University Press.

Houtum, Henk van, and Roos Pijpers. 2007. "The European Union as a Gated Community: The Two-Faced Border and Immigration Regime of the EU." *Antipode* 39 (2): 291–309. https://doi.org/10.1111/j.1467-8330.2007.00522.x.

Howard, Ebenezer. 1902. *Garden Cities of Tomorrow.* London: Swan Sonnenschein.

Hsing, You-tien. 2006. "Land and Territorial Politics in Urban China." *China Quarterly* 187:575–91.

Hsing, You-tien. 2010. *The Great Urban Transformation: Politics of Land and Property in China.* Oxford: Oxford University Press.

Hu, Jintao. 2004. "2004 nian zhongyang jingji gongzuo huiyi" [2004 central economic working conference]. http://www.gov.cn/test/2008-12/05/content_1168928_2.htm.

Hu, Shih. 2013. *English Writings of Hu Shih: Chinese Philosophy and Intellectual History.* Volume 2. Edited by Chih-Ping Chou. Heidelberg: Springer-Verlag.

Hua, Shiping. 1995. *Scientism and Humanism: Two Cultures in Post-Mao China (1978–1989).* Albany, N.Y.: SUNY Press.

Huang, Chun, Liangji Deng, Xuesong Gao, Yi Luo, Shirong Zhang, and Li Liu. 2013. "Rural Housing Land Consolidation and Transformation of Rural Villages under the 'Coordinating Urban and Rural Construction Land' Policy: A Case of Chengdu City, China." *Low Carbon Economy* 4 (3): 95–103. https://doi.org/10.4236/lce.2013.43010.

Huang, Philip C. C. 2011. "Chongqing: Equitable Development Driven by a 'Third Hand'?" *Modern China* 37 (6): 569–622. https://doi.org/10.1177/0097700411419966.

Huang, Xianjin, Yi Li, Ran Yu, and Xiaofeng Zhao. 2014. "Reconsidering the Controversial Land Use Policy of 'Linking the Decrease in Rural Construction Land with the Increase in Urban Construction Land': A Local Government Perspective." *China Review* 14 (1): 175–98. https://doi.org/10.2307/23723006.

Huang, Xiyi. 1998. "Two-Way Changes: Kinship in Contemporary Rural China." In *Village Inc.: Chinese Rural Society in the 1990s*, edited by Flemming Christiansen and Junzuo Zhang, 177–92. Honolulu: University of Hawai'i Press.

Huang, Yasheng. 2008. *Capitalism with Chinese Characteristics: Entrepreneurship and the State.* Cambridge: Cambridge University Press.

Huang Zhong. 2014. "Chengshihua yu 'rucheng' jiti tudi de guishu" [Urbanization and the jurisdiction of "urbanized" collective land]. *Faxue yanjiu* [Legal studies], no. 4: 47–62.

Innes, Judith E. 1996. "Planning through Consensus Building: A New View of the Comprehensive Planning Ideal." *Journal of the American Planning Association* 62 (4): 460–72. https://doi.org/10.1080/01944369608975712.

Jacobs, Jane. 1961. *The Death and Life of Great American Cities.* New York: Vintage Books.

Jessop, Bob, Neil Brenner, and Martin Jones. 2008. "Theorizing Sociospatial Relations." *Environment and Planning D: Society and Space* 26 (3): 389–401. https://doi.org/10.1068/d9107.

Jin, Qiming, and Wei Li. 1992. "China's Rural Settlement Patterns." In *Chinese Landscapes: The Village as Place,* edited by Ronald G. Knapp, 13–34. Honolulu: University of Hawai'i Press.

Johnson, Graham E. 1993. "Family Strategies and Economic Transformation in Rural China: Some Evidence from the Pearl River Delta." In *Chinese Families in the Post-Mao Era,* edited by Deborah Davis and Stevan Harrell, 103–36. Berkeley: University of California Press.

Johnston, Robert A., and Mary E. Madison. 1997. "From Land Marks to Landscapes: A Review of Current Practices in the Transfer of Development Rights." *Journal of the American Planning Association* 63 (3): 365–78. https://doi.org/10.1080/01944369708975929.

Kan, Karita. 2016. "The Transformation of the Village Collective in Urbanising China: A Historical Institutional Analysis." *Journal of Rural Studies,* 47 (Part B): 588–600. https://doi.org/10.1016/j.jrurstud.2016.07.016.

Karl, Rebecca E. 2010. "The Flight to Rights: 1990s China and Beyond." *Telos* 2010 (151): 87–104. https://doi.org/10.3817/0610151087.

Kelliher, Daniel. 1997. "The Chinese Debate Over Village Self-Government." *China Journal* 37:63–86. https://doi.org/10.2307/2950218.

Kennedy, John James. 2002. "The Face of 'Grassroots Democracy' in Rural China: Real versus Cosmetic Elections." *Asian Survey* 42 (3): 456–82. https://doi.org/10.1525/as.2002.42.3.456.

King, Anthony D. 1990. *Urbanism, Colonialism, and the World-Economy.* London: Routledge.

Kipnis, Andrew B. 1997. *Producing Guanxi: Sentiment, Self, and Subculture in a North China Village.* Durham, N.C.: Duke University Press.

Kipnis, Andrew B. 2007. "Neoliberalism Reified: Suzhi Discourse and Tropes of

Neoliberalism in the People's Republic of China." *Journal of the Royal Anthropological Institute* 13 (2): 383–400.

Kipnis, Andrew B. 2016. *From Village to City: Social Transformation in a Chinese County Seat.* Oakland: University of California Press.

Kirkby, R. J. R. 1985. *Urbanization in China: Town and Country in a Developing Economy, 1949–2000 A.D.* New York: Columbia University Press.

Klosterman, Richard E. 1985. "Arguments for and against Planning." *Town Planning Review* 56 (1): 5–20.

Knight, Jack. 1992. *Institutions and Social Conflict.* Cambridge: Cambridge University Press.

Lai, Shih-Kung. 1997. "Property Rights Justifications for Planning." *Progress in Planning* 48:161–246.

Lai, Yani, Edwin Hon Wan Chan, and Lennon Choy. 2016. "Village-Led Land Development under State-Led Institutional Arrangements in Urbanising China: The Case of Shenzhen." *Urban Studies* 54 (7): 1736–59. https://doi.org/10.1177/0042098016629325.

Lai, Yani, Yi Peng, Bin Li, and Yanliu Lin. 2014. "Industrial Land Development in Urban Villages in China: A Property Rights Perspective." *Habitat International* 41 (Supplement C): 185–94. https://doi.org/10.1016/j.habitatint.2013.08.004.

Lampton, David M. 1987. *Policy Implementation in Post-Mao China.* Berkeley: University of California Press.

Latour, Bruno. 2005. *Reassembling the Social: An Introduction to Actor-Network-Theory.* New York: Oxford University Press.

Leaf, Michael. 1998. "Urban Planning and Urban Reality under Chinese Economic Reforms." *Journal of Planning Education and Research* 18 (2): 145–53. https://doi.org/10.1177/0739456X9801800206.

Leaf, Michael. 2002. "A Tale of Two Villages: Globalization and Peri-urban Change in China and Vietnam." *Cities* 19 (1): 23–31. https://doi.org/10.1016/S0264-2751(01)00043-9.

Leaf, Michael, and Li Hou. 2006. "The 'Third Spring' of Urban Planning in China: The Resurrection of Professional Planning in the Post-Mao Era." *China Information* 20 (3): 553–85. https://doi.org/10.1177/0920203X06070043.

Lee, Ching Kwan. 2007. *Against the Law: Labor Protests in China's Rustbelt and Sunbelt.* Berkeley: University of California Press.

Lee, Haiyan. 2011. "The Charisma of Power and the Military Sublime in Tiananmen Square." *Journal of Asian Studies* 70 (2): 397–424. https://doi.org/10.1017/S0021911811000040.

Lee, Keun. 1993. "Property Rights and the Agency Problem in China's Enterprise Reform." *Cambridge Journal of Economics* 17 (2): 179–94.

Lefebvre, Henri. (1970) 2003. *The Urban Revolution.* Translated by Robert Bononno. Minneapolis: University of Minnesota Press.

Leitner, Helga, and Eric Sheppard. 2015. "Provincializing Critical Urban Theory: Extending the Ecosystem of Possibilities." *International Journal of Urban and Regional Research* 40 (1): 228–35. https://doi.org/10.1111/1468-2427.12277.

Lévi-Strauss, Claude. 1963. *Totemism.* Translated by Rodney Needham. Boston: Beacon Press.

Lewis, Mark Edward. 2006. *The Construction of Space in Early China.* Albany, N.Y.: SUNY Press.

Li Keqiang. 2012. "Xietiao tuijin chengzhenhua shi shixian xiandaihua de zhongda zhanlüe xuanze" [The harmonization and promotion of urbanization is an important strategic choice for realizing modernization]. *Xingzheng guanli gaige* [Administration reform], no. 11: 4–10.

Li, Lianjiang, and Kevin J. O'Brien. 1996. "Villagers and Popular Resistance in Contemporary China." *Modern China* 22 (1): 28–61.

Li Peilin. 2005. *Nongmin de zhongjie* [The end of the peasant]. Beijing: Shehui kexue wenxian chubanshe [Social sciences academic press].

Li, Shiyu, and Shuanglin Lin. 2011. "The Size and Structure of China's Government Debt." *Social Science Journal* 48 (3): 527–42. https://doi.org/10.1016/j.soscij.2011.06.003.

Li Yiming. 2013. "Jiti jianshe yongdi liuzhuan yu zizhu xing chengshihua" [The transfer of collective construction land and self-urbanization]. *Hebei jingmao daxue xuebao* [Journal of Hebei University of Economics and Business], no. 3: 23–28.

Liao Yu. 2011. "Renshi yu jiedu huji zhidu gaige de xiangguan wuqu—Yi chongqing huji zhidu gaige wei shijiao" [Interpretation of misunderstandings related to household registration reform—From the perspective of Chongqing's household registration reform]. *Liaoning jing zhuan xuebao* [Journal of Liaoning police academy], no. 6: 70–73.

Lieberthal, Kenneth, and Michel Oksenberg. 1988. *Policy Making in China: Leaders, Structures, and Processes.* Princeton, N.J.: Princeton University Press.

Lin, George C. S. 2007. "Chinese Urbanism in Question: State, Society, and the Reproduction of Urban Spaces." *Urban Geography* 28 (1): 7–29. https://doi.org/10.2747/0272-3638.28.1.7.

Lin, George C. S. 2009. *Developing China: Land, Politics and Social Conditions.* London: Routledge.

Lin, Justin Yifu. 1990. "Collectivization and China's Agricultural Crisis in 1959–1961." *Journal of Political Economy* 98 (6): 1228–52.

Lin, Nan. 1995. "Local Market Socialism: Local Corporation in Action in Rural China." *Theory and Society* 24 (3): 301–54. https://doi.org/10.2307/658072.

Lin, Yi. 2011. "Turning Rurality into Modernity: Suzhi Education in a Suburban Public School of Migrant Children in Xiamen." *China Quarterly* 206:313–30. https://doi.org/10.1017/S0305741011000282.

Liu Hongyan, Xigang Zhu, Peigang Zhang, and Jie Yin. 2005. "Xifang guihua lilun xin sichao yu shehui gongping" [New trends in western planning theory and social justice]. *Chengshi wenti* [Urban problems], no. 6: 90–94.

Liu, Jieyu. 2011. "Life Goes On: Redundant Women Workers in Nanjing." In *China's Changing Welfare Mix: Local Perspectives,* edited by Beatriz Carrillo and Jane Duckett, 82–103. New York: Routledge.

Liu, Serena. 2007. "Social Citizenship in China: Continuity and Change." *Citizenship Studies* 11 (5): 465–79. https://doi.org/10.1080/13621020701605776.

Liu Shouying. 2014. "Zhonggong shiba jie sanzhong quanhui hou de tudi zhidu gaige ji qi shihi" [Land reform and implementation following the third plenum of the 18th Party Congress]. *Fashang yanjiu* [Studies in law and business] 31 (2): 3–10.

Liu, Weidong, Michael Dunford, Zhouying Song, and Mingxing Chen. 2016. "Urban–Rural Integration Drives Regional Economic Growth in Chongqing, Western China." *Area Development and Policy* 1 (1): 132–54. https://doi.org/10.1080/23792949.2016.1151758.

Logan, John R., and Harvey L. Molotch. 1987. *Urban Fortunes: The Political Economy of Place.* Berkeley: University of California Press.

Looney, Kristen. 2015. "China's Campaign to Build a New Socialist Countryside: Village Modernization, Peasant Councils, and the Ganzhou Model of Rural Development." *China Quarterly* 224:909–32.

Looney, Kristen, and Meg Elizabeth Rithmire. 2016. "Urbanization with Chinese Characteristics? China's Gamble for Modernization." Harvard Business School Working Paper 16-083.

Lora-Wainwright, Anna. 2011. "'If You Can Walk and Eat, You Don't Go to Hospital': The Quest for Healthcare in Rural Sichuan." In *China's Changing Welfare Mix: Local Perspectives,* edited by Beatriz Carrillo and Jane Duckett, 104–25. New York: Routledge.

Low, Setha M. 2008. "Incorporation and Gated Communities in the Greater Metro–Los Angeles Region as a Model of Privatization of Residential Communities." *Home Cultures* 5 (1): 85–108. https://doi.org/10.2752/174063108X287364.

Lu, Duanfang. 2006. *Remaking Chinese Urban Form: Modernity, Scarcity and Space, 1949–2005.* London: Routledge.

Lu, Xun. 1990. *"Diary of a Madman" and Other Stories.* Translated by William A. Lyell. Honolulu: University of Hawai'i Press.

Luo, Renfu, Linxiu Zhang, Jikun Huang, and Scott Rozelle. 2007. "Elections, Fiscal Reform and Public Goods Provision in Rural China." *Journal of Comparative Economics* 35 (3): 583–611. https://doi.org/10.1016/j.jce.2007.03.008.

Luo Yixin. 2006. "Gongye fanbu nongye cujin chengxiang xietiao fazhan" [Industry repays agriculture to push forward urban–rural coordinated development]. In *Kexue fazhan guan yu shehuixue qianyan wenti yanjiu* [The scientific development platform and research on questions at the cutting edge of sociology], edited by Shankan He, 64–75. Shanghai: Shanghai shehui kexueyuan chubanshe [Shanghai academy of social sciences press].

Ma Kai, ed. 2006. *Kexue fazhan guan* [Scientific development platform]. Beijing: Renmin chubanshe, dangjian duwu chubanshe [People's press, party-building reading materials press].

Ma, Laurence J. C. 2005. "Urban Administrative Restructuring, Changing Scale Relations and Local Economic Development in China." *Political Geography* 24 (4): 477–97. https://doi.org/10.1016/j.polgeo.2004.10.005.

Ma, Laurence J. C., and Ming Fan. 1994. "Urbanisation from Below: The Growth of Towns in Jiangsu, China." *Urban Studies* 31 (10): 1625–45. https://doi.org/10.1080/00420989420081551.

Man, Joyce Yanyun. 2012. "China's Property Tax Reform: Progress and Challenges." *Land Lines,* April 2012.

Manion, Melanie. 2006. "Democracy, Community, Trust: The Impact of Elections in Rural China." *Comparative Political Studies* 39 (3): 301–24. https://doi.org/10.1177/0010414005280852.

Mann, Susan. 1984. "Urbanization and Historical Change in China." *Modern China* 10 (1): 79–113.

Massumi, Brian. 2002. *Parables for the Virtual: Movement, Affect, Sensation.* Durham, N.C.: Duke University Press.

Mattingly, Daniel C. 2016. "Elite Capture: How Decentralization and Informal Institutions Weaken Property Rights in China." *World Politics* 68 (3): 383–412. https://doi.org/10.1017/S0043887116000083.

Mauss, Marcel. (1950) 2000. *The Gift: The Form and Reason for Exchange in Archaic Societies.* New York: Norton.

McFarlane, Colin. 2011. "Assemblage and Critical Urbanism." *City* 15 (2): 204–24. https://doi.org/10.1080/13604813.2011.568715.

McFarlane, Colin, and Jennifer Robinson. 2012. "Introduction—Experiments in Comparative Urbanism." *Urban Geography* 33 (6): 765–73.

McGee, T. G. 1991. "The Emergence of Desakota Regions in Asia: Expanding a Hypothesis." In *The Extended Metropolis: Settlement Transition in Asia,* edited by Norton Ginsburg, Bruce Koppel, and T. G. McGee, 3–26. Honolulu: University of Hawai'i Press.

Mertha, Andrew. 2009. "From 'Rustless Screws' to 'Nail Houses': The Evolution of Property Rights in China." *Orbis* 53 (2): 233–49. https://doi.org/10.1016/j.orbis.2009.01.008.

Mitchell, J. Clyde. 2011. "Case and Situation Analysis." In *Case Study Method,* edited by Roger Gomm, Martyn Hammersley, and Peter Foster, 165–86. London: Sage.

Mitter, Rana. 2005. *A Bitter Revolution: China's Struggle with the Modern World.* Oxford: Oxford University Press.

Mizoguchi, Yūzō. 2016. "China as Method." *Inter-Asia Cultural Studies* 17 (4): 513–18. https://doi.org/10.1080/14649373.2016.1239447.

Molotch, Harvey. 1976. "The City as a Growth Machine: Toward a Political Economy of Place." *American Journal of Sociology* 82 (2): 309–32. https://doi.org/10.1086/226311.

Morduch, Jonathan. 1995. "Income Smoothing and Consumption Smoothing." *Journal of Economic Perspectives* 9 (3): 103–14. https://doi.org/10.1257/jep.9.3.103.

Morduch, Jonathan, and Manohar Sharma. 2002. "Strengthening Public Safety Nets from the Bottom Up." *Development Policy Review* 20 (5): 569–88.

Morris, David B. 1997. "About Suffering: Voice, Genre, and Moral Community." In *Social Suffering,* edited by Arthur Kleinman, Veena Das, and Margaret M. Lock, 1–24. Berkeley: University of California Press.

Mote, Frederick W. 1977. "The Transformation of Nanking, 1350–1400." In *The City in Late Imperial China,* edited by G. William Skinner, 101–54. Stanford, Calif.: Stanford University Press.

Murphey, Rhoads. 1974. "The Treaty Ports and China's Modernization." In *The Chinese City between Two Worlds,* edited by Mark Elvin and G. William Skinner, 17–72. Stanford, Calif.: Stanford University Press.

Nader, Laura. 1972. "Up the Anthropologist: Perspectives Gained from Studying Up." In *Reinventing Anthropology,* edited by Dell Hymes, 284–311. New York: Pantheon Books.

Naughton, Barry. 1995. "Cities in the Chinese Economic System: Changing Roles and Conditions for Autonomy." In *Urban Spaces in Contemporary China: The Potential for Autonomy and Community in Post-Mao China,* edited by Deborah Davis, Richard Kraus, Barry Naughton, and Elizabeth J. Perry, 61–89. Washington, D.C.: Woodrow Wilson Center Press.

Nelson, Robert H. 1977. *Zoning and Property Rights: An Analysis of the American System of Land-Use Regulation.* Cambridge, Mass.: MIT Press.

Ng, Mee-Kam, and Fulong Wu. 1995. "A Critique of the 1989 City Planning Act of the People's Republic of China: A Western Perspective." *Third World Planning Review* 17 (3): 279–93. https://doi.org/10.3828/twpr.17.3.rk1n81300k6t0g03.

Nolan, Peter, and Gordon White. 1984. "Urban Bias, Rural Bias or State Bias? Urban–Rural Relations in Post-revolutionary China." *Journal of Development Studies* 20 (3): 52–81. https://doi.org/10.1080/00220388408421906.

North, Douglass C. 1981. *Structure and Change in Economic History.* New York: Norton.

North, Douglass C. 1990. *Institutions, Institutional Change and Economic Performance.* Cambridge: Cambridge University Press.

North, Douglass C., John Joseph Wallis, and Barry R. Weingast. 2009. *Violence and Social Orders: A Conceptual Framework for Interpreting Recorded Human History.* Cambridge: Cambridge University Press.

Oakes, Tim. 2019. "China's Urban Ideology: New Towns, Creation Cities, and Contested Landscapes of Memory." *Eurasian Geography and Economics* 60 (4): 400–421. https://doi.org/10.1080/15387216.2019.1668815.

O'Brien, Kevin J., and Yanhua Deng. 2015. "Repression Backfires: Tactical Radicalization and Protest Spectacle in Rural China." *Journal of Contemporary China* 24 (93): 457–70. https://doi.org/10.1080/10670564.2014.953849.

O'Brien, Kevin J., and Rongbin Han. 2009. "Path to Democracy? Assessing Village Elections in China." *Journal of Contemporary China* 18 (60): 359–78. https://doi.org/10.1080/10670560902770206.

O'Brien, Kevin J., and Lianjiang Li. 2000. "Accommodating 'Democracy' in a One-Party State: Introducing Village Elections in China." *China Quarterly* 162:465–89. https://doi.org/10.1017/S0305741000008213.

O'Brien, Kevin J., and Lianjiang Li. 2006. *Rightful Resistance in Rural China.* New York: Cambridge University Press.

O'Callaghan, Cian. 2012. "Contrapuntal Urbanisms: Towards a Postcolonial Relational Geography." *Environment and Planning A: Economy and Space* 44 (8): 1930–50. https://doi.org/10.1068/a44615.

Oi, Jean C. 1992. "Fiscal Reform and the Economic Foundations of Local State Corporatism in China." *World Politics* 45 (1): 99–126. https://doi.org/10.2307/2010520.

Oi, Jean C. 1999. *Rural China Takes Off: Institutional Foundations of Economic Reform.* Berkeley: University of California Press.

Oi, Jean C., and Scott Rozelle. 2000. "Elections and Power: The Locus of Decision-making in Chinese Villages." *China Quarterly* 162: 513–39. https://doi.org/10.2307/656019.

Ong, Aihwa. 1987. *Spirits of Resistance and Capitalist Discipline: Factory Women in Malaysia.* Albany, N.Y.: SUNY Press.

Ong, Aihwa. 2011. "Introduction: Worlding Cities, or the Art of Being Global." In

Worlding Cities, edited by Ananya Roy and Aihwa Ong, 1–26. Hoboken, N.J.: Wiley.

Ostrom, Elinor. 2005. *Understanding Institutional Diversity.* Princeton, N.J.: Princeton University Press.

Oxfeld, Ellen. 1993. *Blood, Sweat, and Mahjong: Family and Enterprise in an Overseas Chinese Community.* Ithaca, N.Y.: Cornell University Press.

Paik, Wooyeal, and Kihyun Lee. 2012. "I Want To Be Expropriated! The Politics of Xiaochanquanfang Land Development in Suburban China." *Journal of Contemporary China* 21 (74): 261–79. https://doi.org/10.1080/10670564.2012.635930.

Park, Albert. 2008. "Rural–Urban Inequality in China." In *China Urbanizes: Consequences, Strategies, and Policies,* edited by Shahid Yusuf and Tony Saich, 41–64. Washington, D.C.: World Bank.

Peake, Linda. 2015. "The Twenty-First-Century Quest for Feminism and the Global Urban." *International Journal of Urban and Regional Research* 40 (1): 219–27. https://doi.org/10.1111/1468-2427.12276.

Peattie, Lisa Redfield. 1987. *Planning, Rethinking Ciudad Guayana.* Ann Arbor: University of Michigan Press.

Pempel, T. J. 1999. "The Developmental Regime in a Changing World Economy." In *The Developmental State,* edited by Meredith Woo-Cumings, 137–81. Ithaca, N.Y.: Cornell University Press.

Pigou, A. C. 1920. *The Economics of Welfare.* London: Macmillan.

Pils, Eva. 2005. "Land Disputes, Rights Assertion, and Social Unrest in China: A Case from Sichuan." *Columbia Journal of Asian Law* 19 (1): 235–92.

Po, Lanchih. 2008. "Redefining Rural Collectives in China: Land Conversion and the Emergence of Rural Shareholding Co-operatives." *Urban Studies* 45 (8): 1603–23. https://doi.org/10.1177/0042098008091493.

Po, Lanchih. 2011. "Property Rights Reforms and Changing Grassroots Governance in China's Urban–Rural Peripheries: The Case of Changping District in Beijing." *Urban Studies* 48 (3): 509–28. https://doi.org/10.1177/0042098010390233.

Po, Lanchih. 2012. "Asymmetrical Integration: Public Finance Deprivation in China's Urbanized Villages." *Environment and Planning A* 44 (12): 2834–51. https://doi.org/10.1068/a44253.

Popkin, Samuel L. 1979. *The Rational Peasant: The Political Economy of Rural Society in Vietnam.* Berkeley: University of California Press.

Pow, Choon-Piew. 2012. "China Exceptionalism? Unbounding Narratives on Urban China." In *Urban Theory beyond the West: A World of Cities,* edited by Tim Edensor and Mark Jayne, 47–64. New York: Routledge.

Pryor, Frederic L. 1973. *Property and Industrial Organization in Communist and Capitalist Nations.* Bloomington: Indiana University Press.

Puett, Michael J. 2002. *To Become a God: Cosmology, Sacrifice, and Self-Divinization in Early China.* Cambridge, Mass.: Harvard University Asia Center.

Purcell, Mark. 2009. "Resisting Neoliberalization: Communicative Planning or Counter-hegemonic Movements?" *Planning Theory* 8 (2): 140–65. https://doi.org/10.1177/1473095209102232.

Ren, Xuefei. 2013. *Urban China.* Malden, Mass.: Wiley.

Ren, Xuefei. 2014. "The Political Economy of Urban Ruins: Redeveloping Shanghai." *International Journal of Urban and Regional Research* 38 (3): 1081–91. https://doi.org/10.1111/1468-2427.12119.

Rigg, Jonathan. 2019. *More Than Rural: Textures of Thailand's Agrarian Transformation.* Honolulu: University of Hawai'i Press.

Rithmire, Meg E. 2015. *Land Bargains and Chinese Capitalism: The Politics of Property Rights under Reform.* New York: Cambridge University Press.

Rittel, Horst W. J., and Melvin M. Webber. 1973. "Dilemmas in a General Theory of Planning." *Policy Sciences* 4 (2): 155–69. https://doi.org/10.2307/4531523.

Robinson, Jennifer. 2002. "Global and World Cities: A View from off the Map." *International Journal of Urban and Regional Research* 26 (3): 531–54. https://doi.org/10.1111/1468-2427.00397.

Robinson, Jennifer. 2006. *Ordinary Cities: Between Modernity and Development.* London: Routledge.

Robinson, Jennifer. 2011. "Cities in a World of Cities: The Comparative Gesture." *International Journal of Urban and Regional Research* 35 (1): 1–23. https://doi.org/10.1111/j.1468-2427.2010.00982.x.

Robinson, Jennifer. 2014. "New Geographies of Theorizing the Urban: Putting Comparison to Work for Global Urban Studies." In *The Routledge Handbook on Cities of the Global South,* edited by Sue Parnell and Sophie Oldfield, 57–70. New York: Routledge.

Robinson, Jennifer. 2016. "Thinking Cities through Elsewhere: Comparative Tactics for a More Global Urban Studies." *Progress in Human Geography* 40 (1): 3–29. https://doi.org/10.1177/0309132515598025.

Robinson, Jennifer, and Ananya Roy. 2015. "Global Urbanisms and the Nature of Urban Theory." *International Journal of Urban and Regional Research* 40 (1). https://doi.org/10.1111/1468-2427.12272.

Rofel, Lisa. 1999. *Other Modernities: Gendered Yearnings in China after Socialism.* Berkeley: University of California Press.

Rosenberg, Lior. 2013. "Urbanising the Rural: Local Strategies for Creating 'New Style' Rural Communities in China." *China Perspectives,* no. 3: 63–71.

Roy, Ananya. 2003. *City Requiem, Calcutta: Gender and the Politics of Poverty.* Minneapolis: University of Minnesota Press.

Roy, Ananya. 2009. "The 21st-Century Metropolis: New Geographies of Theory." *Regional Studies* 43 (6): 819–30. https://doi.org/10.1080/00343400701809665.

Roy, Ananya. 2011. "Slumdog Cities: Rethinking Subaltern Urbanism." *International Journal of Urban and Regional Research* 35 (2): 223–38. https://doi.org/10.1111/j.1468-2427.2011.01051.x.

Roy, Ananya. 2016. "What Is Urban about Critical Urban Theory?" *Urban Geography* 37 (6): 810–23. https://doi.org/10.1080/02723638.2015.1105485.

Sandercock, Leonie. 1998. *Towards Cosmopolis: Planning for Multicultural Cities.* New York: Wiley.

Sandercock, Leonie, and Giovanni Attili. 2010. "Digital Ethnography as Planning Praxis: An Experiment with Film as Social Research, Community Engagement and Policy Dialogue." *Planning Theory and Practice* 11 (1): 23–45. https://doi.org/10.1080/14649350903538012.

Sargeson, Sally. 2004. "Full Circle? Rural Land Reforms in Globalizing China." *Critical Asian Studies* 36 (4): 637–56.

Sargeson, Sally. 2013. "Violence as Development: Land Expropriation and China's Urbanization." *Journal of Peasant Studies* 40 (6): 1063–85. https://doi.org/10.1080/03066150.2013.865603.

Schein, Louisa. 2001. "Urbanity, Cosmopolitanism, Consumption." In *China Urban: Ethnographies of Contemporary Culture,* edited by Nancy N. Chen, 225–41. Durham, N.C.: Duke University Press.

Schön, Donald A. 1983. *The Reflective Practitioner: How Professionals Think in Action.* New York: Basic Books.

Scott, David. 2008. *China and the International System, 1840–1949: Power, Presence, and Perceptions in a Century of Humiliation.* Albany, N.Y.: SUNY Press.

Scott, James C. 1976. *The Moral Economy of the Peasant: Rebellion and Subsistence in Southeast Asia.* New Haven, Conn.: Yale University Press.

Scott, James C. 1985. *Weapons of the Weak: Everyday Forms of Peasant Resistance.* New Haven, Conn.: Yale University Press.

Selden, Mark. 1998. "Household, Cooperative, and State in the Remaking of China's Countryside." In *Cooperative and Collective in China's Rural Development: Between State and Private Interests,* edited by E. B. Vermeer, Frank N. Pieke, and Woei Lien Chong, 17–45. Armonk, N.Y.: M. E. Sharpe.

Shen Lei and Dexiang Zhong. 2007. "Chengzhongcun gaizao sheji shili fenxi" [Analysis of design practice in rebuilding village-in-city]. *Shanxi jianzhu* [Shanxi architecture] 33 (17): 55–56.

Shi, Chen, and Bo-sin Tang. 2020. "Institutional Change and Diversity in the Transfer of Land Development Rights in China: The Case of Chengdu." *Urban Studies* 57 (3): 473–89. https://doi.org/10.1177/0042098019845527.

Shi Nan. 2003. "Chengshi guihua kexue xing yuanyu kexue de guihua shijian"

[The scientific quality of urban planning is grounded in scientific planning practice]. *Chengshi guihua* [City planning review] 27 (2): 8.

Shi Nan. 2004. "Shilun chengshi guihua zhong de gonggong liyi" [On public interest in urban planning]. *Chengshi guihua* [City planning review] 28 (6): 20–31.

Shi Nan. 2005. "Shilun chengshi guihua shehui gongneng de yingxiang yinsu" [Factors influencing the social function of urban planning]. *Chengshi guihua* [City planning review] 29 (8): 9–18.

Shi Nan. 2008. "Lun chengxiang guihua guanli xingzheng quanli de zeren kongjian fanchou" [On the responsibility space of urban and rural planning administration]. *Chengshi guihua* [City planning review] 32 (2): 9–26.

Shi Qinghua and Jianwei Zhuo. 2009. "Nongcun tudi quanshu: Nongmin de rentong yu falü de guiding" [Rural land rights possession: Peasants' identification and legal regulations]. *Guanli shijie* [Management world], no. 1: 89–96.

Shi Yingjun. 2011. "Chengzhongcun gaizao moshi yanjiu" [Research on models of village-in-the-city reform]. *Henan shehui kexue* [Henan social sciences], no. 1: 206–7.

Shirk, Susan L. 1992. "The Chinese Political System and the Political Strategy of Economic Reform." In *Bureaucracy, Politics, and Decision Making in Post-Mao China,* edited by Kenneth Lieberthal and David M. Lampton, 59–91. Berkeley: University of California Press.

Shue, Vivienne. 2017. "Maps, Dreams, and Trails to Heaven: Envisioning a Future Chinese Nation-Space." In *To Govern China: Evolving Practices of Power,* edited by Patricia M. Thornton and Vivienne Shue, 83–120. Cambridge: Cambridge University Press.

Sigley, Gary. 2006. "Chinese Governmentalities: Government, Governance and the Socialist Market Economy." *Economy and Society* 35 (4): 487–508. https://doi.org/10.1080/03085140600960773.

Sigley, Gary. 2009. "Suzhi, the Body, and the Fortunes of Technoscientific Reasoning in Contemporary China." *Positions: East Asia Cultures Critique* 17 (3): 537–66.

Simone, AbdouMaliq. 2010. *City Life from Jakarta to Dakar: Movements at the Crossroads.* New York: Routledge.

Simoons, Frederick J. 1990. *Food in China: A Cultural and Historical Inquiry.* New York: CRC Press.

Sit, Victor F. S. 1996. "Soviet Influence on Urban Planning in Beijing, 1949–1991." *Town Planning Review* 67 (4): 457–84.

Siu, Helen F. 2007. "Grounding Displacement: Uncivil Urban Spaces in Post-reform South China." *American Ethnologist* 34 (2): 329–50. https://doi.org/10.1525/ae.2007.34.2.329.

Skjei, Stephen S. 1976. "Urban Problems and the Theoretical Justification of Urban Planning." *Urban Affairs Review* 11 (3): 323–44.

Smith, Neil. 2008. *Uneven Development: Nature, Capital, and the Production of Space.* 3rd ed. Athens: University of Georgia Press.

Smith, Nick R. 2014a. "City-in-the-Village: Huanggang and China's Urban Renewal." In *Village in the City: An Informal Portrait of South China,* edited by Stefan Al, 29–40. Hong Kong: Hong Kong University Press.

Smith, Nick R. 2014b. "Living on the Edge: Household Registration Reform and Peri-urban Precarity in China." *Journal of Urban Affairs* 36 (S1): 369–83. https://doi.org/10.1111/juaf.12107.

Smith, Nick R. 2018. "Planning Powers as Property Rights in Contemporary China." *Journal of Planning Education and Research,* e-pub before print. https://doi.org/10.1177/0739456X18787623.

Smith, Nick R. 2019a. "Community Self-Organisation in Contemporary China: Efficiency, Equity and Affect in the Process of Institutional Transformation." *International Development Planning Review* 41 (3): 399–418. https://doi.org/10.3828/idpr.2019.12.

Smith, Nick R. 2019b. "One Village, One Product: Agro-industrial Village Corporatism in Contemporary China." *Journal of Agrarian Change* 19 (2): 249–69. https://doi.org/10.1111/joac.12301.

Smith, Nick R. 2020. "Spatial Poetics under Authoritarianism: Graffiti and the Contestation of Urban Redevelopment in Contemporary China." *Antipode* 52 (2): 581–601. https://doi.org/10.1111/anti.12607.

Soja, Edward W. 2014. *My Los Angeles: From Urban Restructuring to Regional Urbanization.* Berkeley: University of California Press.

Soja, Edward W., and Richard J. Tobin. 2007. "The Geography of Modernization: Paths, Patterns, and Processes of Spatial Change in Developing Countries." In *Third World Urbanization,* edited by J. Abu-Lughod and R. Hay Jr., 153–64. London: Routledge.

Solinger, Dorothy J. 1999. *Contesting Citizenship in Urban China: Peasant Migrants, the State, and the Logic of the Market.* Berkeley: University of California Press.

Solinger, Dorothy J. 2011. "Dibaohu in Distress: The Meager Minimum Livelihood Guarantee System in Wuhan." In *China's Changing Welfare Mix: Local Perspectives,* edited by Beatriz Carrillo and Jane Duckett, 36–63. New York: Routledge.

Sopranzetti, Claudio. 2014. "Owners of the Map: Mobility and Mobilization among Motorcycle Taxi Drivers in Bangkok." *City and Society* 26 (1): 120–43. https://doi.org/10.1111/ciso.12030.

Sparke, Matthew, James D. Sidaway, Tim Bunnell, and Carl Grundy-Warr. 2004.

"Triangulating the Borderless World: Geographies of Power in the Indonesia–Malaysia–Singapore Growth Triangle." *Transactions of the Institute of British Geographers* 29 (4): 485–98. https://doi.org/10.1111/j.0020-2754.2004.00143.x.

Stake, Robert E. 1978. "The Case Study Method in Social Inquiry." *Educational Researcher* 7 (2): 5–8.

State Council of the People's Republic of China. 2003. "Guanyu cujin nongmin zengjia shouru ruogan zhengce de yijian" [Opinion on certain policies regarding increasing income for rural people]. http://www.gov.cn/gongbao/content/2004/content_63144.htm.

State Council of the People's Republic of China. 2012. "Guanyu jiakuai fazhan xiandai nongye jin yibu zengqiang nongcun fazhan huoli de ruogan yijian" [Opinion regarding the acceleration of agricultural development and modernization and the strengthening of rural developmental vitality]. http://www.gov.cn/jrzg/2013-01/31/content_2324293.htm.

State Council of the People's Republic of China. 2018. "Guanyu shishi xiangcun zhenxing zhanlüe de yijian" [Opinion regarding the implementation of the rural revitalization strategy]. http://www.gov.cn/zhengce/2018-02/04/content_5263807.htm.

Steinmüller, Hans. 2011. "The Moving Boundaries of Social Heat: Gambling in Rural China." *Journal of the Royal Anthropological Institute* 17 (2): 263–80. https://doi.org/10.1111/j.1467-9655.2011.01679.x.

Steinmüller, Hans. 2013. *Communities of Complicity: Everyday Ethics in Rural China.* New York: Berghahn Books.

Su, Minzi. 2009. *China's Rural Development Policy: Exploring the "New Socialist Countryside."* Boulder, Colo.: First Forum Press.

Sun Peng and Yinbo Xu. 2011. "Woguo jiti jianshe yongdi liuzhuan taishi yu zouxiang panduan" [Judgment regarding the situation and direction of the transfer of collective construction land in China]. *Chongqing shehui kexue* [Chongqing social sciences], no. 10: 45–59.

Sun, Wanning. 2009. "Suzhi on the Move: Body, Place, and Power." *Positions: East Asia Cultures Critique* 17 (3): 617–42.

Tambiah, Stanley J. 1990. *Magic, Science, Religion, and the Scope of Rationality.* Cambridge: Cambridge University Press.

Tan, Qingshan. 2004. "Building Institutional Rules and Procedures: Village Election in China." *Policy Sciences* 37 (1): 1–22. https://doi.org/10.1023/B:OLIC.0000035451.83055.15.

Tang, Beibei. 2015. "'Not Rural but Not Urban': Community Governance in China's Urban Villages." *China Quarterly* 223:724–44. https://doi.org/10.1017/S0305741015000843.

Tang, Wing-Shing. 2019. "Town–Country Relations in China: Back to Basics."

Eurasian Geography and Economics 60 (4): 455–85. https://doi.org/10.1080/15387216.2019.1686407.

Thøgersen, Stig. 2012. "Organizing Rural China: Political and Academic Discourses." In *Organizing Rural China, Rural China Organizing,* edited by Ane Bislev and Stig Thøgersen, 35–50. Plymouth, U.K.: Lexington Books.

Thompson, Edward Palmer. 1963. *The Making of the English Working Class.* London: V. Gollancz.

Thompson, Eric C. 2007. *Unsettling Absences: Urbanism in Rural Malaysia.* Singapore: NUS Press.

Thrift, Nigel. 2004. "Intensities of Feeling: Towards a Spatial Politics of Affect." *Geografiska Annaler: Series B, Human Geography* 86 (1): 57–78. https://doi.org/10.1111/j.0435-3684.2004.00154.x.

Tian Daigui. 2010. *Chongqingshi tongchou chengxiang zonghe peitao gaige tansuo* [Chongqing municipality's experiment in comprehensive urban–rural coordination reform]. Chongqing: Chongqing daxue chubanshe [Chongqing university press].

Tian, Li, Biqing Ge, and Yongfu Li. 2017. "Impacts of State-Led and Bottom-up Urbanization on Land Use Change in the Peri-urban Areas of Shanghai: Planned Growth or Uncontrolled Sprawl?" *Cities* 60 (February): 476–86. https://doi.org/10.1016/j.cities.2016.01.002.

Tian Zhenyu. 2005. "Shenzhen chengzhongcun jianzhu gaizao de mibiao he fangshi" [Goals and methods of architectural rebuilding of villages-in-the-city in Shenzhen]. *Tequ jingji* [Special zone economy], no. 1: 17–21.

Tomba, Luigi. 2009. "Of Quality, Harmony, and Community: Civilization and the Middle Class in Urban China." *Positions: East Asia Cultures Critique* 17 (3): 592–616.

Townsend, Robert M. 1995. "Consumption Insurance: An Evaluation of Risk-Bearing Systems in Low-Income Economies." *Journal of Economic Perspectives* 9 (3): 83–102. https://doi.org/10.1257/jep.9.3.83.

Trappel, René. 2016. *China's Agrarian Transition: Peasants, Property, and Politics.* Challenges Facing Chinese Political Development. Lanham, Md.: Lexington Books.

Tsai, Lily L. 2007. *Accountability without Democracy: Solidary Groups and Public Goods Provision in Rural China.* Cambridge: Cambridge University Press.

Turner, Victor Witter. 1972. *Schism and Continuity in an African Society: A Study of Ndembu Village Life.* Manchester: Manchester University Press.

Upham, Frank K. 2009. "Chinese Property Rights and Property Theory." *Hong Kong Law Journal* 39:611–25.

Walker, Andrew. 2012. *Thailand's Political Peasants: Power in the Modern Rural Economy.* Madison: University of Wisconsin Pres.

Wallace, Jeremy L. 2014. *Cities and Stability: Urbanization, Redistribution, and Regime Survival in China.* Oxford: Oxford University Press.

Wang Dong and Xuming Cai. 2012. "Nongmin zizhu chengshihua yu tudi zhidu gaige" [Villagers' self-urbanization and reform of the land system]. *Tongji yu guanli* [Statistics and management], no. 3: 94–98.

Wang, Fei-ling. 2010. "Renovating the Great Floodgate: The Reform of China's Hukou System." In *One Country, Two Societies: Rural–Urban Inequality in Contemporary China,* edited by Martin King Whyte, 335–64. Cambridge, Mass.: Harvard University Press.

Wang Jinyuan. 2011. "Lun jingyingxing jianshe yongdi de zhengfu caigou—Chengshihua jincheng zhong jiti tudi liuzhuan zhi fali sikao" [A discussion regarding government purchase of operational construction land—Legal considerations regarding the transfer of collective land during urbanization]. *Fashang yanjiu* [Studies in law and business] 28 (3): 45–50.

Wang Lei, Ying Li, and Chao Tian. 2012. "Zhongguo de chengshi qiye zhuyi—Biaoxian xingshi, zhidu jichu yu yingxiang xiaoying" [China's urban entrepreneurialism—Expressions, foundations, and effects]. *Gonggong xingzheng pinglun* [Journal of public administration], no. 2: 43–66.

Wang, Xu. 2003. *Mutual Empowerment of State and Peasantry: Village Self-Government in Rural China.* New York: Nova Science Publishers.

Wang, Ya Ping, Yanglin Wang, and Jiansheng Wu. 2009. "Urbanization and Informal Development in China: Urban Villages in Shenzhen." *International Journal of Urban and Regional Research* 33 (4): 957–73. https://doi.org/10.1111/j.1468-2427.2009.00891.x.

Wang Yong and Guangbin Li. 2009. "Quanli de shehui huigui—lun chengshi guihua de fei shichang quexian" [The return of the rights society—Discussion of the nonmarket flaws in urban planning]. *Guihua shi* [Planners] 25 (2): 56–61.

Ward, Kevin. 2008. "Toward a Comparative (Re)turn in Urban Studies? Some Reflections." *Urban Geography* 29 (5): 405–10.

Watson, Rubie. 1988. "Remembering the Dead: Graves and Politics in Southeastern China." In *Death Ritual in Late Imperial and Modern China,* edited by James L. Watson and Evelyn S. Rawski, 203–27. Berkeley: University of California Press.

Webber, Melvin M. 1963. "Comprehensive Planning and Social Responsibility: Toward an AIP Consensus on the Profession's Roles and Purposes." *Journal of the American Institute of Planners* 29 (4): 232–41. https://doi.org/10.1080/01944366308978072.

Weber, Max. (1946) 2009. *From Max Weber: Essays in Sociology.* New York: Routledge.

Webster, Christopher J. 2009. "Are Some Planning Transactions Intrinsically

Sovereign?" *Journal of Planning Education and Research* 28 (4): 476–90. https://doi.org/10.1177/0739456X08330977.

Webster, Christopher J., and Lawrence Wai-Chung Lai. 2003. *Property Rights, Planning, and Markets: Managing Spontaneous Cities.* Northampton, Mass.: Edward Elgar.

Webster, Christopher J., and Yanjing Zhao. 2010. "Entitlement to the Benefits of Urbanization: Comparing Migrant and Peri-urban 'Peasants.'" In *Marginalization in Urban China: Comparative Perspectives,* edited by Fulong Wu and Christopher J. Webster, 59–71. Basingstoke, U.K.: Palgrave Macmillan.

Weimer, David L., ed. 1997. *The Political Economy of Property Rights: Institutional Change and Credibility in the Reform of Centrally Planned Economies.* Cambridge: Cambridge University Press.

Wen Jiabao. 2003. "Renzhen guanche shiliu da jingshen wei tuijin nongcun xiaokang jianshe er fendou" [Taking seriously implementing the spirit of the 16th Party Congress in order to push forward the construction of rural prosperity]. *Qiushi* [Seeking truth], no. 3: 3–11.

Wen Tiejun. 2000. *Zhongguo nongcun jiben jingji zhidu yanjiu: "sannong" wenti de shiji fansi* [Research on rural China's fundamental economic system: A reconsideration of the era of the "three rural" problems]. Beijing: Zhongguo jingji chubanshe [China economic publishing house].

Wheatley, Paul. 1971. *The Pivot of the Four Quarters: A Preliminary Enquiry into the Origins and Character of the Ancient Chinese City.* Chicago: Aldine.

Wilczak, Jessica. 2017. "Making the Countryside More like the Countryside? Rural Planning and Metropolitan Visions in Post-quake Chengdu." *Geoforum* 78 (January): 110–18. https://doi.org/10.1016/j.geoforum.2016.10.007.

Wildau, Gabriel. 2017. "China Property Tax Languishes as Vested Interests Block Reform." *Financial Times,* June 19, 2017. https://www.ft.com/content/0d18d6b2-45b9-11e7-8519-9f94ee97d996.

Williams, Raymond. 1973. *The Country and the City.* London: Chatto and Windus.

Wilson, Scott. 2002. "Face, Norms, and Instrumentality." In *Social Connections in China: Institutions, Culture, and the Changing Nature of Guanxi,* edited by Thomas B. Gold, Doug Guthrie, and David L. Wank, 163–77. Cambridge: Cambridge University Press.

Wolf, Arthur P. 1974. "Gods, Ghosts, and Ancestors." In *Religion and Ritual in Chinese Society,* edited by Arthur P. Wolf, 131–82. Stanford, Calif.: Stanford University Press.

Wong, Siu Wai. 2016. "Reconsolidation of State Power into Urbanising Villages: Shareholding Reforms as a Strategy for Governance in the Pearl River Delta Region." *Urban Studies* 53 (4): 689–704. https://doi.org/10.1177/0042098015569672.

Wu Dasheng, Nongjian Zou, and Futian Ju. 1988. "Lun xiao chengzhen yu chengxiang xietiao fazhan" [A discussion of small towns and urban–rural coordinated development]. *Shehui xue yanjiu* [Sociological studies], no. 2: 24–35.

Wu, Fulong. 1998. "The New Structure of Building Provision and the Transformation of the Urban Landscape in Metropolitan Guangzhou, China." *Urban Studies* 35 (2): 259–83. https://doi.org/10.1080/0042098984970.

Wu, Fulong. 2002. "China's Changing Urban Governance in the Transition Towards a More Market-Oriented Economy." *Urban Studies* 39 (7): 1071–93.

Wu, Fulong. 2007. "Re-orientation of the City Plan: Strategic Planning and Design Competition in China." *Geoforum* 38 (2): 379–92. https://doi.org/10.1016/j.geoforum.2006.05.011.

Wu, Fulong. 2015. *Planning for Growth: Urban and Regional Planning in China.* New York: Routledge.

Wu, Fulong. 2018. "Planning Centrality, Market Instruments: Governing Chinese Urban Transformation under State Entrepreneurialism." *Urban Studies* 55 (7): 1383–99. https://doi.org/10.1177/0042098017721828.

Wu, Fulong, Jiang Xu, and Anthony G. O. Yeh. 2007. *Urban Development in Post-reform China: State, Market, and Space.* New York: Routledge.

Xiang, Biao. 1999. "Xi, Relations Cluster, and the Formation of a Migrant Community in Contemporary China." *Asian and Pacific Migration Journal* 8 (3): 343–59. https://doi.org/10.1177/011719689900800305.

Xie, Yichun, and Frank J. Costa. 1993. "Urban Planning in Socialist China: Theory and Practice." *Cities* 10 (2): 103–14. https://doi.org/10.1016/0264-2751(93)90042-H.

Xu, Jiang, and Anthony G. O. Yeh. 2005. "City Repositioning and Competitiveness Building in Regional Development: New Development Strategies in Guangzhou, China." *International Journal of Urban and Regional Research* 29 (2): 283–308. https://doi.org/10.1111/j.1468-2427.2005.00585.x.

Xu Juzhou. 2004. "Women chengshi guihua mianlin zhe zhiye daode de wenti" [Questions of professional ethics faced by urban planning]. *Chengshi guihua* [City planning review], no. 1: 22–24.

Xu, Yuebin. 2001. "Family Support for Old People in Rural China." *Social Policy and Administration* 35 (3): 307.

Yan, Hairong. 2003. "Neoliberal Governmentality and Neohumanism: Organizing Suzhi/Value Flow through Labor Recruitment Networks." *Cultural Anthropology* 18 (4): 493–523.

Yang An. 1996. "'Chengzhongcun' de Fangzhi" [The prevention of "villages-in-the-city"]. *Chengxiang jianshe* [Urban and rural development], no. 8: 30–31.

Yang, Mayfair Mei-hui. 1994. *Gifts, Favors, and Banquets: The Art of Social Relationships in China.* Ithaca, N.Y.: Cornell University Press.

Yang, Mayfair Mei-hui. 2004. "Spatial Struggles: Postcolonial Complex, State Disenchantment, and Popular Reappropriation of Space in Rural Southeast China." *Journal of Asian Studies* 63 (3): 719–55.

Yao, Yusheng. 2009. "Village Elections and Redistribution of Political Power and Collective Property." *China Quarterly* 197:126–44. http://dx.doi.org.ezp-prod1.hul.harvard.edu/10.1017/S0305741009000071.

Ye, Jingzhong. 2015. "Land Transfer and the Pursuit of Agricultural Modernization in China." *Journal of Agrarian Change* 15 (3): 314–37. https://doi.org/10.1111/joac.12117.

Ye, Yumin, and Richard LeGates. 2013. *Coordinating Urban and Rural Development in China: Learning from Chengdu.* Northampton, Mass.: Edward Elgar.

Yeh, Anthony Gar-On. 2000. "Foreign Investment and Urban Development in China." In *China's Regions, Polity, and Economy: A Study of Spatial Transformation in the Post-reform Era,* edited by Si-ming Li and Wing-shing Tang, 35–64. Hong Kong: Chinese University Press.

Yeh, Anthony Gar-On. 2005. "Dual Land Market and Internal Spatial Structure of Chinese Cities." In *Restructuring the Chinese City: Changing Society, Economy and Space,* edited by Laurence J. C. Ma and Fulong Wu, 59–79. London: Routledge.

Yeh, Anthony Gar-On, and Fulong Wu. 1999. "The Transformation of the Urban Planning System in China from a Centrally-Planned to Transitional Economy." *Progress in Planning* 51 (3): 167–252. https://doi.org/10.1016/S0305-9006(98)00029-4.

Yep, Ray. 2013. "Containing Land Grabs: A Misguided Response to Rural Conflicts over Land." *Journal of Contemporary China* 22 (80): 273–91. https://doi.org/10.1080/10670564.2012.734082.

Yep, Ray, and Ray Forrest. 2016. "Elevating the Peasants into High-Rise Apartments: The Land Bill System in Chongqing as a Solution for Land Conflicts in China?" *Journal of Rural Studies* 47:474–84. https://doi.org/10.1016/j.jrurstud.2016.07.017.

Young, Iris Marion. 1999. "Residential Segregation and Differentiated Citizenship." *Citizenship Studies* 3 (2): 237–52. https://doi.org/10.1080/13621029908420712.

Yu, Li. 2014. *Chinese City and Regional Planning Systems.* Surrey, U.K.: Ashgate.

Zeuthen, Jesper. 2012. "Rule through Difference on China's Urban–Rural Boundary." *Third World Quarterly* 33 (4): 689–704. https://doi.org/10.1080/01436597.2012.657425.

Zha, Qiang. 2012. "Intellectuals, Academic Freedom, and University Autonomy in China." In *University Governance and Reform: Policy, Fads, and Experience in International Perspective,* edited by Hans G. Schuetze, William Bruneau, and Garnet Grosjean, 209–24. New York: Palgrave Macmillan.

Zhang Dongfang. 2015. “Xiao chanquan fang hefahua yanjiu” [Research on the legalization of small property rights housing]. *Fazhi yu shehui* [Legal system and society], no. 18: 285–87.

Zhang, L., and Simon X. B. Zhao. 1998. “Re-examining China’s ‘Urban’ Concept and the Level of Urbanization.” *China Quarterly* 154:330–81. https://doi.org/10.2307/655894.

Zhang, Li. 2001. *Strangers in the City: Reconfigurations of Space, Power, and Social Networks within China’s Floating Population.* Stanford, Calif.: Stanford University Press.

Zhang, Li. 2012. *In Search of Paradise: Middle-Class Living in a Chinese Metropolis.* Ithaca, N.Y.: Cornell University Press.

Zhang Qiang. 2013. “Zai jiti tudi shang shixian xinxing chengzhenhua” [Realizing new-type urbanization on collective land]. *Beijing guancha* [Beijing observation], no. 10: 28–29.

Zhang, Qian Forrest, and John A. Donaldson. 2010. “From Peasants to Farmers: Peasant Differentiation, Labor Regimes, and Land-Rights Institutions in China’s Agrarian Transition.” *Politics and Society* 38 (4): 458–89. https://doi.org/10.1177/0032329210381236.

Zhang, Tingwei. 2000. “Land Market Forces and Government’s Role in Sprawl: The Case of China.” *Cities* 17 (2): 123–35. https://doi.org/10.1016/S0264-2751(00)00007-X.

Zhang Tingwei. 2004. “Zhuanxing qijian zhongguo guihuashi sanzhong shenfen ji zhiye daode wenti” [Questions of planning ethics and Chinese planners’ three types of roles during the transition era]. *Chengshi guihua* [City planning review], no. 3: 66–72.

Zhang, Yunpeng. 2018. “Grabbing Land for Equitable Development? Reengineering Land Dispossession through Securitising Land Development Rights in Chongqing.” *Antipode* 50 (4): 1120–40. https://doi.org/10.1111/anti.12390.

Zhao Shouliang. 2008. “Lun chengshi guihua zhong xiaolü yu gongping de duili yu tongyi” [The opposition and unity of efficiency and equity in urban planning]. *Chengshi guihua* [City planning review] 32 (11): 62–66.

Zhao Yanjing. 2002. “Cong chengshi guanli zouxiang chengshi jingying” [From managing the city toward operating the city]. *Chengshi guihua* [City planning review] 26 (11): 7–15.

Zhao Yanjing. 2013. “Chengshi guihua zhiye de jingji xue sikao” [Economic thoughts on the urban planning profession]. *Chengshi fazhan yanjiu* [Urban studies] 20 (2): 1–11.

Zhao Yanjing, Zhaoyin Liu, and Shuting Zhuang. 2009. “Shuishou zhidu yu chengshi fengong” [The tax system and the urban division of labor]. *Chengshi guihua xuekan* [Urban planning forum], no. 6: 4–11.

Zhao, Yanjing, and Chistopher J. Webster. 2011. "Land Dispossession and Enrichment in China's Suburban Villages." *Urban Studies* 48 (3): 529–51. https://doi.org/10.1177/0042098010390238.

Zhao, Yaohui. 2003. "The Role of Migrant Networks in Labor Migration: The Case of China." *Contemporary Economic Policy* 21 (4): 500–511.

Zheng Jian. 1997. "'Chengzhongcun' wenti ji duice" ["Villages-in-the-city" problems and countermeasures]. *Dangdai jianzhu* [Modern architecture], no. 4: 20.

Zheng, Shiping. 1997. *Party vs. State in Post-1949 China: The Institutional Dilemma.* Cambridge: Cambridge University Press.

Zheng Yueqin. 2005. "Nongmingong shiminhua jincheng zhong de xinli xingtai he shehui wenhua huanjing fenxi" [Analysis of the psychology and social and cultural environment of migrant workers undergoing urbanization]. *Jingji yu guanli* [Economy and management] 19 (9): 9–11.

Zhou, Daming. 1997. "On Rural Urbanization in China." In *Farewell to Peasant China: Rural Urbanization and Social Change in the Late Twentieth Century,* edited by Gregory Eliyu Guldin, 13–46. Armonk, N.Y.: M. E. Sharpe.

Zhou Erliu and Yulin Zhang. 1991. *Chengxiang xietiao fazhan* [Urban–rural coordinated development]. Nanjing: Jiangsu renmin chubanshe [Jiangsu people's publishing].

Zhou, Jing, and Richard Ronald. 2017. "The Resurgence of Public Housing Provision in China: The Chongqing Programme." *Housing Studies* 32 (4): 428–48. https://doi.org/10.1080/02673037.2016.1210097.

Zhou Yi. 2006. *Zhongguo di yi cun: Huaxi cun zhuan xing jing ji zhong de hou ji ti zhu yi* [Huaxi village: Post-collectivism in a transitional economy]. Hong Kong: Oxford University Press.

Zhou, Yixing, and John R. Logan. 2008. "Growth on the Edge: The New Chinese Metropolis." In *Urban China in Transition,* edited by John R. Logan, 140–60. Oxford: Blackwell.

Zhu, Jieming. 1999. *The Transition of China's Urban Development: From Plan-Controlled to Market-Led.* Westport: Greenwood.

Zhu, Jieming. 2004a. "From Land Use Right to Land Development Right: Institutional Change in China's Urban Development." *Urban Studies* 41 (7): 1249–67. https://doi.org/10.1080/0042098042000214770.

Zhu, Jieming. 2004b. "Local Developmental State and Order in China's Urban Development during Transition." *International Journal of Urban and Regional Research* 28 (2): 424–47. https://doi.org/10.1111/j.0309-1317.2004.00527.x.

Zhu Jieming. 2005. "Shichang jingji xia zhongguo chengshi guihua lilun fazhan de luoji" [The logic of the development of China's urban planning theory under the market economy]. *Chengshi guihua xuekan* [Urban planning forum], no. 1: 10–15.

Zhu, Jieming, and Yan Guo. 2015. "Rural Development Led by Autonomous Village Land Cooperatives: Its Impact on Sustainable China's Urbanisation in High-Density Regions." *Urban Studies* 52 (8): 1395–413. https://doi.org/10.1177/0042098014534736.

Zhu, Jieming, and Hendricus Andy Simarmata. 2015. "Formal Land Rights versus Informal Land Rights: Governance for Sustainable Urbanization in the Jakarta Metropolitan Region, Indonesia." *Land Use Policy* 43 (February): 63–73. https://doi.org/10.1016/j.landusepol.2014.10.016.

Zhu, Keliang, Roy Prosterman, Jianping Ye, Ping Li, Jeffrey Riedinger, and Yiwen Ouyang. 2006. "The Rural Land Question in China: Analysis and Recommendations Based on a Seventeen-Province Survey." *New York University Journal of International Law and Politics* 38:761–839.

Zhu, Yu. 2002. "Beyond Large-City-Centred Urbanisation: In Situ Transformation of Rural Areas in Fujian Province." *Asia Pacific Viewpoint* 43 (1): 9–22.

Zhu, Yu. 2007. "China's Floating Population and Their Settlement Intention in the Cities: Beyond the Hukou Reform." *Habitat International* 31 (1): 65–76. https://doi.org/10.1016/j.habitatint.2006.04.002.

Zhuma Miliang. 2013. "Huji gaige shidian jingyan zongjie yi: Chongqing nongmingong hugai" [Summary of the experience of experiments in household registration reform: Chongqing municipality's household registration reform for rural migrant workers]. http://www.town.gov.cn/csxwlb/shidian/zhuanti2/201305/16/t20130516_748680.shtml.

Zou Deci. 2003. "Lun chengshi guihua de kexuexing" [Discussion of the scientific quality of urban planning]. *Chengshi guihua* [City planning review] 27 (2).

Zukosky, Michael L. 2012. "Quality, Development Discourse, and Minority Subjectivity in Contemporary Xinjiang." *Modern China* 38 (2): 233–64. https://doi.org/10.1177/0097700411410530.

Zweig, David. 1987. "From Village to City: Reforming Urban–Rural Relations in China." *International Regional Science Review* 11 (1): 43–58. https://doi.org/10.1177/016001768701100104.

Index

Page numbers in italic refer to illustrations.

(continued from page ii)

Volume 21
Turkish Berlin: Integration Policy and Urban Space
Annika Marlen Hinze

Volume 20
Struggling Giants: City-Region Governance in London, New York, Paris, and Tokyo
Paul Kantor, Christian Lefèvre, Asato Saito, H. V. Savitch, and Andy Thornley

Volume 19
Does Local Government Matter? How Urban Policies Shape Civic Engagement
Elaine B. Sharp

Volume 18
Justice and the American Metropolis
Clarissa Rile Hayward and Todd Swanstrom, Editors

Volume 17
Mobile Urbanism: Cities and Policymaking in the Global Age
Eugene McCann and Kevin Ward, Editors

Volume 16
Seeking Spatial Justice
Edward W. Soja

Volume 15
Shanghai Rising: State Power and Local Transformations in a Global Megacity
Xiangming Chen, Editor

Volume 14
A World of Gangs: Armed Young Men and Gangsta Culture
John M. Hagedorn

Volume 13
El Paso: Local Frontiers at a Global Crossroads
Victor M. Ortíz-González

Volume 12
Remaking New York: Primitive Globalization and the Politics of Urban Community
William Sites

Volume 11
A Political Space: Reading the Global through Clayoquot Sound
Warren Magnusson and Karena Shaw, Editors

Volume 10
City Requiem, Calcutta: Gender and the Politics of Poverty
Ananya Roy

Volume 9
Landscapes of Urban Memory: The Sacred and the Civic in India's High-Tech City
Smriti Srinivas

Volume 8
Fin de Millénaire Budapest: Metamorphoses of Urban Life
Judit Bodnár

Volume 7
Latino Metropolis
Victor M. Valle and Rodolfo D. Torres

Volume 6
Regions That Work: How Cities and Suburbs Can Grow Together
Manuel Pastor Jr., Peter Dreier, J. Eugene Grigsby III, and Marta López-Garza

Volume 5
Selling the Lower East Side: Culture, Real Estate, and Resistance in New York City
Christopher Mele

Volume 4
Power and City Governance: Comparative Perspectives on Urban Development
Alan DiGaetano and John S. Klemanski

Volume 3
Second Tier Cities: Rapid Growth beyond the Metropolis
Ann R. Markusen, Yong-Sook Lee, and Sean DiGiovanna, Editors

Volume 2
Reconstructing Chinatown: Ethnic Enclave, Global Change
Jan Lin

Volume 1
The Work of Cities
Susan E. Clarke and Gary L. Gaile

NICK R. SMITH is assistant professor of architecture and urban studies at Barnard College, Columbia University.